1012

A Practical Guide to Work

A Practical Guide to Working with TRIPS

Antony Taubman

OXFORD
UNIVERSITY PRESS

OXFORD

UNIVERSITY PRESS

Great Clarendon Street, Oxford ox2 6DP

Oxford University Press is a department of the University of Oxford.
It furthers the University's objective of excellence in research, scholarship,
and education by publishing worldwide in

Oxford New York

Auckland Cape Town Dar es Salaam Hong Kong Karachi
Kuala Lumpur Madrid Melbourne Mexico City Nairobi
New Delhi Shanghai Taipei Toronto

With offices in

Argentina Austria Brazil Chile Czech Republic France Greece
Guatemala Hungary Italy Japan Poland Portugal Singapore
South Korea Switzerland Thailand Turkey Ukraine Vietnam

Oxford is a registered trade mark of Oxford University Press
in the UK and in certain other countries

Published in the United States
by Oxford University Press Inc., New York

British Library Cataloguing in Publication Data

Data available

Library of Congress Cataloging in Publication Data

Library of Congress Control Number: 2011922678

Typeset by Glyph International Private Ltd, Bangalore, India
Printed in Great Britain
on acid-free paper by
CPI Antony Rowe, Chippenham and Eastbourne

ISBN 978–0–19–957520–6

3 5 7 9 10 8 6 4 2

To Roya, for her continuing forbearance and support.
To Harry and Ariane, who will eventually see the point;
probably more so than the author ever could.

Disclaimer

The book is a personal reflection on the practicalities of working with a particular legal instrument and not a work of advocacy or legal interpretation. It was planned and mostly undertaken long before the author's current official appointment and its contents have no connection with his current duties or any other official appointment. **Nothing in this book should be taken as representing an official or authoritative account, and still less a legal interpretation, of any international treaty or other international law.** Nothing in this book should be taken as an official view of the choices taken by any government, nor as an assessment or judgement of any policy, domestic law or official action.

Acknowledgements

Deep appreciation is recorded to the Rockefeller Foundation for the grant of a residency in 2008 which enabled completion of the central passages of the book.

Early groundwork on this monograph was facilitated by a period of study leave granted by the Australian Department of Foreign Affairs and Trade, which is gratefully acknowledged.

Several colleagues have kindly reviewed the proofs to weed out the most egregious errors; but all remaining errors and lapses in judgement are entirely the author's responsibility.

Earlier versions of some passages have been published in the following:

'Rethinking TRIPS: "adequate compensation" for non-voluntary patent licensing' [2008] Journal of International Economic Law;

'Australia's interests under TRIPS dispute settlement: trade negotiations by other means, multilateral defence of domestic policy choice, or safeguarding market access?' [2008] Melbourne Journal of International Law;

'Unfair competition and the financing of public knowledge goods: the problem of test data protection' [2008] Journal of Intellectual Property Law and Practice;

'Thinking locally, acting globally: how trade negotiations over geographical indications improvise "fair trade" rules' [2008] Intellectual Property Quarterly;

'TRIPS jurisprudence in the balance: between the realist defence of policy space and a shared utilitarian ethic' in C. Lenk, N. Hoppe and R. Andorno (eds), *Ethics and Law of Intellectual Property* (Aldershot: Ashgate Publishing, 2007);

'Nobility of interpretation: Equity, retrospectivity and collectivity in implementing new norms for performers' rights', [2005] 12 Journal of Intellectual Property Law 351;

'Collective Management of TRIPS: APEC, New Regionalism and Intellectual Property' in C. Antons, M. Blakeney and C. Heath (eds), *Intellectual Property Harmonisation Within ASEAN and APEC* (London: Kluwer Law International, 2004).

Contents

List of Figures

List of Tables

List of Abbreviations

AB	Appellate Body
CBD	Convention on Biological Diversity
DSB	Dispute Settlement Body
DSU	Dispute Settlement Understanding
GATS	General Agreement on Trade in Services
GATT	General Agreement on Tariffs and Trade
GI	Geographical Indication
GR	Genetic Resource
IP	Intellectual Property
IPR	Intellectual Property Right
ITO	International Trade Organization
LDC	Least Developed Country
MFN	Most-favoured nation
TCE	Traditional Cultural Expression
TK	Traditional Knowledge
UPOV	Union for the Protection of Plant Varieties
WIPO	World Intellectual Property Organization
WTO	World Trade Organization

Introduction

Since its conclusion in 1994, the WTO Agreement on TRIPS (Trade-Related Aspects of Intellectual Property Rights) has been integral to the international legal environment for those working in the field of intellectual property (IP). It has also served as the face of the international IP system for many others, as well: policymakers, analysts, practitioners, activists, commentators dealing with issues as diverse as public health, food security, biodiversity, and access to cultural works; and TRIPS continues to pose systemic questions for international economic law and human rights law.

TRIPS has spawned a vast literature that has closely documented, analysed, and criticised its negotiation, its legal status, and its policy implications, and provides commentary on each of its 73 articles. Leading scholars of TRIPS have produced several excellent systematic commentaries, which any serious practitioner must consult—this book does not have a place in those eminent ranks. Within their formal mandates, the WTO itself and the World Intellectual Property Organization (WIPO), the custodian of several treaties embedded in TRIPS, provide invaluable official information on TRIPS and its diplomatic and legal background. Other international organizations and NGOs actively promote understanding and analysis of TRIPS in relation to public policy and international law.

So why presume to add yet another volume to this growing pile? This book has its origins in numerous conversations with officials, legislators, students, lawyers, journalists, NGO representatives, industry people, trade negotiators, diplomats working on human rights, the environment and public health. For some of these interlocutors, TRIPS took on a monolithic, impenetrable character—at its worst, either a legal trump card that overrules any other set of rules or principles, or an impassable barrier to the formulation of good public policy. In effect, some credited TRIPS with more draconian legal effect than it actually had, and yet dismissed out of hand its positive contribution to public policy.

This book attempts to set the TRIPS Agreement, the actual legal text, realistically within its full practical context. It does not give authoritative commentary or official guidance, and it would be most unwise to rely on the general observations in this book as the basis for any firm legal or policy conclusions. The central ambition for this 'practical guide' is that it should leave the reader with a working understanding of what TRIPS is and is not; what it means to deal with it in a pragmatic way; and above all how to reconcile formal legal compliance with the standards set by TRIPS with the development and implementation of good public policy so as to achieve—in a thoroughly positive sum way—the objectives for improved social and economic welfare that TRIPS itself articulates.

Reading the TRIPS Agreement

TRIPS is not one stand-alone document—to read and understand it as a legal instrument you need to consult several other texts. All these texts are readily accessible. This diagram gives URLs (Web addresses) of the official English versions of the TRIPS Agreement itself, the WIPO treaties that it incorporates or refers to, and GATT/WTO texts that define the legal context of TRIPS and the settlement of disputes under TRIPS.

This book is a general work, not a legal textbook, and any references to treaty provisions are set out in a simplified format—TRIPS:1.1 refers to Article 1.1 of the TRIPS Agreement; Paris:10bis refers to Article 10bis of the Paris Convention, and so on.

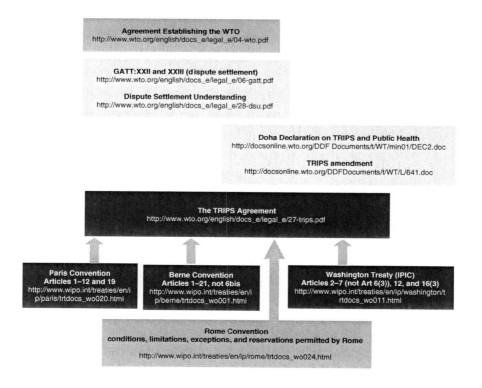

1

What it Means to Work with TRIPS

For more than 500 years, the main objective of the protection of IPRs has been the promotion of industrial creativity to the benefit of a country's social and economic development. Each State, therefore, recognises IPRs according to well-defined public interests. This basic orientation guides, for instance, the system established by the Paris Convention. It also explains and justifies the differences which naturally exist between various national laws dealing with the subject. When the discussion of the issue is moved to trade fora such as GATT, participants should evidently keep in mind this basic principle of public interest implicit in IPR protection.

Delegation of Brazil, Uruguay Round Negotiating
Group on TRIPS—MTN.GNG/NG11/W/30

In 1986, trade ministers responsible for a large share of the global economy met in Punta del Este to launch a wide ranging set of negotiations on rules to govern their trading relations—the Uruguay Round. The international economy differed markedly from today's global market. The Berlin Wall was intact and many countries maintained centrally-planned economies. The internet was a limited tool for academics and researchers, wholly unknown to most of humanity who were oblivious to its potential economic and social impact. But by the time the Uruguay Round came to an end, in 1994, many economies were in transition to market economies and the impact of globalized communications was beginning to be felt. The Uruguay Round itself would dramatically transform the law, politics, and governance of international trade, and would foreshadow the globalized patterns of commerce that we experience today: emphasis on the market and reliance on the private sector to produce public goods; growing liberalization of trade relations; commercial relations that are increasingly blind to national boundaries; scattered chains of production that separate the design and intangible components of a product's value from its physical assembly. And these patterns have been reinforced and accentuated by two dramatic developments since 1986: the spread of the market economy, and the emergence of the internet as a major conduit of commerce, creating a seemingly borderless market and a market in intangible products.

Ministers came to Marrakesh in 1994 to shake hands over the Final Act, the conclusion of the Uruguay Round, putting the seal to an integrated package of trade law treaties that was unprecedented in the scope of issues covered, and the sheer detail of obligations entered into. This 'single undertaking' has been a central part of the international legal landscape since then. Built into this package were the three remarkable outcomes that together form the subject of this book:

(i)   an agreement, the TRIPS Agreement, that effectively recognized that trading partners have a legitimate interest in how well they protect each others' intellectual property (IP);

(ii) a new international organization, the WTO, replacing the makeshift diplomatic assemblage that was the GATT, and administering a complex package of multilateral agreements that built IP integrally into the architecture of trade law; and

(iii) a uniform dispute settlement mechanism, administered by the WTO, that would allow a country to defend its economic interests in the protection of IP rights, through a legalistic, almost judicial, process, rather than the bilateral diplomatic wrangling and use of economic muscle that had come into play earlier when these interests were thwarted in foreign markets.

In short, IP law became a branch of international trade law, as a practical negotiated fact—even though the legal and policy rationale for this move was far from settled (and is still debated today); and this reconception of IP law and of trade interests meant a country's stake in the IP system would be defined, asserted, defended and litigated in the domain of trade law, with unpredictable consequences for IP law and policy, for mainstream trade law, and for the institutions which manage trade relations between nations.

Redefining international IP law in this way and relocating it within a new institutional home was all the more puzzling, since of all the areas of law that the new WTO now covered, it was IP law that was the longest established and deepest rooted internationally, governed as it was by its own multilateral structure. A complex set of treaties on IP had been steadily negotiated and elaborated since the 1880s, when the Paris and Berne Conventions were concluded as some of the earliest of all multilateral treaties, and the predecessors were set up of what grew into a specialized United Nations agency, the World Intellectual Property Organization. Against this longstanding institutional backdrop, what did this latest move now mean? Were there now to be two streams of international IP law—a UN stream and a WTO stream? Would IP as trade law supplant the Paris/Berne/WIPO tradition?

Behind the Acronyms

A glance through the massive literature on TRIPS will disclose a confusing array of jargon and acronyms. Seemingly simple terms can cover over deep legal issues: was 'the GATT' ever a true international organization, or just a legal document; did it ever have legal force; what is it today? Is the WTO a collection of sovereign states or of trading economies? Is it part of the United Nations? What does it mean (if anything) to be a 'signatory' of TRIPS? Even established analysts can show confusion about the complex interplay of treaties, institutions, and negotiating processes that touch on TRIPS. Following is a snapshot of the key terms and institutions.

The World Trade Organization (WTO): an international organization established in 1995 by the Marrakesh Agreement Establishing the World Trade Organization (the 'WTO Agreement'), to provide 'the common institutional framework for the conduct of trade relations among its Members in matters related to' a set of annexed agreements and legal instruments, termed 'Multilateral Trade Agreements', including the GATT, the General Agreement on Trade in Services (GATS), and TRIPS. These Multilateral Trade Agreements do not have a separate legal existence, but are literally annexes to the WTO Agreement.

WTO Members, states and 'separate customs territories': Members of the WTO need not be sovereign nations in the conventional sense; in principle, any state or customs territory that has full autonomy in the conduct of its trade policies can accede to the WTO—this opened the way for WTO membership for the European Communities and for Hong Kong, China, for example, even though they are not recognized as distinct states in international law—neither can join the United Nations in their own right, since the EU is a collection of sovereign nations and Hong Kong is a territory or administrative region within China. Informally, the term 'country' is often

(*cont.*)
used to describe WTO Members as a simpler alternative to the more legalistic 'state or separate customs territory'. The WTO is not a United Nations agency, although it cooperates closely with the UN system.

The General Agreement on Tariffs and Trade (GATT): at first, the GATT was a stand-alone treaty that governed trade relations between its contracting parties, and provided a framework for dispute settlement and for rounds of negotiations to reduce tariffs and other trade restrictions; while it had major political, economic and legal significance, 'the GATT' did not have formal status as a true international organization: as a treaty, it did not even enter into force in a strict legal sense, and in any case was suspended in 1996. Since 1994, a revised GATT has comprised just one component of a more comprehensive body of trade law: it is an Annex to the WTO Agreement, with the same status as the other Multilateral Trade Agreements, such as TRIPS and GATT, that fall under the general umbrella of the WTO. But the GATT brought with it a rich tradition of law and practice that has flavoured and informed relative newcomers such as TRIPS. These two versions of GATT are more correctly termed GATT 1947 and GATT 1994.

The World Intellectual Property Organization (WIPO): the UN specialized agency and principal international organization responsible for intellectual property matters. Its roots reach back to the 1880s, with the establishment of separate bureaux to administer the 1883 Paris Convention for the Protection of Industrial Property, and the 1886 Berne Convention for the Protection of Literary and Artistic Works, the two conventions that still constitute the core instruments of international law on industrial property (patents, trademarks, designs, unfair competition) and on copyright respectively. The two bureaux combined in 1893 to form BIRPI (the French acronym for the United International Bureaux for the Protection of Intellectual Property). BIRPI was transformed into a distinct international organization in 1970 in the form of WIPO, which joined the United Nations system as a specialized agency in 1974. BIRPI, and then WIPO, presided over successive revisions of the Paris and Berne Conventions, and the negotiation of many more treaties dealing with substantive IP standards and administration of IP. Paris and Berne, especially, are incorporated directly within TRIPS, creating a powerful legal linkage between a century of legal evolution within the WIPO-BIRPI ambit and the international trade law epitomized by the Multilateral Trade Agreements of the WTO. The legal instruments and the practical work of WIPO overlap and interact with the WTO and the TRIPS Agreement especially, in many ways. A bilateral WIPO-WTO agreement was concluded in 1995 to further this cooperation.

References: This book is a brief introduction, not a work of legal scholarship. Legal and other references are kept to a minimum. For simplicity, the main treaties are termed 'TRIPS', 'GATT', 'Paris', and 'Berne', and articles within the treaties are cited in the form 'TRIPS:23.1', 'GATT: XX', 'Paris:10*bis*', etc.

Intellectual Property and Trade Law: Marriage of Convenience, or Shotgun Wedding?

The full extent of these outcomes was largely unforeseen in 1986 when the negotiations were launched; but their impact was sealed in 1994, when the Uruguay Round concluded in Marrakesh. Yet this three-way convergence—strong standards for protecting IP, a new international trade organization overseeing those standards, and a rigorous dispute settlement mechanism to deal with frustrated expectations—remains contentious for some critics even today. Some technical, legal issues are still unresolved—debates continue over the proper scope of those obligations, and what it means to comply with them. At the level of policy debate, some free trade theorists and anti-globalization activists seem to form an unlikely coalition in continuing to call for TRIPS to be taken out of the WTO system altogether. They see TRIPS as the product of a shotgun wedding between IP law and trade law, rather than a natural expression of policy convergence between these two areas of law. And debate simmers over what it means to set international standards on IP—TRIPS is purportedly about 'trade-related aspects' of IP: but IP has many other 'aspects' that are swept up by TRIPS—the law of investment, property law, consumer protection law, human rights law, cultural and educational policy, health, the environment and biodiversity, indigenous rights, bioethics, industry policies in sectors such as biotech and information technology—to name just a few of the most topical 'aspects' of IP. Was TRIPS to act as a kind of vector to introduce all these complex legal and political questions into the heart of trade law?

And if there were hopes that concluding TRIPS would reduce political contention over IP protection and articulate a broad consensus . . . well, at times the whole domain of international IP law and policy can seem more controversial and divisive than ever. Once-technical IP matters, then the province of a narrow band of specialists, are now caught up in an ever-widening range of international policy processes: seemingly intractable debates over human rights, biomedical innovation and access to medicines, cultural identity, food security, the environment and the equities surrounding exploitation of genetic resources, the rights of indigenous peoples, internet governance and internet freedoms. Early in its life,

TRIPS was rarely posited as the solution, or even part of a solution, to these intractable issues; more frequently, it was used in debate to symbolize or exemplify all that has gone wrong, or to stand in for the narrow interests of one 'side' in a debate or one industry sector. This state of affairs is evolving, as TRIPS develops a more natural place in the system. For instance, major diplomatic progress was made on the question of TRIPS and access to medicines, although concerns on this score have not fully abated.

Its negotiators did not necessarily see TRIPS as the final word: its original text established a 'built-in agenda' that required future reviews of such questions as geographical indications (is 'Parmesan' an exclusive geographical term or a generic description?; who decides for each country, and how, according to what criteria?); the scope of biotechnology patents (can you patent genes or genetically modified mammals?; how about flu viruses?); cooperation on enforcing intellectual property rights (how to deal with software piracy?), even defining the very legal basis for a dispute under TRIPS (can one country legitimately make a legal complaint that another is frustrating its reasonable expectations regarding IP protection?). Over 15 years after the ink dried on the Marrakesh deal, these questions remained unresolved on some crucial points, despite exhaustive set-piece debates that have lasted longer than the Uruguay Round itself.

On the other hand, at least one pressing issue was resolved with relative promptness—at least for a multilateral process. In 2001, as concern grew about the impact of TRIPS on that most fundamental of policy interests—human health—negotiators were able to establish a landmark Ministerial Declaration, leading to an historic agreement to amend TRIPS to give countries with limited resources greater leverage to secure effective access to medicines: the first, and so far the only, amendment to the hundreds of pages of multilateral trade agreements negotiated in the Uruguay Round. More generally, the introduction of IP into WTO dispute settlement has precipitated a remarkable development: an unprecedented level of precision and depth in legal analysis and legal findings on key issues that reach into the very heart of the delicate policy balances of international IP law—nothing short of the evolution of a richer international jurisprudence of IP.

Once TRIPS was concluded, the focus turned to implementation and compliance—getting domestic laws into line with its requirements. Most developing countries were expected to strengthen their existing laws and introduce new ones to comply with TRIPS by the year 2000. TRIPS therefore made its presence felt as a burdensome to-do list for domestic legislators in those countries, watched closely by foreign interests: for them, 'implementing TRIPS' was a major process of importing complex substantive standards into domestic legislation, drafting many new laws from scratch in unfamiliar areas of law, and creating new enforcement mechanisms

Table 1.1 A Selective Timeline of the Legal Evolution of 'Trade-Related' IP Law

International Intellectual Property Law	International Trade Law	'Trade-Related' Aspects of IP Law
		Bilateral commercial and trade deals throughout the 19th century include provisions on intellectual property, especially trademarks and geographical indications.
1883: signature of the original text of the 'Paris Convention for the Protection of Industrial Property' (subsequently revised or amended in 1900, 1911, 1925, 1934, 1958, 1967, and 1979).		
1886: signature of the original text of the 'Berne Convention for the Protection of Literary and Artistic Works' subsequently revised or amended in 1896, 1908, 1914, 1928, 1948, 1967, 1971, and 1979).		
1891: 'Madrid Agreement Concerning the International Registration of Marks' (revised or amended 1900, 1911, 1925, 1934, 1957, 1967 and 1979)		1891: 'Madrid Agreement for the Repression of False or Deceptive Indications of Source on Goods' (concluded under aegis of the 'Paris Convention'; revised in 1911, 1925, 1934, and 1958)
	1944: Bretton Woods Conference charts the course of post-war multilateral economic governance; envisages International Trade Organization (ITO)	
	1947: Geneva negotiations on charter for the ITO	
	1947: Protocol of Provisional Application of the GATT is signed to give interim effect to elements of the draft ITO Charter	

Table 1.1 *(cont.)*

International Intellectual Property Law	International Trade Law	'Trade-Related' Aspects of IP Law
	1948: Havana Conference concludes the ITO Charter	
	1947–1961: Rounds of tariff reduction negotiations under GATT: Geneva, Annecy, Torquay, Geneva, and Dillon Rounds	
1952: Universal Copyright Convention adopted as a less stringent alternative to 'Berne'		
1961: International Convention for the Protection of Performers, Producers of Phonograms and Broadcasting Organizations (Rome Convention)		
	1964–7: Kennedy Round turns to non-tariff barriers	
1970: 'Patent Cooperation Treaty' (amended or modified 1979, 1984, and 2001)		
	1973–79: Tokyo Round addresses non-tariff barriers	1979: EEC, Japan, US initiate work on anti-counterfeiting in GATT
		1982: draft Agreement on Measures to Discourage the Importation of Counterfeit Goods, circulated as GATT proposal
	1986: Punta del Este Declaration launches Uruguay Round negotiations	1986: Uruguay Round mandate incorporates the first GATT negotiating agenda on IP.
1989: Treaty on Intellectual Property in Respect of Integrated Circuits (Washington Treaty) signed (never enters into force)		

International Intellectual Property Law	International Trade Law	'Trade-Related' Aspects of IP Law
1989: Protocol Relating to the Madrid Agreement Concerning the International Registration of Marks (amended 2006 and 2007)		
		1991: Essential features of TRIPS Agreement largely concluded
1994: WIPO Trademark Law Treaty	1994: Marrakesh Conference signs Final Act of the Uruguay Round	
	1995: Agreement Establishing the WTO and annexed Multilateral Trade Agreements come into effect	1995: TRIPS enters in force
1996: WIPO concludes two 'Internet Treaties': WIPO Copyright Treaty and WIPO Performances and Phonograms Treaty (relevant provisions declared to be 'on par' or consistent with TRIPS)		1996: Majority of TRIPS obligations begin to apply for developed economies
		1996: WIPO and WTO conclude cooperation agreement
		1997: First WTO panel and Appellate Body interpretations of TRIPS obligations
		1997: TRIPS Council begins work on 'built in agenda' on geographical indications
		1998: TRIPS Council begins work on 'built in agenda' on biotechnology and related questions
	1998: Singapore Ministerial: Declaration on Electronic Commerce	
2000: WIPO Patent Law Treaty		2000: The majority of TRIPS obligations begin to apply for developing countries
		2000: Bilateral and regional trade agreements increasingly incorporate IP standards

Table 1.1 (*cont.*)

International Intellectual Property Law	International Trade Law	'Trade-Related' Aspects of IP Law
	2001: Doha Ministerial launches Doha Development Round trade negotiations	2001: Doha Declaration on TRIPS and Public Health
		2002: TRIPS Council Special Sessions commence (negotiating on multilateral GI register)
		2003: Agreement on TRIPS waiver on public health
		2005: Agreement on amendment to TRIPS for public health
2006: Singapore Treaty on the Law of Trademarks		

to make their national systems comply with the letter of the agreement. And there were differences about TRIPS between developed economies, despite the pragmatic alliance and convergence of interests that led them to push for its successful inclusion in the Uruguay Round package—even today, the majority of WTO disputes concerning TRIPS are between developed economies, not the predominantly trend of North versus South that many had earlier expected.

So, on this superficial view, to a sceptical eye, it would seem that TRIPS has sown discord and generated more controversy than it has resolved, and created a heavy burden of compliance that provides little benefit to developing countries; perhaps inclining an observer to sympathize with the calls, still heard, to wind back or even revoke TRIPS. This short book begs to differ absolutely with this view, while respecting the concerns that drive much of the debate about TRIPS. To start with, TRIPS has evolved into a much more interesting and more enabling policy instrument than many early critics expected, and can serve as a guide to fair and balanced public policy, as well as a defence against the excessive influence of sectoral interests and specific actors over domestic policymaking. And developing country negotiators ensured that the text of TRIPS sets an exacting, and in principle very encouraging, rationale and discipline for the protection and enforcement of IP rights: Article 7 of TRIPS stipulates that IP protection should,

contribute to the promotion of technological innovation and to the transfer and dissemination of technology, to the mutual advantage of producers and users of technological knowledge and in a manner conducive to social and economic welfare, and to a balance of rights and obligations.

While this important text essentially captured centuries of past legislative evolution at the national level, never before had the public policy role of IP protection been set out so authoritatively in a major international treaty. By one reading, 'TRIPS implementation' means attaining these ambitious public interest goals through sound policymaking, not simply legislating to achieve passive, formal compliance with the letter of law.

But none of this is new. To the contrary, there is now a massive literature on the law, politics and economics of TRIPS, much of it either critical or revisionist in spirit. Its negotiating history is amply documented, many have analysed and explained how it is or how it should be interpreted and applied, many have offered proposals for revising it and revising the revisions to it, strategies are adumbrated to containing its injurious effects, claims are put forward for TRIPS to be trumped or superseded by preferred international norms and standards. So why add to this copious literature? We should be clear about what this book is not. It is not a comprehensive or authoritative interpretation of TRIPS as a legal text, and it would be a mistake to read it as such. Several leading authors have prepared detailed analyses and interpretative guides to TRIPS, each of them a significant scholar and practitioner, each providing generous illumination, perhaps especially on the points on which they differ. This book does not take a political stance, nor seek to advocate a substantive position: it seeks neither to praise TRIPS nor to bury it. Many diverse polemical views are readily available on the worth, impact and legitimacy of TRIPS, and many more continue to press forward in a generous secondary literature.

This book has a more modest goal. It aims to convey in a practical sense what it is to work with TRIPS, with the text of the treaty as it is and in its actual, functional context. The genesis of TRIPS was a pragmatic initiative, not an idealistic crusade. The major economies had reassessed their economic and trade interests, saw IP protection in foreign markets as critical to those interests, and therefore insisted that their pragmatic need for more effective IP protection be integral to any multilateral trade deal. Developing countries were not won over at the level of principle: many accepted the deal only reluctantly, cautioning against legal harassment upon the conclusion of the treaty, but negotiated hard for the text to include safeguards of *their* interests. Ultimately, TRIPS was accepted as a realist response by one set of negotiators to the realist assertion of pragmatic interests by another set. That same pragmatic spirit infuses the present account of TRIPS: much of the TRIPS literature lacks a truly practical sense of how to pursue defined, legitimate interests within the legal space defined by TRIPS. Perhaps disappointingly from a theoretical or idealistic point of view, trade law is a pragmatic art rather than the abstract dispensation of justice; and if it is to function as a genuine global public good, the first requirement for an international law of IP and trade (IP *in* trade, or IP *as* trade) is to provide a transparent, trusted, and predictable means for managing the inevitable conflicts over IP protection that will arise between trading partners—above all, containing the impact of disputes, so that they do not escalate beyond their proper bounds, and providing robust guarantees against unwarranted intrusions on legitimate domestic policymaking.

TRIPS is an agreement firstly that how national systems protect IP is a legitimate concern in trading relations, and secondly that disagreements between trading partners over IP protection should be resolved according to ostensibly objective and balanced international standards. This means that TRIPS has become a central part of the working environment of many practitioners and policymakers in many fields, including many who are new to IP law and trade law, and many who are sceptical of the current IP system that TRIPS is felt to embody, and are concerned about its impact. But whatever one's political or theoretical preferences, TRIPS is unavoidably *there*, and has to be worked with across a range of fields of public policy. This book therefore explores what it means to work *with* TRIPS, to deal with TRIPS as a practical element of policymaking, legislation, administration, and advocacy. It is not a guide to achieving formal legal compliance as an end in itself—working *for* TRIPS; nor is it a guide to getting around the requirements of TRIPS—working *in spite of* or *against* TRIPS. Much of the art of working *with* TRIPS is to understand the interplay between the international legal standards and national IP laws and their administration. This book therefore explores how good public policy, driven by legitimate domestic interests, need not be in tension with formal compliance with TRIPS standards; it develops the surprising observation that a positive feedback loop can and arguably *should* be established between treaty compliance and good domestic policy. This approach is founded on the following assumptions, which readers may contest or deride—or simply dismiss as naïve or eccentric—but which do at least have the virtue of drawing directly on practical experience.

TRIPS is not a template for legislators, nor a model law

TRIPS is an international agreement between trading partners on what they can legitimately expect of one another as far as IP protection is concerned, and on the actions they can and cannot take when those expectations, inevitably, are significantly frustrated. It is not a model IP law, and for the most part, its text is ill suited to be converted directly into domestic legislation or treated as draft legislation to be directly adapted into domestic law. Apart from legal obligations to comply with TRIPS, it is prudent, and good policy, for domestic policymakers to respect TRIPS standards when passing or revising IP laws, but the essential focus of the legislative process should remain centred on direct national interests and balanced public policymaking rather than simply importing the substantive standards of TRIPS.

'Implementing TRIPS' is more than a legislative exercise

'Implementing TRIPS' has conventionally been viewed as a process of passing or revising domestic laws so as to comply with TRIPS, an essentially passive approach of importing externally determined standards. That made sense in the first years of TRIPS, as many countries scrambled to meet implementation deadlines. But there are richer, more enabling conceptions of implementing TRIPS, which are suited to a more mature phase of its life as an international treaty. In many countries, IP laws are regularly revised and updated through progressive reform as the economic, social, and technological context of IP lawmaking evolves, and court decisions also dramatically shape the practical effect and scope of general principles espoused in IP legislation. Many developing countries first concentrated on doing what was necessary to bring their laws into formal compliance with TRIPS, but have since turned to a second phase of 'TRIPS implementation' which entails tailoring and reforming those laws to adapt them more directly to domestic policy interests within the broad principles and legitimate policy space provided by TRIPS. This is not to flout or to challenge the legitimacy of TRIPS, but represents a more natural and sustainable form of implementing its standards and realizing its implicit and explicit promise that balanced IP protection will yield positive domestic benefits, and not merely benefit foreign nationals (although this is not a zero-sum matter, in any case, as this book will stress). Formulating IP legislation that equally serves domestic policy interests and respects international standards has, after all, been the practice of developed countries for well over a century. The Berne Convention on copyright was first concluded in 1886 and has continued to influence copyright protection in many countries since then—the bulk of TRIPS standards on copyright come straight from Berne, for instance; but passing or revising a copyright law is not simply 'Berne implementation'—it is an act of domestic policymaking guided by the international context and respectful of international obligations.

'TRIPS compliance' means managing trade relations, not avoiding parking tickets

Similarly the idea of 'TRIPS compliance' develops different shades of meaning with the maturing of the regime. Compliance with WTO standards is not like policing a parking lot, where an enforcement officer will issue a ticket and impose a penalty for non-compliance—or a speed camera that will routinely issue a penalty for any infringement. Non-compliance with TRIPS does not bring automatic penalties, and normally does not even yield a formal finding of non-compliance. The only way of reaching an official determination of non-compliance is if another country is concerned about IP protection to the extent that they are prepared to initiate a legal complaint and follow it right through to its conclusion. This happens only rarely. The WTO has 153 members, comprising the bulk of the global economy, and TRIPS sets rigorous standards for an unprecedented range of categories of IP law, as well as their administration and enforcement. Yet between 1995 and 2009 there were only eight distinct findings of non-compliance with TRIPS; all but two (one each on India and China) concerned developed countries.

On the whole WTO Members do seek to comply with TRIPS standards in good faith, and it is both good policy and a formal legal undertaking to do so. But lacunae, grey areas and areas of uncertainty, inevitably continue. Some of these shortcomings or uncertain areas are highly publicized and debated, such as when public health is concerned; others are relatively technical or do not engage major trade interests and are therefore less remarked (such as when a developing country experiences delays in passing a law protecting integrated circuit layouts). Many countries have reported to official WTO bodies that they are still at work preparing or revising necessary legislation, after the formal deadline to do so. Transparency about national laws and legislative processes is in itself an additional form of TRIPS compliance.

Another form of 'TRIPS compliance' is the legal undertaking to use the WTO's multilateral dispute settlement procedures to resolve differences over IP protection, and thus to keep disputes within their proper bounds, testing disagreements against an objective and transparent measure of legitimacy. Differences will inevitably arise with trading partners on the adequacy of one another's IP protection. TRIPS compliance from this perspective means recognizing that TRIPS, within the WTO system, offers a means not only of adjudicating disputes but also in containing the fallout from disputes. Complying with TRIPS therefore means adhering to the multilateral framework to deal with disputes, and using this system to limit the negative impact of disputation by setting a clear ceiling to any retaliation, sanctions or claims for compensation. Unbounded trade disputation can fuel political tensions and create immense economic damage beyond the original scope of any one dispute. This idea of compliance with the WTO legal system is potentially just as significant as questions of legal compliance with specific TRIPS standards. In the exceptional event that a country loses a case and fails to bring its laws into line with TRIPS, the WTO system means that the negative fallout can be kept in proportion and trade retaliation is objective, fair, transparent, and commensurate with the damage caused.

In IP policy terms, it is still a more interesting form of 'TRIPS compliance' to undertake domestic legislation and policymaking as a good faith endeavour to carry out the principles and objectives of TRIPS. Put another way, a strong defence against the complaints of foreign trading partners concerning IP protection is the good faith, transparent and nondiscriminatory domestic policymaking that seeks to achieve the positive, systematic outcomes from IP protection that the text of TRIPS itself articulates. Balanced, fair and effective IP lawmaking is, in a way, a kind of practical interpretation of TRIPS as a treaty.

Good domestic policymaking can be a useful—if informal—guide to TRIPS interpretation

TRIPS now influences the formulation of IP legislation across the globe—both in the countries that are already members of the WTO, and in the countries seeking to join; TRIPS is now the principal yardstick for international legitimacy of national IP laws and systems. But the standards of TRIPS are for the most part very general in character, while national laws are typically more detailed, focussed, and complex. So to assess whether a domestic law is 'compliant' with TRIPS requires more than interpreting and clarifying TRIPS standards: as the AB observed in the first major case on TRIPS, *India – Pharmaceutical Patents*, it is necessary to examine the laws themselves; otherwise, only the country concerned could assess whether its own laws met its obligations to other countries under TRIPS. As the AB pithily commented, 'this, clearly, cannot be so'. But TRIPS was not negotiated in the abstract: the standards it sets out for IP protection are them-selves drawn for the most part from national laws and legal procedures, a kind of distillation of the accumulated experience of legal development in national systems, principally Europe and North America, laws that were shaped through centuries' attempts to find dynamic policy balances in important areas of public policy. So to interpret the standards of TRIPS will—explicitly or implicitly—entail looking back through the experience of national legislative development, a kind of accumulated understanding as to what amounts to good policy settings and equitable procedures. But TRIPS cannot be interpreted by simply referring to those very laws that it is meant to serve as a benchmark for—otherwise interpreta-tion would be an entirely circular affair, and there would be no objective basis for dispute settlement between two countries. This apparent paradox arises especially when looking at terms such as 'reasonable'—TRIPS uses such terms when setting international standards; but it is hard to understand those standards in practice without looking at what has been done at the domestic level; and yet these terms need to be interpreted objectively so as to assess whether a country's laws comply with them or not.

To complicate matters, TRIPS is a complex blend of legal systems—different traditions of domestic IP law, the separate evolution of international IP law over more than a century, the law of international trade and dispute settlement, and broader public international law. An absorbing scholarly debate continues over the correct methodology for interpretation: how to read the text of TRIPS, and how much latitude it leaves, or should leave, for national laws. At one level, interpreting the text of TRIPS is a fascinating exercise in legal theory; often, debates over interpretation are tinged by political, ideological or pragmatic considerations. Specialist lawyers and writers continue to debate the scope of key provisions of TRIPS, and the degree of latitude that countries have, or should have. And the only legally significant or binding form of interpretation is that which is conducted by a dispute settlement panel or the AB; the WTO members can collectively agree on an authoritative interpretation of TRIPS, although this has never been done. But, aside from both scholarly debate and dispute settlement, one important practical act of 'TRIPS interpretation' is the very drafting of a law or regulation that is intended to comply with TRIPS. Formal legal compliance with TRIPS is not, of course, the end of the story—it is meant to deliver practical benefits in the real world. Except in an abstract sense, IP is not directly 'protected' by TRIPS. IP is protected by national laws that give effect in diverse ways to the standards of TRIPS. Delivering on the intended public welfare benefits of TRIPS therefore occurs most immediately at the level of national law. This means that the balance of rights and obligations that TRIPS calls for can ultimately only be attained through the grant, administration, and enforcement of IP at the national level.

In the most general terms, to interpret TRIPS means clarifying in practice the very general rules about what kind of material should be protected as IP; rules about what kinds of limitations and exceptions to protection are legitimate; and rules about how IP should be administered and enforced. Ultimately, these ideas can only be worked out with reference to the existing body of practical experience— what makes a work sufficiently 'original' to merit copyright protection; what is the nature of 'legitimate interests' of IP that exceptions should not 'unreasonably prejudice'; what kind of administrative burden for right holders is excessive or discriminatory—such questions cannot be answered purely in the abstract, but in some way or other, directly or indirectly, will be guided by lessons of accumulated practice over time. This means that national IP laws are in themselves a kind of interpretation of TRIPS standards. Putting it another way, if, as TRIPS says, IP protection should produce 'social and economic welfare' and 'a balance of rights and obligations', then to find the answer of how this can be delivered, one cannot delve endlessly into the text of TRIPS itself—one has to look at the operation of national IP laws, and how they are exercised and administered. Therefore, the most compelling form of 'interpreting' TRIPS is to pass and administer laws that are formally compliant with TRIPS but also illustrate clearly how its general principles and standards can be brought into practice, and how the expected balance of interests and welfare outcomes can be delivered in the real world. The domestic legislator and administrator has to be seen as an active participant within the interpretative community that determines the practical impact of TRIPS implementation—not as a separate, passive recipient of externally determined outcomes. In the longer term, the most important form of 'TRIPS interpretation' is not the detailed legal analysis that trade lawyers undertake when resolving a dispute. It is the 'TRIPS interpretation' that policymakers and legislators undertake when seeking to shape workable, effective and fair systems of IP protection that produce the public goods that are expected of them, while also complying formally with TRIPS standards—more than abstract legal analysis, this work adds to the pool of common wisdom that helps guide the evolution of legal standards and ultimately shapes their interpretative context.

Domestic Lawmaking as TRIPS Interpretation

The idea that national policymakers are interpreters of TRIPS, and not merely passively complying with its obligations, is a challenging idea, but one that goes to the heart of grasping what it means to work practically with TRIPS. Whatever formal legal construction is made of the treaty language of TRIPS, on many key issues there will inevitably be some informal feedback from national laws and the choices made at the domestic level.

TRIPS is part of a complex body of international law, the law that governs relations between states. TRIPS defines standards that define what trading partners can legitimately expect of one another as to how IP is protected. But the protection itself effectively takes place at the level of national law: TRIPS itself says WTO Members 'shall give effect to the provisions of this Agreement.' And it explicitly provides that they 'shall be free to determine the appropriate method of implementing the provisions of [TRIPS] within their own legal system and practice.' So domestic law and institutions—laws, regulations, IP offices, courts—give effect to the standards and principles of TRIPS; it is ultimately up to them to deliver on the objective that IP protection should produce public benefits and a balance of rights and obligations. This means that assessing a country's compliance with TRIPS mostly involves looking at national laws and how they are implemented within that country. But this also means that when you try to interpret the standards and principles of TRIPS, you are inevitably

(*cont.*)

influenced or guided by experience and legal traditions at the national level. It can sound paradoxical, or logically circular: to clarify and inform what TRIPS obliges countries to do, we need to look at what countries have actually done. Consider, for instance, the following questions that are central to interpreting key TRIPS standards:

- What is an 'invention' (the essential concept of patent law); what makes it new, inventive or useful?
- When is remuneration 'equitable' or 'adequate' when third parties are authorized to use protected IP?
- When does prejudice to a right holder's legitimate interests become 'unreasonable'?
- What is the 'normal exploitation' of a protected work?
- When are 'procedures and formalities' for obtaining IP 'reasonable'?
- When is a competitor's use of valuable data 'unfair commercial use'?
- When is use of a a descriptive term 'fair' in the context of trademark rights?
- What qualities make a design 'new or original'?
- What are 'reasonable commercial terms and conditions' for the grant of a voluntary licence under a patent?

These concepts grew out of legal evolution mostly at the national level and were later codified in TRIPS. It is therefore difficult for anyone reading the text of TRIPS to shut out the accumulated experience at the national level that has shaped these concepts. Yet TRIPS is a distinct layer of international law created to adjudicate disputes between countries as to the adequacy of their laws' protection of IP. It would be pointless to assert that any exception to IP rights is 'reasonable' simply because one country's courts have allowed it; or to argue that a definition of a patentable 'invention' is consistent with TRIPS purely because it is present in one country's patent law. There would be no objective international basis to settle disputes on these central questions. Yet it would be unrealistic to interpret these concepts in total isolation, without at least seeking informal guidance from practical experience.

This apparent paradox can be resolved by looking at the practice of lawmaking and international dispute settlement. National laws are of central importance in giving real, practical effect to the objectives of IP protection as espoused by TRIPS. Domestic legislators and policymakers form a vast, informal interpretative community, clustered around core international standards, accountable to and informed by one another as they seek to ensure that national IP laws both advance their intended policy objectives and meet the legitimate expectations of trading partners. We will see, in looking at TRIPS law, how dispute settlement panels have undertaken objective textual analysis of key TRIPS standards, while at the same time cross-referencing or confirming their readings against actual national experience. They have also surveyed national approaches when seeking to determine whether a particular issue is a legal one, to be settled under TRIPS, or is a matter of policy, yet to be resolved between WTO members.

The following pages will explore what these seemingly abstract concepts mean in practice for those who wrestle with the challenge of bridging between two goals:

- ensuring sound, welfare-enhancing domestic policy settings, to meet the objectives articulated by TRIPS and the public benefits it indicates should flow from IP protection, and
- meeting the treaty-backed and potentially legally-enforced expectations of and obligations to trading partners, as essentially defined by TRIPS.

This book explores one central idea, with strong practical consequences: these two goals need not be in fundamental tension with one another; to the contrary, a good faith effort to attain one of these goals is more likely than not to serve as a sustainable way of meeting the other goal. We cannot dismiss the possibility, or even the reality, of eventual tension or conflict between the two goals, and pragmatic policymakers need to assess the costs and benefits of strategies for dealing with any such conflict. But to presume that there is fundamental or inherent tension between the two may be a self-fulfilling and self-defeating prediction that in itself becomes a barrier to beneficial policy outcomes, and may obscure TRIPS-compliant options that are effective in advancing the public benefit. The book takes this idea further: developments in technology, patterns of trade, and perceived economic interests, make the interaction between IP law and trade law inevitable, and create an objective need for a systematic reconciliation between the two. Even if TRIPS itself was the result of a distinct negotiating process, nonetheless a balanced, policy-rich approach to IP has a natural place within the law governing countries' trade relations.

An essential ingredient for this outcome is clarity, and confidence, in the reading of TRIPS as a legal text—what in this book is termed a 'practical jurisprudence'. Clarity of the scope of legal obligations is key to freedom of action for the policy-maker. To see how this can matter, consider the field of public health. 2001 saw the most significant development under TRIPS since the Uruguay Round concluded.

Trade ministers met in Doha to launch the next round of trade negotiations—the Doha Round. But they also issued a stand-alone Ministerial Declaration on TRIPS and Public Health which responded to growing public concern about the impact of TRIPS on access to medicines—public health being the kind of public policy objective that the IP system is expected not only to avoid obstructing, but should actively promote. The Doha Declaration served a fascinating function: it brought the political understanding of TRIPS into line with its actual legal scope, so as to clarify the flexibilities that policymakers had available; it linked the interpretation of TRIPS as a legal instrument with positive opportunities to pursue policies that aim to serve public health. It was at once a political declaration that gave guidance on how TRIPS should be interpreted as a legal text and articulated the flexibilities open to countries at the national level. Under Doha, legal clarity, precision on treaty interpretation, and making explicit what had been legally implicit, all came together to open up positive opportunities for sound domestic policy as well as for more settled trading relationships.

Public health is, understandably, a pressing public priority, and has dominated debate about TRIPS in the near-decade since Doha. But the same general approach—finding a clear and coherent place for IP in the trade law system—applies to many policy areas that TRIPS touches upon: whether they concern broad policy interests such as education and cultural exchange, or particular sectors of development interest such as textiles, indigenous knowledge systems or information technology. This book aims to promote consideration of what it means in practice to pursue national interests in this way by briefly sketching out ways of formulating a systematic understanding of the law and practice of TRIPS, an idea of TRIPS that can be put to work for practical ends.

Outline of TRIPS Disputes

A highly distinctive feature of TRIPS law and practice is the formal dispute settlement process of the WTO. This system subjects the main legal texts of international IP law to far closer scrutiny than ever before, producing case law or 'jurisprudence' of unprecedented detail and precision in the international IP law. This book will discuss a number of these disputes. For ease of reference, Table 1.2 lists all TRIPS-related cases raised under the WTO dispute settlement system. In some, TRIPS was only one aspect of a wider complaint, and the non-TRIPS issues are not mentioned (one dispute, DS152, did not directly concern TRIPS compliance, but rather addressed one Member's national measures for monitoring and enforcing TRIPS obligations in other Members). See the key below for more details.

Table 1.2 Outline of TRIPS Disputes

Full title (*short title*)	Member initiating case ('complainant')	WTO dispute number	Outcome	TRIPS/WTO non-compliance?	Intellectual property issues
Argentina—Certain Measures on the Protection of Patents and Test Data	United States	DS196	MAS	-	Protection against unfair commercial use of test data submitted for regulatory use; scope of biotechnology patents; provisional court orders for infringement and the burden of proof for infringement of process patents; patent rights over products produced by patented processes and imports; safeguards for compulsory licences; transitional patents.
Argentina—Patent Protection for Pharmaceuticals and Test Data Protection for Agricultural Chemicals	United States	DS171	MAS	-	Patent protection or exclusive marketing rights for pharmaceutical products; protection of test data during transition period for TRIPS implementation.
Brazil—Patent Protection	United States	DS199	MAS	-	'Local working' requirements for patents, and possibility of compulsory licensing if not produced locally.
Canada—Patent Term	United States	DS170	AB	Yes	Term of patents already in force when TRIPS comes into effect.
Canada—Pharmaceutical Patents	European Communities	DS114	Panel	Yes	Exceptions and limitations to rights under a patent; discrimination between fields of technology in patent system.

Table 1.2 (*cont.*)

Full title (*short title*)	Member initiating case ('complainant')	WTO dispute number	Outcome	TRIPS/WTO non-compliance?	Intellectual property issues
China—Measures Affecting Financial Information Services and Foreign Financial Information Suppliers	European Communities	DS372	MAS	-	Whether measures affecting foreign suppliers of financial information enabled suppliers to protect secret and commercially valuable information lawfully within their control.
China—*Measures Affecting the Protection and Enforcement of Intellectual Property Rights*	United States	DS362	Panel	Yes	Thresholds for trademark counterfeiting and copyright piracy to be subject to criminal procedures and penalties; disposal of infringing goods confiscated by customs authorities; criminal procedures and penalties for unauthorized reproduction or unauthorized distribution of copyrighted works; and copyright protection and enforcement for material not authorized for publication or distribution within China.
Denmark—Measures Affecting the Enforcement of Intellectual Property Rights	United States	DS83	MAS	-	Availability of provisional measures available in civil infringement proceedings.
European Communities— Trademarks and Geographical Indications (Australia)	Australia	DS290	Panel	Yes	National treatment in the protection of geographical indications, and the relationship of geographical indication protection with pre-existing trademarks.

Case	Respondent	DS	Status		Measure
European Union and a Member State—Seizure of Generic Drugs in Transit (Brazil)	Brazil	DS409	-	-	Seizure of generic drugs while in transit in the EU, covered by patent rights in the EU but not in original country or final destination.
European Union and a Member State—Seizure of Generic Drugs in Transit (India)	India	DS408	-	-	-
European Communities—Trademarks and Geographical Indications (US)	United States	DS174	Panel	Yes	National treatment in the protection of geographical indications, and the relationship of geographical indication protection with pre-existing trademarks.
European Communities—Enforcement of Intellectual Property Rights for Motion Pictures and Television Programs	United States	DS124	MAS	-	Enforcement of copyright over TV broadcasts of motion pictures and television programmes.
European Communities—Measures Affecting the Grant of Copyright and Neighbouring Rights	United States	DS115	MAS	-	Same measure as DS82 (respondent Ireland).

Table 1.2 (*cont.*)

Full title (*short title*)	Member initiating case ('complainant')	WTO dispute number	Outcome	TRIPS/WTO non-compliance?	Intellectual property issues
European Communities—Patent Protection for Pharmaceutical and Agricultural Chemical Products	Canada	DS153	-	-	Discrimination as to field of technology in patent term extensions.
Greece—Enforcement of Intellectual Property Rights for Motion Pictures and Television Programs	United States	DS125	MAS	-	Same measure as DS124 (respondent EC).
India—*Patents* (*US*)	United States	DS50	AB	Yes	Provisional arrangements pending the introduction of patents on pharmaceutical products ('mailbox' case).
India—*Patents* (*EC*)	European Communities	DS79	Panel	Yes	Provisional arrangements pending the introduction of patents on pharmaceutical products.
Indonesia—Autos	United States	DS59	Panel	No	Whether benefits for motor vehicles bearing a unique Indonesian trademark owned by Indonesian nationals discriminates against national treatment principle vis-à-vis foreign-owned trademarks and their owners.

Case	Complainant	DS No.	Status	Description
Ireland—Measures Affecting the Grant of Copyright and Neighbouring Rights	United States	DS82	MAS	Copyright protection of translations of official works, architectural works, and anonymous and pseudonymous works; ownership of rights in film, and recognition of bodies established to protect the rights of unknown authors of unpublished works; limitations and exceptions to copyright; rental rights for phonograms; unauthorized recording of performances; criminal procedures and penalties for copyright piracy on a commercial scale; protection of pre-existing material.
Japan—Measures Concerning Sound Recordings	United States	DS28	MAS	Protection of past performances and existing sound recordings.
Japan—Measures Concerning Sound Recordings	European Communities	DS42	MAS	Protection of sound recordings (as for DS28).
Pakistan—Patent Protection for Pharmaceutical and Agricultural Chemical Products	United States	DS36	MAS	Patent protection for pharmaceutical and agricultural chemical products and exclusive marketing rights in such products.

Table 1.2 (*cont.*)

Full title (*short title*)	Member initiating case ('complainant')	WTO dispute number	Outcome	TRIPS/WTO non-compliance?	Intellectual property issues
Portugal—Patent Protection under the Industrial Property Act	United States	DS37	MAS	-	Patent terms to be at least 20 years.
Sweden—Measures Affecting the Enforcement of Intellectual Property Rights	United States	DS86	MAS	-	Provisional measures *inaudita altera parte* in civil proceedings to secure evidence of infringement of IP rights.
United States—*Section 110(5) Copyright Act*	European Communities	DS160	Panel	yes	Exceptions and limitations to copyright and related rights.
United States—*Section 211 Appropriations Act* (also *Havana Club*)	European Communities	DS176	AB	yes	National treatment in the enjoyment of trademark rights; ownership entitlements on IP.
US—Section 301 Trade Act	European Communities	DS152	Panel	na	Use of multilateral dispute settlement system to determine violation of trade obligations and to authorize retaliatory measures.
United States—Section 337 of the Tariff Act of 1930 and Amendments thereto	European Communities	DS186	-	-	National treatment and non-discrimination in the enforcement of IP rights.
United States—US Patents Code	Brazil	DS224	-	-	Patent rights on inventions made with federal assistance.

Key:

Title: The title of a case identifies the Member whose measure is at issue in the dispute (the 'respondent'), as well as the measure itself. Cases that proceed to the panel phase are given a short title for convenience. Only short titles are given here, when available, in italics.

Complainant: The WTO Member initiating the complaint.

WTO Dispute Number: Each dispute is given a unique serial number, in order of the original complaint being lodged with the DSB. This can be used to obtain all documents concerning the dispute from the official document portal: <http://www.wto.org/english/docs_e/docs_e.htm> accessed 26 October 2010.

Outcome: Disputes may be resolved through a mutually agreed solution ('MAS'), a finding by a dispute settlement panel specially composed to consider the matter ('Panel'), or an appeal from a panel finding on points of law to the Appellate Body ('AB'). Other cases may be effectively suspended before moving to the Panel phase.

TRIPS/WTO non-compliance: did the Panel or AB conclude that a measure was non-compliant with WTO obligations regarding TRIPS? 'Yes' in this column normally means non-compliance in one or several aspects, but not *all* the elements of the original complaint. In other cases, non-compliance with other WTO obligations was found, and is not covered here.

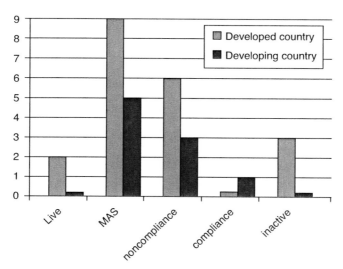

Figure 1.1 Outcomes of TRIPS Disputes: Comparison of Complaints against Developed and Developing WTO Members (as at November 2010)

TRIPS can also be invoked in dispute settlement regarding WTO obligations in other sectors. When a Member is found not to comply with a recommendation to bring its laws into compliance with WTO obligations in other areas, the complaining Member can, in certain circumstances, seek approval to withdraw TRIPS obligations as a form of retaliation to induce compliance with WTO obligations. Members have requested such 'cross-retaliation' under TRIPS in three cases as set out in Table 1.3:

Table 1.3 Disputes Involving 'Cross-Retaliation'

Dispute	Complainant	WTO dispute number	Field of trade
US—Gambling	Antigua and Barbuda	DS285	Cross-border supply of gambling and betting services.
EC—Bananas III (Ecuador)	Ecuador	DS86	Access to market for agricultural products.
US—Upland Cotton	Brazil	DS267	Subsidies on upland cotton.

2

TRIPS Law and TRIPS Politics: Legal Clarity and Policy Flexibility

The absence of adequate protection in the case of intellectual property has led to considerable distortions in trade in certain sectors. The GATT can and must act in parallel with other institutions in framing principles and rules relating to the trade aspects of intellectual property. Our aim in this area . . . must be to create a favourable, dynamic climate which will give a fresh boost to the world economy.

Willy De Clercq, Member of the European Commission,
Punta del Este, 1986

Among the new obligations which we consider as a major concession is the agreement on intellectual property. In order for us to implement the agreement fully, we require technical assistance from our developed trading partners. As we make our adjustment, what we need most is technical cooperation and not legal harassment.

S.B. Joedono, Trade Minister of Indonesia, Marrakech 1994

Intellectual property does not belong in the WTO, since protecting it is simply a matter of royalty collection . . . The matter was forced onto the WTO's agenda during the Uruguay Round by the pharmaceutical and software industries, even though this risked turning the WTO into a glorified collection agency.

Jaghdish Bhagwati, 'From Seattle to Hong Kong,' Foreign Affairs (2005)

TRIPS in the Spotlight

TRIPS is the best known of all international treaties on IP, and certainly the most controversial. For some critics, TRIPS was seen, perhaps inevitably but inaccurately, to symbolize a whole philosophy of how knowledge should be managed—privatization of knowledge, encroachments on the public domain, setting corporate profits and private rights ahead of public welfare. And a vigorous debate continues over legal, political, and economic issues raised by TRIPS, as well as its relationship with human rights and development. But TRIPS is also part of the practical working environment for many who deal with IP law and policy. Such 'TRIPS practitioners' form a diverse group, in contrast to earlier generations of specialists in IP law—they include trade and IP lawyers, economic analysts, legislators, trade negotiators, government officials in numerous policy fields, lobbyists and advocates, and civil society organizations concerned with a host of current issues from the digital divide to public health. It seems everyone has a view about TRIPS, what it does, and what it should and should not do; and these views are as diverse as the practitioners who hold them.

TRIPS was not negotiated as an end in itself but as a means of bringing greater order, transparency, predictability and even fairness to the way governments do business with each other in progressing their interests on IP, especially when those interests are felt to diverge and these differences sharpen to the point of disputation. For this mechanism to work in practice means taking a calm, realist, objective view of TRIPS, and detaching it as a legal instrument from the values, preconceptions, and political agendas that various actors associate with it. It means looking for bedrock principles and legal common ground amidst the tremendous diversity of views that TRIPS has aroused.

TRIPS has had unprecedented impact on the IP laws of many nations, and the prospect of dispute settlement can magnify its influence—one conventional view is that 'trade sanctions' are what sets TRIPS apart from the century-old tradition of international IP law it grew out of. But TRIPS is not the oppressive monolith and rigid set of punitive standards that early critics feared it was; to some extent its true legal character and scope are still up for grabs, and is in the hands of practitioners of TRIPS law (some of whom are unaware that they *are* 'TRIPS practitioners').

TRIPS still raises unresolved foundational questions about what it means to incorporate IP standards into trade law. It is unwise to be too certain, too early, about the true nature and exact legal scope of TRIPS obligations. TRIPS is a hybrid legal text set within a complex legal setting, with unexpected implications that are only now being fully understood. Whether familiarity breeds contempt is one matter; but contempt rarely breeds familiarity. And effective use of TRIPS—using it, practically and effectively, to advance and defend legitimate interests—does require familiarity with its provisions and maintaining a confident measure of its actual legal effect.

Intellectual Property and Trade Law: A Shotgun Wedding?

TRIPS is often first known for the controversy surrounding it: anti-globalization activists and free trade theorists, normally poles apart, unite to condemn it; for those who contest the legitimacy of the WTO and the justice of the modern IP system, it is almost a perfect storm, combining the supposed power of the WTO to impose sanctions with intrusive rules that reach well behind the border into areas of public policy (health, food, the environment, education) normally thought to be the sovereign domain of domestic regulators—seemingly the very opposite of the 'free trade' ethos that the WTO is thought to embody. For some, therefore, TRIPS is the black sheep of the WTO flock—the genetically modified organism, perhaps, a transgenic hybrid of trade law and the law of IP.

But TRIPS has garnered more political credibility and legal coherence as trade law—and has taken on a more diverse and interesting role—as its real legal function is better understood. As a trade weapon, it can be used as much as a shield as a sword—it is used to defend domestic policy choices as much as to impose outcomes on others, and it is used by developing countries to leverage access to markets in the major developed economies. Its curiously unsettled nature—the unfamiliarity of IP standards implanted within the trade law system—perhaps fairly reflects the uncertainties for the trade law system that are posed by contemporary economic trends. The establishment of TRIPS coincided with changes in ways of doing business that made it possible to trade purely in the content of knowledge and cultural works: what Negroponte called an economy of 'bits' and not 'atoms', an 'economy of verbs'; what was for Rifkin an 'economy of granters of access,' an economy in which knowledge creation is not an external factor but central to productivity, where valuable trade is not just something you can drop on your foot, and where valuable commercial transactions may be structured in terms of granting access to content rather than as physical goods changing hands.

One business alone—the iTunes Store—has sold over twelve billion songs, around two transactions for each person on earth. A similar software outlet, Apple's App Store, was launched in 2008; two years later over seven billion applications had been downloaded. An entirely new market for musical works—mobile phone ring tones—was at one point estimated to make up 10 per cent of the music market. Each one of these transactions represents a licence to use packets of disembodied information shipped around the internet, with no physical goods changing hands. When you 'buy' a song on iTunes, you effectively pay money to have the contents of your flash memory or hard drive rearranged; how you use this digital download is restricted by a contractual agreement and by IP law, and often also by technological protection. Legal scholars debate the true nature of this transaction, but one thing is clear—you haven't purchased the song as such, and you don't 'own' it the way you own a physical object. In each of these transactions, people part with money for access to digital content and rights to use it. A massive trade in rights of access and use—in other words, trade in IP *as such*. For IP is essentially the set of laws that entitle you to say whether or not, and if so how, I can use inventions, designs, creative works, or distinctive signs, that you have created. If I 'buy' your song or your app, you are simply agreeing to let me use it in accordance with a licence under your copyright.

This kind of digital transaction has more dramatically highlighted the intangible content of trade, and enabled a kind of pure trade in IP. But in one form or another IP has been intertwined with trade, and trade politics, for many years. In substance, TRIPS was not a dramatic break with the past; it was

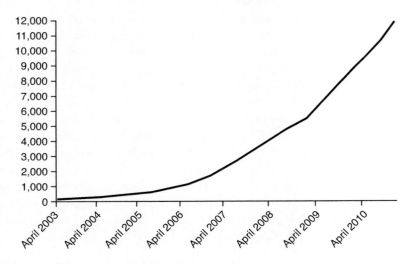

Figure 2.1 Trade in Intellectual Property? Transactions on the Apple iTunes Store (cumulative total (millions))
Data source: www.apple.com

more a culmination of a long trend—its legal and policy roots reach well back into the 19th century, and the first recognition that the knowledge component of international commerce demanded a multilateral response in the form of the Paris and Berne Conventions, first concluded in the 1880s. Some of today's toughest debates over TRIPS echo back well over a century. The late 19th century saw intensive wrangling over issues with continuing resonance today, such as the scope of the subject matter that patents should cover, the compulsory licensing of patents and whether patent rights should allow true exclusivity or should only operate as a right to claim royalties, and the proper scope of protection of geographical indications—what forms of descriptive and evocative use of geographical terms are legitimate in commerce, and what should be suppressed. The *Madrid Agreement for the Repression of False or Deceptive Indications of Source on Goods* of 1891 was an early multilateral treaty on 'trade-related aspects of IP' and on how IP should be enforced.

For the most part, the actual standards of TRIPS are reasonably conservative in character—at least for most developed countries, whose laws and legal systems the TRIPS standards were essentially modelled upon. Equally, TRIPS is silent on some key issues that preoccupy policymakers today, such as IP on the internet, domain names, patent quality, and the protection of traditional knowledge systems and biodiversity. Even so, TRIPS revolutionized the international governance of IP, and precipitated a massive wave of IP legislation and institution-building, predominantly for those developing countries which had not already introduced the kind of comprehensive IP protection that TRIPS mandated.

TRIPS in the WTO

The Final Act of the Uruguay Round put an end to some eight years of multilateral trade negotiations. This work was contained in the Agreement Establishing the World Trade Organization (the WTO Agreement), which in turn incorporated a hefty bundle of detailed trade agreements. It forged a new framework of rules governing how most of the world's economies would do business with one another, and a new institution to oversee those rules. This complex package of legal texts included some striking features that were not foreshadowed when the negotiations were launched in Punta del Este in 1986:

- *The invention of the World Trade Organization itself*, as a stand-alone international organization, with legal identity and the responsibility of managing the rules of international trade.

The original negotiating mandate did not foresee the creation of a new organization. The idea emerged during the negotiations, reviving post-war plans for an International Trade Organization that had earlier been quietly shelved. Trade rules had been governed through a looser arrangement, the GATT, which had been provisionally in force for some 40 years and did not constitute a separate organization. Even at a late stage in the Uruguay Round negotiations, the GATT Director General felt the creation of a new organization was a 'nebulous' idea, lower in priority than the conclusion of GATT negotiations. Yet the creation of this new institution, the WTO, gave international economic law a stronger institutional presence, a decisive shift from its earlier improvised, informal character, towards a formal, legalistic structure—a shift, in effect, from a diplomatic forum to a legal regime.

- *A single mechanism for settling disputes* over the full range of trade rules covered by the WTO Agreement, including conventional trade in physical goods, trade in services, and intellectual property.

It was no foregone conclusion that a single legal framework would cover disputes over the wide and disparate range of trade interests included in the WTO rules—again, late in the negotiations, this remained a 'delicate political question', with doubts expressed whether 'cross-retaliation from goods to services, or to intellectual property rights . . . is feasible and desirable.' The actual outcome, a single dispute mechanism, meant that, when countries dealt with their differences over trade, diverse interests in different sectors would be closely intertwined, leading to unexpected consequences. Developed countries could use the inducement of access to traditional markets to push developing countries to strengthen their IP protection. But developing countries were equally given a new form of trade leverage—meaning they could use IP to leverage access for agricultural products in rich country markets.

- *A comprehensive agreement covering the protection of intellectual property* under national law—the TRIPS Agreement.

The original Uruguay Round mandate to negotiate on IP aimed to 'clarify' existing trade law provisions and to 'elaborate as appropriate new rules and disciplines.' There was a special focus on 'international trade in counterfeit goods,' as this was felt to be an illegitimate form of cross-border trade. But what emerged from the negotiations was much broader, an agreement that was by far the most comprehensive yet struck on IP protection. It incorporated much of the existing international law of IP, broadened it, and set it in the newly established institution and dispute settlement system created by the WTO. IP law became a form of trade law, as a negotiated outcome, whether or not that was a neat theoretical fit.

These three developments resulted from negotiating dynamics. None was inevitable at the time the negotiations started, but they have since solidified into firm, positive features of the international legal landscape. This transformation radically changed the international face of IP law. And it redefined how governments managed their trade relations in the steadily more sensitive and controversial realm of the knowledge economy.

What Aspects of Intellectual Property Rights are 'Trade-Related'?

To work within this integrated framework means looking objectively at the international law as it operates today. And it means squarely tackling a legal and political conundrum posed by these developments, one that theoreticians, trade diplomats and activists are still wrestling with: what is the *trade* aspect of the IP system, and what is the IP aspect of the trade law system? How can TRIPS be reconciled, in a workable way, with other areas of international IP law, a contested arena now sprawling across a wide array of law and policy—human rights, health, the environment, the internet, education, research and development? IP law has irrevocably broken out of the narrow, specialized domain it once occupied—but what does this mean for practitioners? If international IP law is now up for grabs for an ever widening circle of legal traditions and systems, from human rights law to classical trade law, how can it effectively function to provide a predictable and transparent basis to settle disputes?

While it was an agreement purportedly on *trade-related aspects* of intellectual property rights, TRIPS seemed to cover so many aspects of IP law that it was hard to see any distinctive 'trade-related' flavour that would set it apart from the long-established treaties on IP that it built upon. TRIPS incorporates the Paris and Berne Conventions, respectively on industrial property and on copyright and related rights, IP treaties on IP that date back to the 1880s and are among the first true multilateral agreements. The Uruguay Round negotiators agreed upon standards that made extensive use of these existing materials, and even its new standards drew heavily on working texts earlier drafted in various processes convened by WIPO, the specialized agency of the United Nations responsible for IP, which is also the custodian of the Paris and Berne Conventions. This major overlap between the standards of TRIPS itself and the pre-existing framework of international IP law left open the question of what were the specially 'trade-related' aspects of IP that TRIPS was meant to deal with.

In fact, TRIPS is best understood as, simply, an agreement that IP *is* trade-related—as a political and economic fact. It recognized pragmatically that a contemporary trade deal was not possible unless it went some way towards reconciling expectations on the protection of IP. It was a direct, realist, response to the stark reality that industrialized countries saw IP protection as central to their trade interests, and were prepared to exercise economic leverage, including through trade disputes, to promote those interests. The raw fact that the major economies of the world pursued and defended their IP interests *as trade interests*, created a practical need for the international rule of law. Even as the WTO/TRIPS architecture was settling into place, the then head of the GATT put it bluntly: 'unless we establish clear multilaterally agreed rules and disciplines in these new areas, disputes would invariably be left in the hands of those advocating unilateral or bilateral action.'

TRIPS and the New Economy

Accounts of the negotiation of TRIPS point, accurately enough, to the extensive strategizing and lobbying that produced an outcome that went well beyond earlier GATT work on IP and trade, which had concentrated on trade in counterfeit goods. The outcome was an agreement covering the full sweep of IP law, ranging from biotech patents to performers' rights, and areas such as trade secrets that had never before been codified in international treaties. TRIPS is therefore a clear example of the positive creation of international law through the deliberate assertion of specific national interests; the text of TRIPS came about not as the scholarly codification of an abstract set of principles, but as a direct consequence of the assertion of specific trade interests. But to focus on these diplomatic dynamics can belie the deeper, broader legal roots of many of the provisions of TRIPS. And, since its conclusion, TRIPS has evolved considerably as a legal instrument, as its legal, political, economic and technological environment evolves, and as countries identify and pursue their interests within the WTO/TRIPS system in unforeseen ways.

So now, a quarter-century since negotiations started, it is time to set TRIPS apart, as a legal text, from the original impetus and specific interests that drove IP into the WTO, and to work with it as an integral part of the trade law system, as a practical means of organizing and conducting trade relations in an economic environment that values intangible content as much as tangible matter. In fact, to paraphrase Voltaire, if TRIPS didn't now exist, it would still be necessary to invent it.

This is because IP issues have become intrinsically intertwined with conventional trade, and managing trade relations means managing expectations on IP protection. And to achieve this effectively, a sound, non-discriminatory bedrock of multilateral rules should be a strong preference to improvized collections of bilateral dealmaking.

Consider what was happening at the same time as TRIPS was being concluded:

- Technological change, and the pure trade in knowledge products: Greater connectivity through information and communications technology led to increasing disembodiment of commercial activity, removing physical constraints on transactions. From the early nineties, the internet grew rapidly as a medium for doing business, finally detaching the value of intellectual works—like songs, news articles, and software—from the physical media that carried them, creating a growing trend towards transactions purely in knowledge products. Trading in bundles of newsprint, polycarbonate CDs, magnetic tapes, or vinyl discs was no longer necessary as a kind of proxy for transactions in the actual content consumers wanted—the software, the news article, or the musical work. Many now choose to purchase knowledge products as such, free of any physical carrier, and changing the nature of international trade in these products.

- Intangibles and economic growth: From the mid-eighties, economic theory sought to redress a longstanding gap in the analysis of economic growth, with the emergence of so-called 'new growth theory'. The development of new technology and human capital had been considered as external ('exogenous') when modelling economic growth; new growth theory included these factors as 'endogenous' and sought to build them into economic model. This work, according to one of its principal authors, 'suggests that the most important job for economic policy is to create an institutional environment that supports technological change.'[1] Gordon Brown, then Shadow Chancellor (Finance Minister) of the United Kingdom, was lampooned for citing this 'post neo-classical endogenous growth theory' in a speech in 1994. But several months after this speech, in January 1995, the United Kingdom was legally bound by TRIPS, the first multilateral trade agreement to recognize directly the intangible component of economic growth.

- IP entering economic strategies: As policymakers placed increasing stock on innovation and technological development as a central ingredient in economic development—seeing technology and human capital as a factor of production, alongside the classical factors of land, labour and capital stock—closer attention

---

[1] Paul M. Romer, 'Beyond Classical and Keynesian Macroeconomic Policy' [1994] Policy Options, July–August.

was paid to how it should be managed. The United States, faced with evidence of failure effectively to utilize public-funded research, decisively shifted from a policy of leaving publicly-funded research in the public domain or for government agencies to develop, towards a strategy that actively used the IP system and market-based mechanisms for technology diffusion. Many other countries, both developed and developing economies, take a careful, strategic approach to knowledge management as an integral part of their economic infrastructure. IP law and policy, and the settings struck in national laws, are a crucial component of this infrastructure.

TRIPS came about because of the kind of pragmatic calculations that trade negotiators are asked to make. The leading industrialized economies, facing a post-industrial future as the bulk of manufacturing capacity moved, seemingly inexorably, to the developing world, felt that their economic interests and future commercial advantage lay in the knowledge component of trade. Developing countries had experienced demands for stronger IP protection backed by the threat of unilateral trade sanctions. Many were apprehensive that their freedom to set policy and to manage their own IP systems would only worsen without a clear benchmark for defining what claims for IP protection their trading partners could legitimately claim, and without a sure multilateral framework for resolving differences. The dominant economies saw IP infringements as illegitimate trade and as unfair competition, eroding their commercial edge; for them, any multilateral trade deal would require their trading partners both to legislate so as to confirm that this trade violated legally recognized rights, and actively to create the practical means to suppress infringing trade—so they pursued both a norm-setting agenda and an enforcement agenda. For developing countries, a major negotiating objective for TRIPS was to reduce the operation of unilateral sanctions and to embed IP disputation into an objective, rules-based dispute settlement system, so it would not just be economic strength that determined what was right and what kind of trade retaliation was appropriate.

Thus, like many international agreements, TRIPS was a contrivance, a contingent deal; a pragmatic response to political needs; the least imperfect outcome that could be agreed in practice to accommodate diverse interests around the table, and not the ideal text that any one negotiator wanted. It was not an abstract, structured exercise in reforming trade law to give effect to the lessons of new economic theory. Theoretical preferences range from insistence that IP should be kept out of trade law altogether; to calls for an IP agreement that is directly embedded in public international law, subordinate, for instance, to the law of human rights and the environment; to demands for a tighter, more prescriptive IP agreement closer in character to comprehensive harmonized international legislation on IP. None of these were achieved in the package signed in Marrakesh, and it is mistaken to define or interpret the actual negotiated result according to such political or theoretical preferences: the deal was what was actually on the table.

Even so, such pragmatic negotiating outcomes are not haphazard deals drawn up in isolation; they draw their substance from well-established legal principles and accumulated practice, and indeed are entirely capable of reconciliation with broader public international law and with sound domestic policy. The principles and standards of TRIPS are based on centuries of legal evolution, nationally and internationally, that produced broadly compatible standards and principles for IP protection. IP law and policy has been guided by a complex mix of social and economic factors, both domestic and international, and has long been influenced by countries' trade relations and by imported legal models and traditions. And there is a clear link between the lessons of economic analysis and the pragmatic interests pursued in trade negotiations: the growing perception, on the part of industry lobbyist, trade negotiator and economic theorist alike, that the knowledge component of economic growth and of commercial transactions could no longer be seen as 'exogenous' but had to be factored in to trade relations.

Resistance to TRIPS

But TRIPS was not a consequence of an easy political consensus, and continues to face two forms of resistance: a fundamental theoretical and systemic claim that IP standards have no part in any trade deal; and a critique that the actual standards set in TRIPS are unfairly weighted against developing countries and were extracted under economic coercion.

Under the GATT, the treaty that had largely defined multilateral trade law between World War II and the creation of the WTO, 'trade' meant trade in goods, and tangible goods at that—stuff you can drop on your foot. This conception of trade excluded a huge proportion of the value of international transactions, and the sources of economic growth; and this mismatch was growing, as the intangible component of economic transactions grew faster than trade in physical goods. The WTO package deal therefore included the General Agreement on Trade in Services (GATS), the first multilateral agreement on this form of intangible trade, which constitutes the bulk of economic activity in most developed countries.

And the package included TRIPS, which presented a more confronting challenge as to what trade law should be about.

Further, TRIPS stands in *apparent* conflict with the conventional understanding of trade negotiations moving towards greater 'liberalization'—the move towards fewer barriers between two willing parties to a transaction, progressed through negotiations aimed at dismantling government interference in trade. Instead, TRIPS positively requires governments to step in and set constraints on certain economic activity, under an obligation to suppress a kind of 'illegitimate trade'— trade that infringes IP rights. Rather than imposing a ceiling on government regulation, as classical trade law does, TRIPS set a floor or minimum standard.

TRIPS therefore affronted or perplexed many veteran trade negotiators: IP protection was not seen as a natural part of trade law and trade negotiations. They saw it as indeed 'exogenous' to international trade law—a means of reaching behind the border to intrude in domestic regulatory issues, akin to the regulation of process and production methods through international trade, another area of increasing controversy and complexity in trade law—a traded product was no longer considered as frozen in the present and isolated from its origins, but was rather as the embodiment of various inputs, some legitimate (fairly licensed technology, authorized trademarks), and some illegitimate (environmentally harmful fishing methods, misappropriated know how).

So the anti-globalization movement showed rare unity with free trade theoreticians in disparaging TRIPS. Many advocates of developing countries' interests put the view that TRIPS was an intolerable burden, and a last-ditch attempt by the post-industrial industrialized world to preserve precious comparative advantage. According to various commentators, TRIPS is responsible for 'heartless exploitation of the poor and suffering'; by this view it also undermines biodiversity and enables biopiracy, prevents access to essential medicines, uses ideas to extort payment, favours rent seeking over competitive commerce, transfers massive amounts of wealth from poor countries to rich ones, ends national sovereignty, is 'clearly anomalous within GATT', and creates the disturbing precedent of incorporating domestic regulatory standards in international trade rules. Commentators saw it as an historic turning point: '[t]he principles of common heritage, free flow and national sovereignty along with the NIEO [new international economic order] agenda meet their Waterloo in TRIPS.' Its perceived coercive effect drew particular criticism. In 2000, as Indonesia's major obligations under TRIPS came into effect, *Warta Ekonomi*, a leading Indonesian economic journal, depicted TRIPS as a destructive hammer, paired with a whip, crushing compact discs with the headline 'A Million People are Criminals.'

The sense that IP standards did not fit within a trade law system went back to the launch of the Uruguay Round negotiations. Developing countries had argued for a negotiating mandate solely focussed on counterfeit goods, reflecting earlier work in the GATT, and even upon the conclusion of the negotiating mandate, India said that protection of IP rights was 'not within the jurisdiction of [GATT]' and that negotiations should be limited to 'avoidance of discriminatory restrictions and disguised barriers to trade arising out of measures relating to intellectual property protection.' Just days before the Uruguay Round was launched, the Non-Aligned Movement Summit in Harare had formally declared IP to be beyond the legal competence of the GATT.

From a Politics of TRIPS to the Practice of TRIPS

Yet TRIPS is now embedded within the international legal system. It is essential for many to develop a practical, working understanding of TRIPS—how it functions, what it does and does not do, how to read and interpret it, how to use it to pursue interests and defend choices, and how to face down those with competing versions of TRIPS. This applies for those with an intrinsic interest in IP law and an academic fascination with the curious construct of an IP treaty within a trade law regime; but it equally applies to those who need to take account of it and work with it pragmatically, even—for some—grudgingly. Practitioners of international IP law are not a narrow priesthood of like-minded legal experts, but form a diverse and growing community wrestling with ever broader policy issues and legal questions. Their ranks include government officials, trade negotiators, civil society and industry NGOs, activist academics, policy researchers, private firms, and legal practitioners. TRIPS now formally binds over 150 members of the WTO and directly influences their national laws; it is a legal benchmark for around 30 more countries which seek to join the WTO; it is also a point of reference or source of law for scores of regional and bilateral agreements—TRIPS 'normalized' the incorporation of IP protection into trade agreements and trade relations generally, with strong implications for hundreds of bilateral and regional trade deals concluded since the Uruguay Round. Numerous, diverse industry and civil society organizations, and many thousands of legal advisors and academics, are now working with the central legal texts that define the international IP regime, namely TRIPS and the pre-existing law that it assimilated.

The practice of international IP law is not confined to precise legal questions and pure questions of treaty interpretation. These questions are central, and important, but have to be understood and applied within the far broader context of trade negotiations and international political relations, IP policymaking and development strategies in the new economy, the ethical and human rights dimensions that increasingly shape the operational context of IP law and policy, and the character of the international institutions that can determine actual choices far more than strict legal constraints. Practitioners need to understand the interplay between political considerations, trade interests, and the purely legal interpretation which characterizes international dispute settlement in this domain.

To work effectively with TRIPS therefore requires a realist approach. This means making use of TRIPS and the law and legal system it is embedded within as they exist, not as one might wish them to be. This does not, however, mean that practitioners are simply passive recipients of externally imposed standards. The domestic policymaker who implements the general norms of TRIPS is, in an important sense, an authoritative interpreter of TRIPS standards; over time, domestic policy choices made in good faith will, if indirectly, affect the way TRIPS is read and interpreted. In other words, implementing TRIPS is not just a one-way process of receiving and complying with establishing norms; implementing TRIPS is a dynamic process, whereby the accumulation of domestic choices for law and regulation over time shape the expectations of trading partners and also indirectly colour the background of formal treaty interpretation.

The role of the domestic lawmaker and policymaker is crucial. Ultimately, the most momentous act of 'TRIPS interpretation' is the passing of domestic laws which give actual, practical effect to the relatively abstract legal formulations and broad expectations articulated by the treaties; and it is only through domestic laws that the effects, good and bad, of IP law treaties are actually felt. So to develop a practical jurisprudence of TRIPS, to build a workable reading of its text, is to defend legitimate policy choices, and the freedom to make those policy choices, in an environment where such choices can be scrutinized closely by trading partners.

Effective domestic policymaking is greatly facilitated by clarity about TRIPS standards, about such questions as what material is eligible for IP protection and what need not be protected; what exceptions and entitlements for users of IP are permissible; and what procedural safeguards are required for enforcement and regulatory curbs on IP. When a government takes tough policy choices in the regulation of IP, this can irritate trading partners, affront sectoral interests, and curtail perceived rights or entitlements. The scale and significance of IP policymaking, and its growing economic and social impact, make this kind of dissension more or less inevitable. Respect for IP is considered a critical trade interest by many major economies. In turn, failure to protect IP is considered an effective denial of market access for many firms. The law of TRIPS sets objective limits to what trading partners can expect from one another, and TRIPS dispute settlement procedures cap the capacity to retaliate when those expectations are not met. Thus a clear legal grasp of TRIPS law and the practical consequences of dispute settlement form an invaluable aid in making sustainable and beneficial policy choices. But setting out such a pragmatic way of working with TRIPS has provoked two lines of criticism: that to explain TRIPS is to defend it or to legitimize it; and that to analyse the practicalities of TRIPS is to encourage non-compliance with it.

'Defending TRIPS'

This book stems from many conversations which have highlighted the value of objective understanding of what it means to work with TRIPS in practice, as against broader political debate. At a conference on HIV-AIDs in 2001, I outlined a 'practical jurisprudence' of TRIPS. This sounds like legal jargon, but a 'practical jurisprudence' simply means a systematic and coherent approach to reading the text of TRIPS in the light of its full legal context, but with certain practical needs in mind, when weighing choices for domestic IP law. In this case, my task was to show how a straightforward reading of the treaty would leave open scope for countries to take a range of actions to secure affordable medicines, especially through permissible exceptions to patent rights—some of what are now termed 'TRIPS flexibilities'. The essential idea was that an objective reading of TRIPS text enabled greater legislative freedoms than an overly political or theoretical approach would allow. A widely-voiced view at the time was highly critical of TRIPS—with claims even that it was 'the root of all evil'. Its critics argued that it should be rescinded or excised from the WTO package altogether: as the *New Internationalist* opined that year, 'Take TRIPs Out: Restore National Patent Protection Systems: We demand the removal of [TRIPS] from the WTO,' in *WTO: Shrink It or Sink It*.

Afterwards, participants consoled me privately, suggesting that I had been asked to do the unthinkable, to 'defend TRIPS', when everyone knew it was indefensible at a basic moral level. I was startled—not because of the depth of feeling, nor the sense of passion and urgency—this was, after all, a conference on how to address deep structural inequities in responses to a devastating pandemic. But I was struck by the idea that an objective account of how to read a treaty's text to find practical ways to put medicines in the hands of those who needed them was seen as a tactic to 'defend' the treaty. To my mind, devising programs to address urgent health needs was paramount, so practical choices had to be made for national health policy; the international legal context was only one consideration among others, and had to be kept clearly in context. To maintain clarity and focus, one needed a sober, practical reading of the legal text concerned, and an assessment of the likelihood of a dispute being taken, and the consequences of any dispute settlement action. Confidence in compliance with treaty standards translates directly into political sustainability of policy choices. This does not mean taking a partisan stance on the treaty as a whole, nor reflecting on its origins and negotiation. It means building confidence that certain choices can be made free of the prospect of trade retaliation, even if there may be differences over their wisdom and impact as policy options. It is therefore not a matter of 'defending TRIPS,' but using TRIPS *to* defend—especially to defend legitimate domestic policy choices.

'Getting around TRIPS'

In discussing realistic ways of working with TRIPS, I have encountered a second, very different, criticism: that such a pragmatic approach encourages non-compliance with TRIPS, that it concerns political strategies to escape the legal obligations of TRIPS. By this view, TRIPS is a kind of international IP statute that should be policed carefully for infringing activity, stressing compliance as an end in itself. But TRIPS has two broad functions: first, it is an international treaty governing relations between trading partners, a means of organizing and managing relations on IP matters, and keeping differences within reasonable bounds; and second it espouses broader policy goals for IP protection that domestic authorities are responsible for delivering upon. It will rarely be enough, to yield the intended benefits of TRIPS, simply to write laws that are formally compliant with the treaty—to check the compliance boxes and then calmly await for the benefits to ensue—without making the system work in practice.

Practitioners know that 'TRIPS implementation' means much more than passive, reactive compliance with its provisions, doing just enough to stay out of trouble with powerful trading partners:

- Looking outward to a country's trading relations, 'implementing TRIPS' can also mean using it as intended within the WTO regime to define, objectively and explicitly, the expectations that countries can rightly demand of one another so far as IP protection is concerned, and to resolve, in measured and transparent way, the disputes that inevitably arise when expectations are thwarted;
- Looking inward to domestic policymaking, 'implementing TRIPS' can mean using its standards as a benchmark and general guide for a balanced national system of IP protection that respects legitimate expectations but does not overprotect IP, actively promoting the public interest; in essence, this means

delivering in practice on the public policy objectives that TRIPS itself sets for IP protection—a social economic welfare, through a balancing of rights and obligations.

The Limits to International Lawmaking

Such enticing public benefits—utilitarian benefits in the form of enjoyment of fruits of innovation, and equity and balance of interests in the way the system works—cannot result purely from the functioning of an international treaty. The treaty guides and shapes national laws and administration to some extent but does not deliver concrete outcomes that directly affect people. What ultimately matters is how national systems put these general principles and broad international standards to work. TRIPS is not a kind of model IP law, to be pasted into the national statute books. As an international legal text, TRIPS cannot and should-not stand in alone for a balanced, equitable and effective national IP system. TRIPS leaves open many important choices for domestic law and policy, and as a legal text it cannot stand in for the important work of legislators, judges, and regulators within national systems. It is therefore crucial to keep the treaty system in perspective, and TRIPS in its proper place. At the national level, laws have to be constitutional, but the constitution doesn't predetermine every last rule and regulation—the constitution defines the space that the lawmaker can legitimately work within. Equally, to be defensible against challenge from other countries, national laws should be consistent with TRIPS obligations. There is also a strong objective case that TRIPS-consistency of laws is a good guarantee that a national system will display procedural fairness, transparency, and non-discrimination; will achieve effective balances between rights and obligations and between public and private interests; and will be broadly compatible with the IP systems of trading partners. But the treaty does not define the full content of the laws, nor predetermine their practical impact.

Domestic legislation can naturally test the boundaries of a nation's constitution. Indeed, much of the detail of constitutional law is constructed through contested cases, through the resolution of disputes that deliver new case law and new insights in areas of policy importance. The same applies for the boundaries set for international treaties—treaty language, as negotiated, is general in character, sometimes even deliberately ambiguous, so that wrangling over treaty interpretation, informally or through formal dispute settlement, can be what really sheds light on the nature of those treaty commitments. Where it really counts, a practical jurisprudence of international IP law is built through the progressive resolution of disagreement and discord, gradually building a workable conception of what is legitimate and what is not. Conflict, disagreement, even passionate debate is inevitable over the proper scope of IP regulation—this is, after all, how IP doctrines have mostly been hammered out in national laws and in domestic courts over many years, through the steady accumulation of case law. Indeed, some contestation may be welcomed, as it helps to advance a clearer understanding of what choices are legitimate and beyond challenge—provided, ultimately, that there is a reasonably fair, stable, and predictable means of resolving such disputes, structured by legitimate and balanced principles and procedural safeguards. Arguably, that is what TRIPS aspires to be; and its fairness and effectiveness will only be enhanced by greater precision as to its precise legal character and scope.

The key to achieving these outcomes is to be very clear about what TRIPS obliges, and what it does not—at least as clear as can be achieved in the knowledge that some provisions are very broad or uncertain in scope. The greater the precision of legal understanding, the greater will be the freedom to operate in setting national policy directions. The best term for this kind of systematic understanding of TRIPS law is 'a practical jurisprudence'. Such an approach to understanding TRIPS should:

- be sufficiently well founded in law, practice, and policy to give robust and useful practical guidance to the domestic policymaker and legislator, whose choices are ultimately the only act of TRIPS interpretation and implementation that practically matters from the point of view of concrete public interest; and
- give sufficient recognition to the practicalities, practice, and legal requirements of formal dispute settlement, given that actual and reliably predictable outcomes of dispute settlement proceedings are ultimately the only legal considerations that should constrain the domestic policymaker and legislator.

A practical TRIPS jurisprudence must also keep the treaty in perspective. In the debate swirling around TRIPS, proponents and opponents of TRIPS alike can greatly overstate its true legal effect. Sometimes, it is as though an 'oral jurisprudence' of TRIPS had evolved, a kind of traditional narrative, in the hothouse of public debate, lobbying, and advocacy. This perceived legal impact would reach beyond the actual scope of the agreement as a legal text creating rights and obligations between sovereign international entities. Alternatively, this legal discourse would invent loopholes for sheer expediency. The resulting uncertainty could create greater obstacles to sustainable domestic policy choice than a cool legal reading of TRIPS would actually entail. Several misconceptions have clouded objective analysis:

- an assumption that TRIPS law was identical to what proponents of strong TRIPS standards had sought, overlooking the public policy safeguards that were carefully included in the course of negotiations;

- the conception of TRIPS as a kind of mandatory template for domestic legislative drafters, a rote to-do list for national parliaments, rather than one component of a complex mechanism for regulating and setting bounds to bilateral disputes between international trading partners—while domestic IP policymaking and legislation must draw on a broader set of policy and legal sources to be effective;
- the concern that any technical non-compliance with TRIPS would immediately trigger automatic trade sanctions, rather than seeing TRIPS as part of a practical set of mechanisms for dealing with trade disputes and containing their impact.

Access to Medicines and the Compulsory Licensing Debate

The debate over access to medicines, culminating at the 2001 WTO Ministerial Conference in Doha, exemplifies why it is crucially important to detach political debate from a clear look at legal standards: to a large extent, the debate concerned political demands to have the freedom to do what was already legally permissible. Patent rights are not absolute, and are not meant to be: patents are a utilitarian instrument of public policy. Among other limitations, governments and judicial authorities can make 'government use orders' or issue 'compulsory licences'. Such authorizations permit third parties to use the patented invention without the consent of the patent owner. There has been long controversy, reaching back into the 19th century, as to whether a patent should remain a truly exclusive right, and when, and on what grounds, it should become simply an entitlement to receive a fair royalty payment against others' use of the patented insertion.

A full review of this heated debate is not attempted here. Strong policy differences continue even today as to the value and effectiveness of compulsory licensing of patents on pharmaceuticals: some argue that it should be actively, even routinely, pursued as a means of promoting access to treatments; others argue that systematic use of compulsory licensing would thwart the essential function of the patent system in bringing new treatments to the public. Most countries have provisions in their patent laws that legally permit compulsory licensing and government use orders; the debate pivots over how freely or routinely they can or should be used in practice, and the policy implications and health impact of too little or too much resort to this kind of intervention; in short, a richer debate about when it is good policy to use legal options, rather than wrangling over legal questions in isolation.

Early TRIPS negotiating proposals sought to curtail the legitimate scope of compulsory licensing, and to limit the substantive grounds on which a government could issue compulsory licences. These proposals did not prevail. The actual, agreed treaty text essentially left open the substantive grounds and the legal or policy basis for such authorizations under national law. Negotiators settled for a codification of procedural safeguards to prevent the arbitrary and unfair exercise of the power to grant such non-voluntary authorizations. Yet, in later debate, as health policy experts turned to the TRIPS Agreement often for the first time, original negotiating goals to curtail compulsory licensing were conflated and confused with the actual negotiated outcomes. Thus some observers tacitly assumed that TRIPS had, in effect, either banned all such measures, or had dramatically restricted the substantive grounds for their issuance. And when national authorities contemplated such measures, they were reported to be 'flouting' international trade law: the Wall Street Journal reported in February 2001 that 'Brazil May Flout Trade Laws To Keep AIDS Drugs Free For Patients'.

How can such a misconception evolve? Partly because concern at the routine compulsory licensing of pharmaceutical patents (together with the non-availability of patents on pharmaceutical products in many countries) was, indeed, a major impetus for the inclusion of IP standards within the Uruguay Round. And after the conclusion of TRIPS, some industry interests and concerned governments continued to argue against using the compulsory licensing as a routine tool of public policy—they saw this either as a poor policy choice or as contrary to their interests, or as both. But, at times, this debate created an impression that compulsory licensing, per se, was in breach of international trade law. Early in this debate, some advocates who urged the compulsory licence as a means of promoting access to patented drugs, seemed to take this perspective at face value. An early assumption was that proponents of reduced grounds for compulsory licensing had actually got what they may have wanted from the treaty negotiations, even though, in fact, public policy safeguards and clear flexibilities had been deliberately and carefully included in the final, adopted text. Another herring of a different shade of red was the idea that a country had to declare a state of emergency to entitle it to issue a compulsory licence or to authorize government use; debate swirled around the question of what circumstances entitled a government to proclaim a 'national emergency or other circumstances of extreme urgency'; learned, well-meaning but redundant and misleading parallels were drawn with emergency safeguards under other areas of trade law. A calm reading of the plain black-letter text of TRIPS would have mostly settled these questions, but the intensity of the debate created a need for a political solution to reinforce the legal reality.

Addressing this state of affairs, the 2001 Doha Declaration on TRIPS and Public Health articulated what had been implicit in TRIPS, and what had already been successfully negotiated by developing countries during the Uruguay Round: freedom to determine the substantive grounds for compulsory licensing. The Doha Declaration therefore served the interesting function of adjusting a received or 'oral' jurisprudence of TRIPS, a perceived or asserted legal scope attributed inaccurately to the treaty language, so as to align it more accurately with the black letter law of TRIPS as a legal text: to synchronize political perceptions of the law with its actual legal reach. Doha provided a political gloss on the text of TRIPS by referring to a 'right to grant compulsory licences' and 'the freedom to determine the grounds upon which such licences are granted'. By doing so, the Declaration did not rewrite TRIPS; it simply made explicit what was implicitly there, so as to dispel avoidable confusion and contention. It did not resolve the policy debate as to whether and when compulsory licensing was a good idea; but it did help to remove legalistic distractions and clarified when governments could choose this option in the confidence that an already difficult decision would not incur trade retaliation.

Illustrating the difference between political perceptions and actual legal constraints, the Doha negotiations also identified a true legal problem that had to be addressed by modifying, or at least waiving, existing legal standards. TRIPS required compulsory licences granted be predominantly for the domestic market. But countries with limited manufacturing capacity could not effectively use compulsory licensing as an intervention for public health, because they would have to import pharmaceuticals rather than make them at home. Under TRIPS, foreign producers could not make pharmaceuticals under compulsory licences predominantly to serve the domestic needs of these countries. To address this concern, it was considered necessary to rewrite the black letter law of TRIPS: accordingly, Doha also led to the creation of a tailored mechanism (termed the 'Paragraph 6' or Article31*bis* mechanism). Negotiations yielded first a waiver, then a legal exception, to the TRIPS requirement that these authorizations be granted predominantly for the domestic market. WTO Members agreed on the first and hitherto the only formal amendment to the entire Uruguay Round package of WTO trade law: in itself a testament to the perception that fundamental interests are at stake.

Power to the Policymakers

Despite the significant adjustments made during the access to medicines process, and the latent flexibilities for domestic policymakers that this process brought to light, some commentators and observers continue to contest the legitimacy of TRIPS. The intensity of debate over TRIPS, and its often polarized character, can obscure its inherent fluidity as a legal text, and its proper interaction with domestic policy. The domestic legislator plays a key role as a practical interpreter of the text of TRIPS: at one level, passing domestic IP laws entails making a practical legal judgement as to what measures will resist any likely challenges as to their treaty consistency, but, in a more constructive way, is also the only effective means of delivering the positive benefits expected from treaty standards. Political debates and wangling over legal readings of TRIPS, as well as focusing on TRIPS compliance as an isolated end in itself, can all divert attention from the vital task of developing a positive public-interest conception of TRIPS implementation, and putting TRIPS to work as an effective means of promoting public welfare. TRIPS should serve as a stable legal platform for the domestic policymaker to explore policy choices, ranging over public health policy, management of biodiversity, education and cultural policy, information technology, and economic development. Choices in these policy domains are contested by a widening range of domestic and foreign constituents—not all of whom will be content with any pathway taken—and a sober reading of TRIPS should provide a level of confidence that legal challenges and trade retaliations can be contained, allowing a stronger focus on quality policymaking.

'Impossible things' about TRIPS

So working effectively with TRIPS entails clarity about what it actually is, as against what it is perceived to be, and detaching its legal effect from its political context. The White Queen, in Lewis Carroll's 'Through the Looking Glass', claimed to be able to believe 'as many as six impossible things before breakfast.' As a practical exercise in distinguishing TRIPS as a legal text from its political background, consider the following 'impossible things about TRIPS'—unexpected aspects of TRIPS that challenge some common assumptions about its legal effect.

• TRIPS is a 'fair trade' agreement. This observation will be seen as paradoxical and provocative, especially to those who advocate a more just international trade system under the political banner of 'fair trade' and who have singled out TRIPS for criticism. Actually this comment only concerns the formal structure and basic logic of TRIPS, not its content or the value system it embodies. TRIPS is founded on the idea that there is a form of 'legitimate trade'—trade that does not infringe IP rights—that governments are bound to respect, in contrast with an obligation to take action against 'illegitimate trade', or trade that infringes IP, particularly counterfeit trademark goods and pirated copyright works, and that there is a proper place in the trade law system for measures to suppress unfair competition and dishonest trade practices. TRIPS therefore inverts the logic of mainstream trade law which sets a ceiling to government intervention in trade, and instead requires governments to take positive steps to prevent a form of trade that is seen as illegitimate or unfair, at least in terms of IP law.

- TRIPS is conservative. Described as a revolution, TRIPS contains relatively few true novelties when it comes to the substantive standards it requires of national systems, at least from the point of view of most developed countries. Its flexibilities may have to be unearthed, but the text retains a deep background of policy flexibility in IP law, carried over from the foundational international treaties of Paris and Berne. To make a sweeping generalization, TRIPS was for the most part a codification of a typical level of protection in the developed world in the late 1980s—it forged few genuinely new legal standards for IP protection. There are, of course, major exceptions to this observation; and a number of developed countries encountered genuine policy and fundamental doctrinal difficulties with TRIPS implementation and compliance. Its revolutionary qualities lie not in the formal substance of its standards, but how those standards are applied, interpreted, and enforced, and how far developed country standards should affect developing countries' choices; in short, how they influence actual governmental behaviour, rather than their inherent content.

- TRIPS codified the social function of IP. TRIPS emerged as a product of give and take in the negotiating logic of the Uruguay Round, rather than as an idealized collective policymaking endeavour. Its conclusion and implementation are viewed by some commentators as a consequence of the realist exertion of the economic interests of developed economies. Yet precisely because developing country negotiators sought to preserve valuable policy space, it is the first international IP treaty explicitly to articulate a strong ethic of public welfare and basic equity as the policy basis and very rationale of IP protection.

- TRIPS is a cost and a benefit. The negotiating history of TRIPS creates a paradox, a paradox that can never be teased out theoretically on paper or in the academic symposium, but that only the nimble and informed domestic policymaker can resolve in practice. The paradox is that TRIPS was negotiated as a trade 'concession', but it can—indeed *should*—be implemented for economic and social gain. Most developing countries negotiated and complied with TRIPS as a negotiating concession, construing it as an economic burden shouldered only to secure offsetting gains from access to agricultural, textile, and other industrial markets under the package deal of the Uruguay Round. Few would have unilaterally adopted the full standards of TRIPS without external inducements. Yet TRIPS is, on the face of it, intended to promote social and economic welfare, and a balance of rights and obligations. Thus, compliance with TRIPS is presented both as a costly negotiating trade-off and as a beneficial act of public policymaking. WTO dispute settlement exhibits this paradox more generally—even if trade liberalization is a negotiating 'concession,' it is still, according to classical trade theory, in the mutual interest of all parties. When a country wins a trade dispute and the losing party fails to comply with the outcome, it is entitled to 'suspend concessions' (ie impose retaliatory sanctions), which in theory would itself impose economic costs on the victorious complainant. This paradox may be resolved in the context of TRIPS by dismantling the conception of the Agreement as a monolithic set of provisions, as a form of multilateral legislation for domestic laws, and seeing it in context as an international treaty governing trade relations, setting general standards and defining domestic elbow room, and thus one ingredient only in a complex domestic legislative process that encompasses and accommodates many overlapping interests, so that 'compliance' takes on many shades in the detailed practice of domestic IP policymaking.

- Trade retaliation cuts both ways: Early in the life of TRIPS, some assumed that failure to comply with TRIPS to the letter would trigger immediate, draconian trade sanctions; yet, over 15 years into its life as a regime, and with many instances of apparent non-compliance, the only 'sanction' for breaching TRIPS was an arbitrated compensation agreed between the US and the EU, the two dominant developed economies within the WTO. By contrast, three developing countries—Ecuador, Antigua, and Brazil—have proposed TRIPS-related sanctions in the course of WTO dispute settlement in their efforts to leverage access for their agricultural and services exports (see Table 1.3).

- Multilateralism bred bilateralism. TRIPS was seen by many negotiators as a cure for unilateralism or bilateralism in settling IP-related trade disputes. It also set up policy processes to deal with core outstanding issues in a multilateral forum. Yet, after substantive TRIPS provisions entered into force for most countries a strong upswing in bilateral trade negotiations had the effect of extending or revising multilateral standards through bilateral agreement, and creating bilateral dispute settlement mechanisms. Developed countries had been expected to continue pursuing their interests in multilaterally advancing norms under TRIPS, but mostly chose the bilateral path instead. Instead, some five years after TRIPS entered into force, developing countries were pursuing norm-setting goals under TRIPS, notably in the field of GR and TK.

In the late 1980s and early 1990s, in the absence of established international rules governing the appropriate scope and limits to patents on pharmaceuticals, several developing countries had to balance IP and public health issues (including patentability of medicines) against continued access to export markets in areas of comparative advantage as one basis for economic development (another factor in public health). Experience showed how unilateral measures, rooted in the domestic law of the *demandeur* state, could be invoked in developed country markets, with the effect that punitive tariffs would curb sensitive and valuable imports from developing countries if their domestic IP regimes were considered to be inadequate—according to an essentially unilateral, external standard of what is adequate or appropriate. Actual cases of sanctions were very rare (although there was one instance in the late 1980s of failure to protect pharmaceutical patents leading to the imposition of punitive tariffs, in turn influencing domestic legislative changes). Yet the degree of bilateral monitoring, and the potential for targeted trade sanctions and more general damage to a cooperative trading and political relationship, meant that unilateral standards of adequacy or acceptability of IP protection could be highly persuasive. Given the substantial nature of the trade interests involved, and the inevitability that they will be asserted and defended, a realist analysis at least suggests that bilateral diplomatic channels to settle disputes will lead to asymmetric and unilateral outcomes.

Upon the adoption of TRIPS, at Marrakech in 1994, Indonesia expressed a wider apprehension about 'legal harassment' over TRIPS and called instead for technical cooperation. The background of concern led to the potentially paradoxical outcome that TRIPS was both constructed as a multilateral refuge from bilateral 'legal harassment' and yet served as a means of legitimizing and giving multilateral force to such leverage.

These tensions are resolved by recognizing the legitimate role of the domestic policymaker. Precisely because TRIPS does reach to an unprecedented degree into domestic policymaking, the very policy choices, the framing of equitable considerations and how they are resolved, that arise at the domestic level reach back into the interpretative context of TRIPS. Beyond the domestic environment, and the good-faith and legitimate endeavours undertaken there to harness and to bound exclusive rights in the expectation of broader welfare outcomes, there is no alternative forum for determining and implementing on a practical plane some of the important policy balances and policy provisions that define the essential architecture of TRIPS. Rather than insisting on an exclusive cleavage between domestic policy space and the formal imposition of international legal obligations, active exploration of beneficial and equitable welfare outcomes within the domestic policy environment is both a higher form of treaty implementation and is in itself a more compelling and legitimate means of treaty interpretation, one that can lend justice and validity to the standards embodied in the treaty.

3

Situating TRIPS Within the WTO: In Practice and in Theory

The TRIPS Agreement is one of the new agreements negotiated and concluded in the Uruguay Round of multilateral trade negotiations. The TRIPS Agreement brings intellectual property within the world trading system for the first time by imposing certain obligations on Members in the area of trade-related intellectual property rights.

Appellate Body, India – Pharmaceutical Patents

Of course, the Duc was agitated about Hollywood's belief that it had invented the 'French kiss' . . . I patted his back and said that I agreed with him and he calmed down, grateful that I had understood. Although I fear there was something to do with the World Trade Organisation and protection of the French film industry in his point which I missed.

Frank Moorhouse, Loose Living

The WTO is more than a multilateral trading system. It has accumulated issues that are non-trade and not in its mandate. An example – the prime example – is TRIPs. This is not a liberalisation device, it's a protectionist device. . . . '

Martin Khor, Third World Network

Structurally, TRIPS is integral to the WTO—its legal instruments, its policy bodies and negotiating processes; its dispute settlement mechanism; its review systems;

and its interaction with other organizations. Conceptually, its place is less clear: there are teasing foundational questions about how to situate IP protection within a trade law system. But a working grasp of both its structural and conceptual place is essential for the effective practice of TRIPS law. In turn, this requires a systematic understanding of how the WTO functions. Even though TRIPS has strong legal and conceptual links with other legal traditions, ultimately TRIPS law and practice is a subset of WTO law and practice.

Since its inception, the WTO itself has attracted debate and controversy. This contention is, in part, a measure of its real-world impact; but the concerns voiced about the WTO also respond to broader trends, well beyond its actual legal or institutional reach. The WTO can serve as a proxy for wider concerns and anxieties about economic and cultural globalization and systems of international governance. Just as for TRIPS itself, the practitioner has to distil the actual legal and political scope of the WTO as an organization from the far broader international and political contexts in which it is often invoked. And as for TRIPS, as one approaches the WTO with practical ends in mind, initial preconceptions about its actual role and function have to give way to a more diverse and nuanced view of how it operates.

To the general observer, the WTO presents two powerful faces that consume the bulk of the political bandwidth devoted to the organization and its operations:

- the multilateral *negotiations* ('rounds') on new rules to govern trade relations between WTO Members, especially the Doha Development Round, which has run through most of the present decade; and
- the formal procedures for settling *disputes* between members concerning—and especially the prospect of 'sanctions' for transgressions of the rules.

Looking at negotiations on new rules and at the enforcement of existing rules, concerns can run deeply that trade interests and economic considerations will trump or exclude the social, environmental, and cultural interests that are often closer to the immediate lives and sense of well-being of many—even, or especially, in periods of economic uncertainty. Again, these concerns mirror critiques of TRIPS—that, firstly, as a set of negotiated rules governing access to and dissemination of knowledge, cultural works, and technology, TRIPS gives priority to sectoral industrial interests, centred on the developed world; and that, secondly, its enforcement is used to impose values and interests that are essentially commercial in character and associated with powerful interest groups.

To stand back from the immediate political fray, however, the WTO as an international institution presents more diverse facets to the world, undertakes a much wider range of activities, and engages with a wider set of interests and values than a first encounter might suggest. Depending on how you encounter it and what your interests are, the WTO can be considered from several points of view:

- Law: the WTO administers a comprehensive body of international trade law, especially the array of treaties packaged together under the Final Act of the Uruguay Round, but also in the heritage of GATT law, the growing body of WTO case law, other materials such as Ministerial Declarations, and the plurilateral agreements that smaller subsets of WTO Members have negotiated—this includes the TRIPS Agreement as a legal text in itself, but also the case law decided under TRIPS and the broader legal context for TRIPS interpretation and dispute settlement practice;
- Global governance: the WTO provides an institutional framework for the great majority of the world's countries to work collectively on a host of economic and trade issues, and to manage their trade relations—as its membership is open to separate customs territories as well as recognized states, it gives economic players such as the European Union and Hong Kong, China separate seats at the table, unlike general United Nations practice;
- Trade negotiations: the WTO provides forums for negotiating new or revised norms, whether fully multilateral (involving all WTO Members) or plurilateral in membership (involving a subset of Members): for instance, current negotiations on a multilateral register for GIs;
- Transparency: the WTO undertakes a series of peer-review processes both of the overall trade policy of its members (through the Trade Policy Review Mechanism), and of specific elements of law and regulation, such as the transparency and peer review processes created under TRIPS concerning IP systems in WTO members;
- Information: the WTO publishes extensive information about national laws, regulations and standards; trade statistics; trade policies; and economic, policy and legal analysis—for example, the TRIPS transparency obligations have yielded a unique resource of practical information about IP laws, administration and enforcement in most of the WTO's 153 members;
- Expertise: the WTO provides technical and analytic expertise and capacity building, and works in partnership with other agencies offering capacity building and technical assistance in fields of economic policy and development—again, there is a distinct TRIPS aspect to this function, which includes a specific agreement with WIPO to cooperate in providing technical assistance; and
- Dispute prevention and settlement: the WTO offers several avenues for dispute settlement to enable the orderly, transparent and rules-based resolution of disputes arising between trading partners; any dispute about compliance with

WTO rules must be resolved through the multilateral mechanism established by the WTO, and any retaliation for non-compliance with WTO rules must be vetted by the multilateral system to ensure it is appropriate and suitably bounded.

The Functions of the WTO:
Article III of the *Agreement Establishing the WTO*

1. The WTO shall facilitate the *implementation, administration and operation,* and further the objectives, of this Agreement and *of the Multilateral Trade Agreements,* and shall also provide the framework for the implementation, administration and operation of the Plurilateral Trade Agreements.
2. The WTO shall provide the *forum for negotiations* among its Members concerning their multilateral trade relations . . .
3. The WTO shall administer the Understanding on Rules and Procedures Governing the *Settlement of Disputes* (. . . 'Dispute Settlement Understanding' or 'DSU'). . . .
4. The WTO shall administer the *Trade Policy Review* Mechanism (. . . 'TPRM'). . . .
5. With a view to achieving *greater coherence in global economic policy-making,* the WTO shall cooperate, as appropriate, with the International Monetary Fund and with the International Bank for Reconstruction and Development and its affiliated agencies.

Legally, the WTO is structured as a hierarchy of agreements within one integrated whole; and its governance mirrors this structure closely: thus, an overarching political body directs and oversees the work of numerous subsidiary bodies that deal with the issues covered by specific agreements. Ministers representing national governments signed the Final Act at Marrakesh that brought the WTO into existence and turned the negotiated texts into international law; and ministers continue to meet, in principle every two years, in sessions of the Ministerial Conference that constitutes the highest political body of the WTO. The Conference takes decisions on negotiating mandates, and adopts their outcomes; it has issued declarations (including the Doha Declaration on TRIPS and Public Health) and has the capacity to approve amendments to WTO agreements. The bulk of the more routine work of the WTO is conducted by national representatives, typically their Geneva-based ambassadors, meeting regularly as the WTO General Council. The General Council exercises the functions of the Ministerial Conference in the intervals between its sessions: so, for instance, the only amendment to the WTO Multilateral Trade Agreements agreed so far, the public health amendment to TRIPS, was adopted by the General Council in 2005, exercising the functions of the Ministerial Conference.

Apart from its regular work, the General Council meets separately in two distinct modes, both directly relevant to the practical operation of the TRIPS Agreement:

- it convenes as the Dispute Settlement Body (DSB), responsible for the over-sight of the dispute settlement mechanism of the WTO, thus administering all the disputes taken by members concerning WTO agreements including all disputes about TRIPS;
- it convenes as the Trade Policy Review Body, undertaking peer review assess-ments of all WTO members to enhance transparency in, and understanding of, their trade policies and practices, including their intellectual property systems and policy settings.

The Trade Negotiations Committee, an additional body established by the Doha Ministerial Conference, operates under the authority of the General Council, and supervises continuing negotiations in line with the mandate set for the Doha Round.

Making dispute settlement work well, and making sure it is both fair and balanced, and *perceived* to be fair and balanced, were major objectives of the Uruguay Round negotiations. Built into the architecture of the WTO, therefore, are structural and procedural safeguards to make dispute settlement less politi-cal and more judicial in character. When the General Council meets as the DSB, it does not pass judgement on the merits of complaints, but oversees an objective set of dispute settlement procedures. Should one WTO Member wish to pursue a complaint against another, and consultations do not resolve the matter, the DSB establishes a distinct panel which hears the two sides and reports on the dispute; unless the case is settled or withdrawn, the panel draws up recommendations which the DSB then is bound to adopt (unless the DSB is unanimous in rejecting them). From this initial finding, a separate appeal process is available to the Appellate Body (the 'AB'), a distinct element of the WTO system which is kept carefully independent from the political processes of the WTO; it serves as a standing body of senior legal experts who hear appeals on points of law raised in WTO disputes. The DSB appoints AB members and channels appeals to it, but the AB functions independently of the DSB in under-taking its legal work.

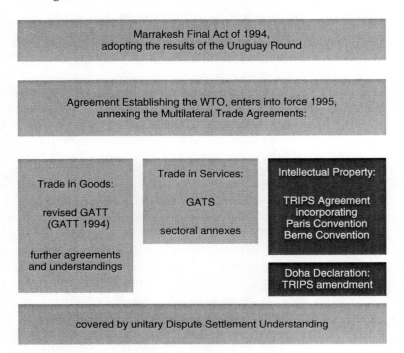

Figure 3.1 Simplified WTO Legal Structure

The next layer of governance below the General Council also closely mirrors the legal structure of the WTO and its trade rules. So, just as the Multilateral Trade Agreements—including the GATT, GATS, and TRIPS—are annexes to the WTO Agreement, the specialized bodies that administer those agreements—the Council for Trade in Goods, the Council for Trade in Services and the Council for TRIPS—are subsidiary bodies operating under the guidance of the General Council, and through it the Ministerial Conference. A glance at both its legal context and its governance within the WTO illustrates how, as a practical matter, TRIPS is firmly embedded in the fabric of multilateral trade law and its governance, following the decision in the course of the Uruguay Round to build IP into a unitary system of trade rules and the multilateral management of trade relations.

This 'embedded' quality of TRIPS has immediate and far-reaching consequences for practitioners, in terms of law, litigation and the conduct of negotiations. It means that TRIPS can be adhered to, interpreted, enforced, contested, monitored, and renegotiated only as one element of the overall package of trade law. It means that any amendment to TRIPS, or any proposed authoritative interpretation of

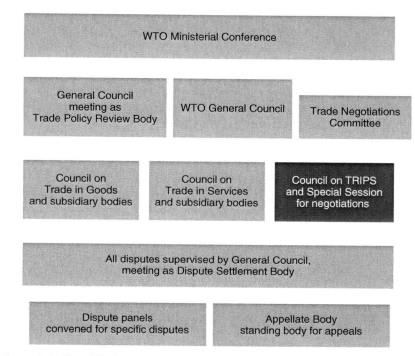

Figure 3.2 Simplified WTO Governance Structure

its text, must be passed from the Council for TRIPS to the General Council; the TRIPS Council has no independent legal authority to interpret or amend 'its own' agreement. All WTO members are automatically members of both the TRIPS Council and the General Council, with equal rights, so any recommendations of the TRIPS Council are likely to be adopted at the higher level. However, the hierarchy of these decision-making bodies is an important reminder of the wider political and legal context within which the WTO must consider any IP issues.

The very obligation to comply with the provisions of TRIPS has a legal basis in the overarching WTO Agreement. It requires each WTO Member to 'ensure the conformity of its laws, regulations and administrative procedures with its obligations as provided in the annexed Agreements' (XVI: 4): the AB has therefore decided that' if a provision of an "annexed Agreement" [such as TRIPS] is breached, a violation of Article XVI: 4 [of the WTO Agreement itself] immediately occurs'. And from a practical perspective, an even more momentous choice was to incorporate TRIPS as one of the 'covered agreements' under the common Dispute Settlement Understanding that establishes detailed procedures for handling disputes over the agreements. Uruguay Round negotiators consciously set aside the option to tailor a distinct dispute settlement mechanism specifically for TRIPS—that model was on the table but was not taken up. Incorporation of TRIPS within the dispute settlement system alongside the other trade agreements means, for example, that,

- the very cause of action for TRIPS disputes—the legal basis for lodging a complaint against another WTO member about IP protection—is not found in TRIPS itself, but in the GATT; the TRIPS article on dispute settlement simply provides that GATT: XXII and XXIII 'as elaborated and applied by the [DSU] shall apply to consultations and the settlement of disputes under [TRIPS]'.
- interpretation of TRIPS as a legal text is shaped and coloured by the background law of the WTO, and the legal heritage of the GATT dispute settlement practice dating back prior to the WTO Agreement itself; this legal background has been used, for instance, in the practice of dispute settlement when considering such questions as how to interpret the core non-discrimination principles of TRIPS.
- complaints about non-compliance with TRIPS have been mixed with complaints about failure to meet obligations under other trade agreements, illustrating that the trade interests that countries bring to the table in disputes are not neatly confined to one category or another: one dispute covered trademark aspects of Indonesia's national car programme alongside a range of conventional trade in goods and services trade issues; another dispute concerned issues of non-discrimination in the protection of geographical indications (GIs), and dealt with TRIPS and GATT provisions side by side.
- disputes about TRIPS have clarified some broader interpretative questions, and thus fed back legal understanding into 'mainstream' WTO law; for instance, one of the first cases to go to the AB concerned TRIPS provisions on patent protection—and this provided the opportunity for the AB to make far-reaching rulings on how WTO law should be interpreted and to clarify how domestic legislation should be considered in assessing compliance with international legal obligations.

Situating TRIPS in the WTO: Values, Ideology, and Theory

Beyond this functional account, the WTO is often perceived to embody a set of values and ideologies, and to function as a vehicle for pushing a particular economic model: in effect, it is viewed as a Geneva branch of the 'Washington consensus', that is the trade arm of the institutions of neo-liberalism—in other words, very generally, favouring liberalized markets and a reliance on the private sector to deliver public goods. This characterization is perhaps influenced by the mandate of the WTO to 'provide the common institutional framework for the conduct of trade relations among its Members', and its general focus on progressive trade liberalization—the goal, captured in the preamble to the WTO Agreement, of contributing to certain objectives 'by entering into reciprocal and mutually advantageous arrangements directed to the substantial reduction of tariffs and other barriers to trade and to the elimination of discriminatory treatment in international trade relations'.

But looking further at the 'objectives' that this institution is intended to progress, the non-commercial public interest objectives of public policy are included: trade and economic relations should aim to raise standards of living, ensure full employment and growth in real income; and expand production of and trade in goods and services,

while allowing for the optimal use of the world's resources in accordance with the objective of sustainable development, seeking both to protect and preserve the environment and to enhance the means for doing so in a manner consistent with their respective needs and concerns at different levels of economic development.

The objective of the original GATT, negotiated in the immediate post war era, referred to the 'full use of the resources of the world'; but, as the AB itself has pointed out, this objective 'was no longer appropriate to the world trading system of the 1990s', and was modified to refer to sustainable development and environmental protection. The AB remarked that this language reflected 'the intentions of negotiators of the WTO Agreement' and that 'it must add colour, texture and shading to . . . interpretation of the [annexed] agreements'. The basic assumption is indeed that trade and economic activity is on the whole beneficial and desirable; but not a sense that trade is an end in itself, nor that trade relations should be regulated from a narrow theoretical or ideological base; the more recent recognition of environmental concerns, for instance, reflects a broader shift in the political and cultural context of international trade relations.

TRIPS itself, within the WTO system, epitomizes the complexities that arise when trying to bridge between the management of trade relations and an engagement with a wider set of policy concerns and interests, as well as international legal principles and the institutions that embody those principles. It is no accident that the only agreed amendment to the entire WTO corpus of trade agreements since 1995 has been to TRIPS, and to deal with that most fundamental of public policy interests—public health. And questions continue as to whether TRIPS presages a healthy, timely broadening of the trade agenda to reflect transformations of the economy, or whether it amounts to an undesirable intrusion of legal principles and commercial interests into the governance of trade relations, that threatens the health of the overall system.

Contesting the Idea of TRIPS

In practice, TRIPS is already well embedded into the practical functioning of the organization and the settlement of trade disputes. Yet critics continue to argue that TRIPS is an anomaly within the WTO system. They contend that IP is a constraint on trade, and that pressure on trading partners to strengthen IP protection is a new-age kind of protectionism. By this conception of the WTO, it should have no business in establishing such standards for domestic regulation. Eminent trade economist Jagdish Bhagwati accepted as a legitimate development the novel incorporation of services into the trade law system, in the form of GATS. But by sharp contrast he likened the incorporation of TRIPS to,

the introduction of cancer cells into a healthy body. For virtually the first time, the corporate lobbies . . . had distorted and deformed an important multilateral institution, turning it away from its trade mission and rationale, and transforming it into a royalty collection agency.

Criticism of TRIPS may be levelled either at its standards *as such* and their direct economic and social impact, or at its systemic consequences—the very idea of building obligations to protect IP into trade law, potentially transforming the essential character of institutions such as the WTO. In thinking through these critiques—which any active TRIPS practitioner will need to do, when working on wider legal and policy questions—and in analysing the place of TRIPS within the WTO, clarity is needed on both aspects—what is the direct effect of TRIPS obligations, and how does TRIPS influence the trade law system— and on the distinction between them. Both aspects are highly significant, but for practitioners they have different consequences. TRIPS did set standards for IP protection that were unprecedented in scope and rigour, although the actual legal text is not what any specific lobbyist or interest group wanted, and it is not an inflexible model law. But the broader legal context of TRIPS also redefined both how IP standards would be interpreted and what it means to comply with these standards. Initially, critics felt that this new 'trade-related' version of IP would focus IP law and policy to serve a narrow base of commercial interests, and exclude traditional public interest concerns. But, in practice, the incorporation of IP into this wider legal context has opened up new interpretative contexts and new avenues to incorporate public policy interests and legal concepts drawn from other fields of public law. Equally, TRIPS has influenced the character of trade law within and beyond the WTO—numerous bilateral and regional agreements now incorporate provisions on IP whereas in the past these ordinarily would not have dealt with substantive IP law.

Roots of the WTO

At its inception, multilateral trade law had little scope for the positive protection of IP. The elements of the post-war economic order were developed in 1944 at the Bretton Woods Conference; this yielded the International Bank for Reconstruction and Development (IBRD—the World Bank) and the International Monetary Fund (IMF); these were to be supplemented by an International Trade Organization (ITO) to deal with trade relations. In 1947, the United Nations Conference on Trade and Employment adopted the Havana Charter for the ITO, establishing a broad mandate for this new body. In considering the role of the WTO, it is critical to recall that the motivation for multilateral governance of trade grew not from vague utopianism or economic fundamentalism, but as a firmly realist response to two ruinous wars and an intervening period of economic crisis and political instability. In working through the legal complexity, institutional labyrinths, vaunting rhetoric, byzantine dealmaking, and seemingly endless procedural welter of the international system, it is easy to overlook this primary, central impulse. Trade barriers, experience of discriminatory dealings in trade relations, perceptions of exclusion, and fears of lack of sustainable access to essential resources fuelled economic crisis and political breakdown that stoked the outbreak of war.

One of the principal actors in this period set out this rationale in words that are frequently quoted, but for sound reasons:

you could not separate the idea of commerce from the idea of war and peace . . . wars were often largely caused by economic rivalry conducted unfairly . . . unhampered trade dovetailed with peace; high tariffs, trade barriers, and unfair economic competition, with war. Though realizing that many other factors were involved, I reasoned that, if we could get a freer flow of trade—freer in the sense of fewer discriminations and obstructions—so that one country would not be deadly jealous of another and the living standards of all countries might rise, thereby eliminating the economic dissatisfaction that breeds war, we might have a reasonable chance for lasting peace.

But another kind of realism—realism about what is manageable in domestic politics—tempers such global ambitions for open trade. International commitments may be used to lock in sound policy settings and to defend them against sectoral interests in domestic politics; but, equally, international outcomes must be sold back home. And, over time, it became clear that the United States would not ratify the Havana Charter, owing to concerns about its impact on sovereignty and its potential intrusions on domestic policymaking. Hence the Havana Charter was not implemented and the ITO failed to materialize.

The Havana Charter had covered a wide sweep of economic governance issues, including employment, commodity agreements, restrictive business practices, international investment and services. Its section on restrictive business practices dealt with the anti-competitive misuse of IP, a theme still of policy interest today in the continuing debate about how best to balance competition policy and the IP system to achieve the objectives of TRIPS. The political climate turned against this ambitious charter. However, a pragmatic approach to multilateral trade governance enabled the effective implementation of the GATT, which was harvested from the negotiations on general principles governing trade and on substantial tariff reductions based on reciprocal concessions. To deal with domestic concerns about ratification, the original GATT was brought into being as an interim measure: it was essentially the chapter on Commercial Policy extracted from the Havana Charter, brought into force through a Protocol of Provisional Application (which entered into force in 1948), ostensibly pending the entry into force of the full ITO Charter (which finally faltered in 1950).

The evolution of the GATT is a telling case study of the nature of international law and multilateral governance: despite its interim, almost improvized, nature as an international instruments, and its 'provisional' application, the GATT provided the framework for multilateral negotiations and dispute settlement on trade up to the creation of the WTO in 1995. Eight rounds of trade negotiations followed the conclusion of the GATT, focusing at first on tariffs on industrial products and quantitative restrictions, and later on non-tariff measures such as safeguards, subsidies, anti-dumping, and technical barriers to trade. This period also saw the evolution of the dispute settlement mechanism, and a growing body of jurisprudence on trade disputes, maturing from an informal, essentially diplomatic, approach into the more legalistic system that now prevails when two countries seek to settle disputes.

The Uruguay Round was the final trade round under the GATT as such, and concluded in April 1994 with a Ministerial Conference at Marrakesh which adopted TRIPS as a part of a large package of trade agreements, collectively forming the Final Act of the Uruguay Round. While this outcome went much further than earlier rounds in its scope and institutional formality, there are strong elements of continuity between the GATT system before and after the Uruguay Round. The Round consolidated and formalized a set of trends that had developed over the life of the GATT since the immediate postwar negotiations—trends towards a more legalized and less diplomatic approach to dispute settlement, and towards recognizing many factors other than import tariffs that can distort a fair competitive relationship between domestic and foreign firms. And even TRIPS itself, despite its apparent novelty within the trade law system, has stronger links with the GATT system than may meet the eye.

Intellectual Property under the GATT

Comprehensive, mandatory standards on IP protection were no part of the original conception of the ITO; IP protection was considered foreign to the GATT for much of its history. In fact, the chief reference to IP in the GATT is as an *exception* to its rules. GATT:XX stipulates that the provisions of the GATT should not get in the way of measures to protect patents, trade marks and copyrights, and to prevent deceptive practices, unless those measures amount to 'arbitrary or unjustifiable discrimination' or 'a disguised restriction on international trade'. This exception was clarified under the pre-WTO GATT when the US Tariffs Act was challenged. This law was amended in 1988 to allow the International Trade Commission, an agency of the US Federal Government, to take action against imports that infringed IP rights and threatened damage to US industry interests, under the general rubric of suppressing unfair competition.

It is a fundamental principle of trade law—albeit one with significant exceptions—that foreign traders' goods should not be discriminated against and should be treated no less favourably than domestically produced goods: the principle of national treatment. And despite the GATT:XX exception, the US system of IP protection was found to have breached the national treatment requirement of GATT, because it gave US goods better treatment than foreign-sourced goods. Even though the mechanism had a legitimate objective (that of protecting IPRs), the particular approach taken was found to fall within the definition of a 'measure that constitutes a means of arbitrary or unjustifiable discrimination between countries where the same conditions prevail, or a disguised restriction on international trade'. This case underscored that IP protection was not a kind of trump card that excluded the operation of the basic trade law principles of non-discrimination, and that IP laws had to be implemented and enforced in harmony with these principles.

Yet the essential impulse under the GATT was to negotiate and then consolidate improved conditions for non-discriminatory market access for goods—initially lowering tariffs, and then through the progressive dismantlement of non-tariff barriers. This meant, in principle, ever lower levels of government interference in trade. Yet TRIPS is about insisting that governments actively intervene to prevent certain forms of commercial practices—illegitimate infringements of IP rights. An apparent contradiction then arises between:

- the creation and protection of exclusive rights under the IP system: these rights by definition act to restrict commercial activity and require the active intervention of government in trade, in particular the provision of legal means to halt the importation of infringing goods, and
- the liberalizing trend in international trade, effected through the progressive reduction of governmental barriers to trade (tariffs, quotas and discriminatory regulatory restrictions) through mutual agreement, and the de facto elimination of barriers to trade through the application of technologies which are creating virtual global markets

Within the WTO system, this contrast is most neatly captured by comparing TRIPS to the Agreement on Technical Barriers to Trade (the TBT Agreement): this agreement is, in effect, a 'maximum standard' or a ceiling on government regulation. Under the TBT, 'technical regulations should be no more trade-restrictive than necessary to achieve a legitimate objective'—in other words, government regulation should in principle be effected by the least trade-restrictive measure. Regulation to achieve any legitimate objective is not *mandated* by the agreement— you can be consistent with the TBT by choosing not to have any technical regulations at all; but when you choose to introduce regulations they should not be discriminatory or unnecessarily restrictive to trade.

By contrast, TRIPS has extensive, mandatory obligations concerning the availability, administration and enforcement of IP. The section on border control measures in effect requires a distinct layer of government regulation on international trade, which must cover at least counterfeit trade mark and pirated copyright goods, but can cover other IP-protected goods as well. Unlike the TBT, you are in breach of TRIPS if you do not take positive steps to give effect to its standards. Rather than limiting the scope of government regulation, TRIPS insists upon it. Further, as it is a 'minimum standard' agreement, rather than setting a ceiling, it imposes a floor: compliance with its standards is required, but they can be exceeded, since TRIPS:1.1 provides that, 'Members may ... implement in their law more extensive protection than is required by 'TRIPS]'. Teasing out and reconciling these apparent contradictions is the central challenge of locating IP standards within trade law in a workable manner.

The very idea of TRIPS—IP law as trade law—provokes some fundamental questions:

- What is 'trade' anyway? What kind of international commercial transactions should be recognized as suitable to be regulated through trade law—in particular, does the transformation of economic life and the impact of technology mean that alongside trade in physical goods, trade law should also deal with transactions concerning the intangible, knowledge-based component of trade and transactions essentially concerning rights of access to protected material? In short, are iTunes downloads also a kind of international trade, alongside shipments of physical CDs?
- What is international trade law *for*? Is the objective to advance 'free trade' as an end in itself—the longstanding Bretton Woods goal of progressive, nondiscriminatory liberalization; or is there a deeper idea of encouraging 'legitimate trade'—not eliminating all barriers to trade for the sake of it, but removing regulations that create distortions and unfairness in international trade? Given the intense debate over 'free trade' versus 'fair trade', this question goes well beyond the challenge of accommodating TRIPS within the trade law system—it goes to the heart of ideas of economic theory, and even how global justice and fairness should drive the evolution of trade law.

To the critics of TRIPS, reconciling IP standards with classical liberal trade law is fundamentally a theoretically unsound proposition: they stand poles apart. Yet the original GATT did give a very slender hint of how to reconcile these ideas—in acknowledging the need to suppress misleading indications of the origin of goods, as a basic requirement for fairness in commerce. One of the central areas of IP law concerns the protection of distinctive names, signs and other indications—trade names, trademarks, GIs. The law of distinctive signs has its roots in the law of unfair competition and fair trading, reflecting the public policy interest in preventing misleading and deceptive behaviour in the marketplace . This area of IP law has the strongest intuitive base for the general public—effecting a fundamental norm against deceiving or misleading the consumer.

Suppressing unfair trade was a negotiating objective at the first conference to work on the Paris Convention, in 1880. The evolution of Paris over the following century gradually strengthened the scope of this obligation, and has focused especially on trade that infringes trademarks and trade names (Paris:9), acts that directly or indirectly falsely indicate where goods come from or falsely identify the commercial entity linked to goods (Paris:10), and 'unfair competition' in general, defined as 'any act of competition contrary to honest practices in industrial or commercial matters', including acts that create confusion or mislead the public regarding traded goods (Paris:10*bis*). This standard is directly applied as a TRIPS obligation, and also helps shape the standard in TRIPS for protection of GIs.

Perhaps the first fully 'trade-related' multilateral agreement on IP, the 'Madrid Agreement for the Repression of False or Deceptive Indications of Source on Goods' was concluded in 1891: it aimed at preventing the importation of goods with false or misleading indications. The same interests were pursued at the Versailles peace conference, and in the League of Nations, as an element of 'equitable treatment for the commerce of all Members' in its covenant. International law gradually developed a common, but very general standard of 'legitimacy' in international trade. The Paris Convention now articulates a widely accepted obligation actively to suppress trade that unfairly usurps or damages the reputation of other traders as a means of damaging their competitive position. Determining what is 'unfair' is difficult, and to some extent subjective and dependent on cultural and economic differences, but the general principle is firmly established.

Now consider how the GATT, the central text of international trade law, deals with a similar concept. GATT:IX concerns national rules governing marks of origin on traded goods. It mostly aims, in line with the general thrust of trade law, to set a ceiling on national regulations on origin marking, requiring them not to be discriminatory among trading partners and not to be too burdensome. But it recognizes that consumers should be protected against fraudulent or misleading indications, not unlike the Paris idea of unfair competition. Unlike multilateral IP law (and the future TRIPS), it doesn't specifically require laws to be passed. But it creates a positive international obligation to cooperate 'with a view to preventing the use of trade names in such manner as to misrepresent the true origin of a product, to the detriment of such distinctive regional or geographical names of products of the territory of a [country] as are protected by its legislation.' To be sure, it differs from a core 'IP' or 'GI' approach, but it does broadly reflect some concepts found in Paris, and in later TRIPS rules on GIs, such as restricting obligations to names already protected in the country of origin (compare TRIPS: 24.9). An obligation to 'accord full and sympathetic consideration' to 'requests or representations' regarding product names almost contains a hint of the current TRIPS negotiations on a multilateral register of GIs.

A pre-WTO dispute panel considered this provision under the GATT. The case pivoted on the general GATT principle of national treatment, but it also considered whether it was legitimate commercial activity for Japanese producers to use English, French or German terms, such as *Chateau* or *Reserve* or *Village*. This case—decided under the mainstream trade law of GATT—dealt with issues relevant to GI protection that still confront the WTO today. It illustrates how the original GATT requires some action to preserve an idea of legitimacy or fairness in commercial activity—and that this requirement has surprising resonances with the long evolution of the idea of 'unfair competition' in the Paris Convention.

What, then, is the proper context for TRIPS within an international trade law system? How should the doctrines of IP law be reconciled with the broad tenets and functions of trade law? One approach is to focus on the common idea that certain commercial activities are considered illegitimate; that when countries negotiate on the rules that should govern their trade relations, they accept that certain trading activities are unfair or illegitimate, and that they have a positive obligation either to suppress such activities or at least to introduce legal mechanisms enabling them to be suppressed under domestic law by interested parties. Among such illegitimate or unfair activities are infringements of IP rights, considered as such according to standards of protection set at a reasonable level and consistent with broad international practice and the background law of IP.

IP law is a complex set of legal ideas, and forms of protection and exploitation of IP vary greatly. But there is one, simple central idea that is common to IP law: for certain, well-defined subject matter, one should have the right to object to certain, defined uses that another makes of the protected material, or to set conditions for how that other party uses it. IP standards then determine in great detail what subject matter should be so recognized, what kind of uses of it should be potentially constrained, and what should be the consequences of such misuse. These detailed standards are guided, elaborated and revised, mostly under domestic law, according to basic public policy considerations.

Table 3.1 Embedded Ideas of Legitimate Trade and Public Policy in IP Law

Field of IP	What is protected?	Against what illegitimate acts?	Why?
Copyright law	Literary/artistic works	Unauthorized public use, commercial reproduction	Promote creative industries, cultural freedoms, educational policy
Patent law	Inventions	Unauthorized uses, particularly on commercial scale	Competition through technological innovation, technology dissemination, incentive to invest
Distinctive marks and signs	Trademarks, GIs, trade names	Misleading or deceptive uses, unfair use of others' reputation	Consumer information, fair trading, competition
Design law	Industrial designs	Commercial use and reproduction	Fair competition, innovation through original design
Undisclosed information	Trade secrets, test data	Unfair commercial use, breach of confidentiality	Repress illicit and unfair commercial activity, promote production of test data and new products

The point of entry—or, from a critic's point of view, the thin end of the wedge—for IP standards within trade law is acceptance that standards against unfair competition need to be enforced both for the market to serve the public interest and for international trade relations to meet political expectations: an economic and a political rationale. Building on the idea that trade law can require the suppression of confusing or deceptive marking or description of goods, and the misleading invocation of a competitor's reputation, a more elaborate case can be built that other accepted forms of IP infringement are also illegitimate and should be suppressed to maintain a balanced and fair marketplace that similarly promotes public welfare. That bare assertion begs enormous questions, including what forms and levels of IP protection are fair and appropriate, and what amounts to an improper suppression of legitimate commercial activity—a question that has been the central challenge of IP lawmaking for some four centuries. We know that this debate will never be fully resolved even within a single jurisdiction, and that ideas of what amounts to an appropriate level of protection will evolve under the influence of economic, technological, and social change. So, in articulating a common approach to what amounts to legitimacy in trade, TRIPS expresses general principles and broad expectations as to how IP protection should be carried out, without venturing into the closer details that are found in national laws and regulations and in the detailed findings of courts and administrative authorities. TRIPS therefore defines a level of 'legitimacy' in trade and clarifies what a trading nation can reasonably expect in terms of access to IP protection for its nationals in foreign markets—lack of discrimination, procedural fairness, and a reasonable standard of protection.

Is TRIPS a 'Market Access' Agreement?

Trade negotiators see their central task as negotiating market access, and they typically choose a mix of two general approaches. Under the 'managed trade' or 'fix outcome' model, they cut deals on specific targets—import quotas or other directly measurable levels of access especially in politically sensitive areas. A 'rules-based' or 'fix rules' approach aims at agreeing on common standards that will give firms a reasonable opportunity to compete in foreign markets. Rules-based negotiations originally created market access by lowering tariffs and then by decreasing other regulatory barriers, on a non-discriminatory ('most favoured nation') basis. Trade deals do not, on the whole, remove barriers altogether but aim to ensure that regulations are reasonable and are applied without discrimination.

Underlying the rules-based approach is the central idea that firms should have a fair opportunity to compete.

For some of its harsher critics, TRIPS is the ultimate 'managed trade' deal: a special favour for the industry sectors that lobbied for it; nothing to do with market access. But TRIPS is most usefully viewed as a set of non-discriminatory principles that clarify and augment—even bring up to date—the idea that trade rules should give all traders a fair opportunity to compete, so that the public benefits from the enhanced competition. IP law draws its roots from the law of competition and protection of the freedom to ply one's trade, and the idea of a transparent and fair market place. The roots of patent law in many countries are found in the Statute of Monopolies passed by the English Parliament in 1623. This law aimed to eliminate harmful monopolies and illegitimate restraints on trade based 'upon misinformations and untrue pretences of public good', while consciously carving out patents of invention as legitimate exceptions to this general rule. Along similar lines today, the public policy rationale of IP law is the recognition that innovation—whether in technology, design, creative works, or branding—is an important form of competition that serves the public interest. Competition policy aims to limit excessive market power through promoting rivalry and the entry of new firms. Innovation is a vital ingredient of effective rivalry and market entry. Recent 'endogenous' theories of economic growth accept that innovation must be incorporated integrally within explanations of how the market functions; contrasting with the classical growth model which focused on the accumulation of capital and labour, and treated growth of productivity through technological development as a given, or as 'exogenous' to the theory of growth.

TRIPS becomes a stronger candidate for a genuine trade agreement once we recognize that innovation is a key aspect of market access and competitive rivalry, and once the knowledge component of economic activity is systematically integrated into mainstream trade law. Many firms rely on innovation and their distinctive reputation to compete, in turn advancing the overall welfare of society. A reasonably sure legal framework is required to support this competition. Systematically undermining the competitive edge that a firm sustains through innovation and distinctive reputation is effectively to deny market access to that firm.

Of course IP can be used in undesirable ways to suppress competition. To create absolute, unbounded and impervious IP rights would be the kind of anti-competitive sectoral protectionism that some critics of TRIPS can assume it to be. But to preclude IP protection outright, or systematically to negate its effect in practice, would deny the public much of the benefits from the competitive effect of innovation. Thus policymakers have long sought a balance, captured in the Jacobean Statute of Monopolies and now exemplified in the objectives for IP protection articulated in TRIPS:7.

Stronger recognition of competitive interests in innovation also shaped the political environment, generating demand for trade rules on IP. Effectively denying IP protection, or systematically negating its effect, thwarts legitimate expectations of market access for trading partners. This can spur a realist assertion of concrete economic interests, in the form of trade retaliation. In turn, such unilateral measures in defence of IP interests kindles demand for objective and predictable standards on IP protection to be agreed multilaterally, so as to avoid the welfare costs of more random, power-based resolution of disagreements.

TRIPS took shape, therefore, as a way of defining what amounts to a fair competitive relationship in international trade, by incorporating into trade law the kind of economic interests that IP law has long recognized. A close look at the legal rationale of dispute settlement illustrates that the true cause of action in TRIPS dispute settlement is not non-compliance as such—the legal basis for taking a complaint is the nullification or impairment of expected benefits relating to IP protection. In practice, failure to comply with TRIPS is considered, prima facie, to deny expected benefits under TRIPS, and it is very difficult to overcome this assumption. But at the level of principle, it is important to clarify that TRIPS compliance is not insisted upon as an end in itself, and is not the essential grounds of a dispute—the basic function of dispute settlement under TRIPS is therefore to preserve entitlements to a fair or legitimate competitive relationship between competitors, inasmuch as these concern appropriate IP protection at an objectively agreed common level which is available without discrimination and without unreasonable burdens, such entitlements bring strictly defined by the provisions of TRIPS itself rather than any more politicised or uncertain claims.

Ultimately, then, a stronger conceptual footing for TRIPS within the body of WTO trade law can be found if a suitable level of IP protection is accepted both as a legitimate claim in international trade relations and as an important element of effective market access and a fair opportunity to compete, when the idea of 'competition' is not static, but includes capacity to innovate and to establish a distinctive reputation in the marketplace.

4

A Practical Anatomy of TRIPS

The TRIPS regime is a treaty that establishes a public international law regime which is intended to reinforce the protection of IPRs through the establishment of minimum standards and to commit states to provide adequate enforcement mechanisms and access to justice to IPRs holders. Though TRIPS will lead to the gradual harmonization of IPRs laws as regards its basic principles, the agreement does not qualify as a uniform law which supersedes the territorial character of national IPRs systems and which simultaneously produces the same effect in the territories of all WTO Members.

Andres Moncayo von Hase

We stress the importance of IPRs related to trade . . . Nevertheless . . . [TRIPS] should not become a subterfuge for restrictive and anti-competitive practices . . .

De Mario Reyes Chavez, National Secretary for
International Economic Relation, Bolivia

The Hybrid Structure of TRIPS

The actual text of TRIPS itself comprises a preamble and seven parts. Its provisions cover the substantive standards for IP protection, but also set out underlying principles that govern the IP system, and define how the rights are exercised, administered and enforced so as to achieve that welfare-enhancing balance of interests that its principles espouse. But TRIPS is more than the legal text that meets the eye. First, it is not a stand-alone treaty: there are no 'signatories' to TRIPS itself. It is one element of a composite legal text, subordinate to an integrated institutional structure. Second, TRIPS imports provisions from WIPO treaties beyond the scope of the WTO altogether, and gives them separate legal effect distinct from their own legal status. Third, its hybrid quality means that the text of TRIPS is not a bare set of words, but a text with deep roots, influenced by four streams of legal tradition: the broad principles of international IP law; international trade and economic law, epitomized by the GATT and the case law of the WTO; public international law on human rights, the environment and other fields of global policy interest; and national traditions of IP lawmaking and administration. And TRIPS, in turn, feeds back into each of those legal traditions. Further, TRIPS has been subject to later developments—the Doha Declaration, an agreed amendment, and dispute settlement findings. So the text of TRIPS that its negotiators signed at Marrakesh is only one part of the law of TRIPS.

The full 'text' of TRIPS is also much more than the words to be found in Annex 1C of the Uruguay Round package. Figure 4.1 is a *simplified* illustration of the composite texts that define TRIPS standards. Accordingly, it is not possible to read and interpret TRIPS without directly consulting the substantive texts of other international IP conventions—especially Paris and Berne, but also on more specialized subjects Rome and Washington (IPIC). Most importantly, TRIPS incorporates all the substantive law of Paris and almost all of Berne, even though these treaties have distinct legal status, are separately administered by WIPO, and legally bind most countries independently of any obligations within the WTO (by 2010, 173 countries had adhered to Paris, and 164 to Berne; the WTO had 153 members). So TRIPS requires compliance with the standards of WIPO treaties, even when Members have separately chosen to adhere to them directly or when, by reason of their legal status, they are ineligible to sign them (eg the European Communities and Hong Kong, China, are both Members of the WTO directly bound by TRIPS, but neither can directly adhere to Paris and Berne).

Some uncertainty clouded the status of these treaties as part of the 'text' of TRIPS, until clarifications were developed during dispute settlement. These uncertainties were not legal curiosities but went to the heart of what TRIPS required as a treaty, as these two questions illustrate:

- Were the 'new' provisions of TRIPS itself on a higher level and considered to be later in time than the earlier provisions introduced into TRIPS from Paris and Berne? No. The Panel in *US—Section 110(5) Copyright Act* confirmed that the imported provisions of Berne applied directly as an integral part of TRIPS; further, the 'new' provisions of TRIPS and the introduced provisions of Berne 'entered into force at the same point in time', so there was no application of the legal principle that a later treaty supersedes an earlier treaty on the same point, and there is no legal hierarchy between 'pure TRIPS' and 'Berne within TRIPS'.

- Must TRIPS explicitly mention an area of IP explicitly for it to part of a Member's obligations? No. A dispute settlement panel, in *US—Section 211 Appropriations Act*, decided that TRIPS did not cover the protection of trade names even though Paris did, since this area of IP was not specifically listed in the TRIPS text. The AB overturned this finding, and ruled that the relevant Paris obligation did apply directly to WTO Members and was not 'conditioned' by its incorporation within TRIPS—so, as for Berne, Paris obligations are not in a lower category than TRIPS provisions on the same matter.

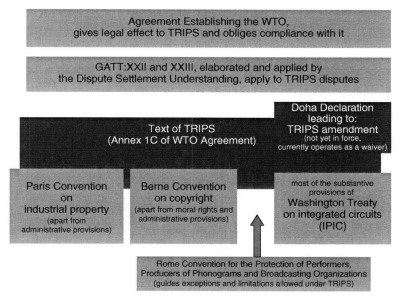

Figure 4.1 The Texts of TRIPS

The Legal Effect of TRIPS

TRIPS binds all members of the WTO—no reservations are possible. It is not possible to adhere separately to TRIPS without joining the WTO. But its obligations came into effect over time.

(cont.)

January 1, 1995	The WTO Agreement comes into force, bringing TRIPS into force, as one of the annexed agreements.
January 1, 1996	Developed country WTO Members obliged to give full effect to TRIPS provisions; all WTO members obliged to respect non-discrimination principles.
January 1, 2000	Developing countries (apart from LDCs) and economies in transition obliged to give full effect to TRIPS provisions, apart from extension of product patents.
January 1, 2005	Developing countries (apart from LDCs) and economies in transition obliged to extend patent protection to all technologies covered by TRIPS.
January 1, 2006	Original deadline for LDCs to comply with TRIPS provisions.
July 1, 2013	Revised deadline for LDCs (apart from pharmaceutical patents); further extension possible upon request.
January 1, 2016	LDCs due to introduce patents for pharmaceutical products.

The obligation to comply with TRIPS is found in the Agreement itself—'Members shall give effect to the provisions of this Agreement'—but ultimately stems from the WTO Agreement ('Each Member shall ensure the conformity of its laws, regulations and administrative procedures with its obligations as provided in the annexed Agreements')—so that a failure to comply with TRIPS is also a breach of the WTO Agreement; WTO dispute settlement has confirmed this.

Accession: when a country joins the WTO, an agreement is struck on the terms of accession—the 'Protocol of Accession'—which specifies the timing for that country's obligations, including under TRIPS, and refers also to more detailed understandings about an acceding member's approach to fulfilling its obligations and the timeline for giving effect to TRIPS. Accession is a kind of contractual deal involving extensive negotiations on the terms of joining the WTO; while this mostly concerns trade in goods and services, acceding countries may also agree on additional obligations relating to IP, apart from the specific obligations of TRIPS. Such additions are considered integral to the WTO Agreement for that Member.

Box 4.1 The Content of TRIPS

Preamble

Part I: General provisions and basic principles

Part II: Standards concerning the availability, scope and use of IP rights

1. Copyright and Related Rights

2. Trademarks

3. Geographical Indications

4. Industrial Designs

5. Patents (*includes plant variety protection*)

6. Layout-Designs (Topographies) of Integrated Circuits

7. Protection of Undisclosed Information (*includes test data protection*)

8. Control of Anti-Competitive Practices in Contractual Licences

Part III: Enforcement of IP rights

1. General Obligations

2. Civil and Administrative Procedures and Remedies

3. Provisional Measures

4. Special Requirements Related to Border Measures

5. Criminal Procedures

Part IV: Acquisition and maintenance of IP rights and related inter-partes procedures

Part V: Dispute Prevention And Settlement

Part VI: Transitional Arrangements

Part VII: Institutional Arrangements; Final Provisions

The Content of TRIPS

The preamble

The preamble of TRIPS is not empty rhetoric, and merits careful reading. It sets the context for TRIPS standards, without making law in itself. Dispute settlement panels and the AB itself have therefore used the preamble as a touchstone for confirming their readings of the operational text. For instance, in *EC—Trademarks and Geographical Indications*, the panel observed that,

the object and purpose of the TRIPS Agreement, as indicated by Articles 9 through 62 and 70 and *reflected in the preamble*, includes the provision of adequate standards and principles concerning the availability, scope, use and enforcement of trade-related intellectual property rights. (emphasis added)

The preamble looks back at the political difficulties that ultimately led to the decision to build a stronger foundation of multilateral rules to settle disagreements on IP, and looks forward to the gradual reconciliation of IP law with trade law. Thus, uniquely among the WTO package of agreements, the TRIPS preamble cites the importance of 'reducing tensions by reaching strengthened commitments to resolve disputes on trade-related intellectual property issues through multilateral procedures'. This reference to 'tensions' gives a measure of the political background of the negotiations—not even the original GATT, born as it was from ruinous trade rivalry and a world war, is so explicit about the link between stronger multilateral rules on trade and the reduction of tensions. TRIPS aims at establishing 'effective and expeditious procedures for the multilateral prevention and settlement of disputes between governments', a continuous reminder of the essential, practical legal function of TRIPS.

The preamble also suggests that infringements of IP are a form of 'distortion' of trade, while recognizing that IP protection should not itself become a barrier to legitimate trade—note, again, this reconciliation of IP law and trade law in the idea that trade law has a proper role in determining that certain forms of trade are not legitimate and can and should be suppressed, but that such 'suppression' should not overreach itself and interfere with legitimate trading activities. The preamble recalls that national IP systems are intended to serve public policy objectives, including development and technological objectives. The preamble sets TRIPS rules squarely in the context both of the foundational principles of the GATT, and the existing IP treaties, reflecting the historic role of TRIPS as a bridge and a synthesis between these two established streams of international law.

Part I: General Provisions and Basic Principles

This Part sets out the scope and essential policy basis of TRIPS. Importantly for TRIPS practice, it determines the scope of 'intellectual property' covered by TRIPS obligations—as we have seen, the AB has clarified that this covers the categories specifically listed in Part II (see the outline in Box 4.1), but also trade names which are included in Paris. Other categories are also mentioned in TRIPS, such as plant variety protection. This meant, for example, that Members must protect trade names in a non-discriminatory way even though they are not mentioned explicitly in the text of TRIPS itself. This Part clarifies that the key non-discrimination obligations under TRIPS have a wide scope, including 'matters affecting the availability, acquisition, scope, maintenance and enforcement' of IP rights, not merely, therefore, concerning substantive standards alone but how they are administered and enforced. Some forms of IP are not included in this scope—such as the distinct, *sui generis* protection of traditional knowledge (TK) that a number of countries are introducing; this protection could, in principle, be reserved for domestic TK holders (although when IP measures covered by TRIPS—such as GIs, unfair competition and confidentiality—are used to protect aspects of TK, the normal rules on non-discrimination would apply).

Non-discrimination

What does non-discrimination mean in practice? Two broad principles apply:

- 'national treatment': foreign nationals must enjoy at least the level of treatment enjoyed by domestic nationals (the 'trade law' version of this principle) or just the same as that enjoyed by domestic nationals (the Paris/Berne version); so if domestic patent holders are entitled to extend their patent terms beyond the 20 years TRIPS requires, then so must patent holders from any WTO Member.
- 'most favoured nation (MFN)': an 'advantage, favour, privilege or immunity' granted to the nationals of any other country must be 'accorded immediately and unconditionally to the nationals of all other Members'; so if a bilateral deal is done to offer patent term extensions to nationals of one country, the same benefit should flow through to nationals of all others that are in the WTO.

The provisions on non-discrimination represent the most important convergence of the trade law of GATT and the IP law of Paris and Berne. In fact, the original version of Paris, in 1883, basically only required national treatment, as well as a 'right of priority' which was a practical means of non-discrimination (it gave foreign nationals a reasonable period to lodge applications in other countries based on their home filing). A country could be technically compliant with the original Paris Convention and not have a patent system at all—because foreign nationals were not discriminated against; but as soon as patents were available for domestic nationals, they had to be available on essentially the same terms to those from other Paris Convention countries (in fact, Paris legally constituted a 'union' of nations for the purpose of protecting industrial property). National treatment in IP laws should not be taken for granted: it has not always been available, and many hold an intuitive view—a kind of 'IP mercantilism'—that granting IP rights to foreigners is an economic loss, and should only be extended to them if they bargain their way into the domestic system on the basis of reciprocal concessions. And indeed there remains a residue of this kind of reciprocal bargaining in the IP treaties, notably concerning copyright terms. Even so, national treatment is firmly established as a core principle of international IP law, stemming from concerns in the globalizing marketplace of the 1870s that failure to grant IP rights to foreigners amounted to a form of unfair competition—in brief, just the same concerns that drove the TRIPS negotiations over a century later in a later phase of globalization.

The GATT version of national treatment applies to goods, rather than IP right holders, but the same broad idea applies. The AB has clarified that GATT:III obliges Members to 'provide equality of competitive conditions' for imported as against domestically produced goods. How IP is administered and enforced affects those competitive conditions: in fact, as we have seen, pre-WTO GATT case law covered concerns about IP protection that discriminated against the goods of foreign traders. GATT:XX allows exceptions to national treatment where necessary for IP protection, but this does not entitle a Member to discriminate unreasonably against imported goods. And since TRIPS has effectively merged IP and trade law, several cases have addressed national treatment concerns under both GATT and TRIPS in parallel: when the EU was found to impose an 'extra hurdle' on foreigners seeking protection of GIs, this was a breach of national treatment under both TRIPS and GATT, based on the failure to provide 'effective equality of opportunities'—recalling the essential thrust of incorporating IP within trade law. But these are still distinct, and complementary, ideas of fairness in trading opportunities. The Panel contrasted the GATT idea of national treatment—'equality of conditions of competition between products'—with the TRIPS version—'effective equality of opportunities for nationals with regard to the protection of IP rights'. In practice, these two distinct legal ideas overlap.

The MFN principle is, by contrast, new to multilateral IP law, even though the AB has termed it 'one of the cornerstones of the world trading system' and 'in a word, fundamental'. IP treaties typically left more latitude for deals that gave nationals of one country a better level of treatment than another country—on matters such as term of protection and protection afforded to performers, phonogram producers, and broadcasters. TRIPS leaves open these existing exceptions, but does impose in general a wide-ranging obligation to extend benefits granted to one trading partner automatically to all other WTO Members.

Reflecting the relatively high level of completion of TRIPS as a trade agreement, there are remarkably few exceptions to the basic principles of national treatment and MFN—contrast TRIPS, for example, with the GATT, which allows a country to give much better market access to other members of customs unions and free trade areas than it affords to other countries; and the GATS which enables Members to reserve service industry sectors from the obligation to apply national treatment to market access for services. The United States responded to a finding of discrimination in the market for online gambling by seeking explicit to exclude that sector from its GATS commitments. TRIPS exceptions to MFN are very narrow and limited, and the impact of this stringent approach has grown since TRIPS was concluded, as many bilateral and regional trade deals now establish higher levels of IP protection than TRIPS requires. One reading of the MFN principle would mean that such improved protection should flow through to all WTO Members, and not just be limited to parties to a bilateral or regional pact. So if A and B agreed amongst themselves to offer patent term extensions to one another's nationals, then this reading of the MFN principle would oblige them to make this extended protection available to nationals of every WTO Member. This has been termed the 'ratchet' effect of bilateral dealmaking coupled with the multilateral MFN principle, a matter of intense debate and controversy given that the bulk of IP norm-setting in the past decade has occurred in bilateral and regional forums.

Objectives and principles

Articles 7 and 8, in this Part, are pivotal elements of TRIPS—Article 7 ('Objectives') establishes the objectives of IP protection under TRIPS and Article 8 ('Principles') clarifies the space for national authorities to pursue public policy objectives consistently with TRIPS. Article 7 is an authoritative statement of the public policy role of the IP system, unprecedented in multilateral law. To recall, it specifies that IP should be protected and enforced to promote innovation and the transfer and dissemination of technology, 'to the mutual advantage of producers and users of technological knowledge and in a manner conducive to social and economic welfare, and to a balance of rights and obligations'. This provision formalizes ideas, long present in IP law, of equitable balance, of entitlements and responsibilities, even of an IP right as a kind of social contract. It serves as a valuable reminder to domestic policymakers of the underlying purpose of the IP system—not merely in creating the legal basis of rights, but also in the practice of granting, administering and enforcing them. A teasing, but important, legal question arises as to how it should be used to interpret and define more specific provisions of TRIPS, such as the rules on limitations and exceptions, but it is not necessary to buy into this formal interpretative debate to recognize this article as an invaluable benchmark for IP policymakers.

Article 8, on first reading, is circular and appears almost redundant—it seems to say TRIPS allows countries to take certain measures provided that they are consistent with TRIPS. But the logic of this provision has come into focus as TRIPS is analysed more as a component of trade law. The question has been raised whether there are general exceptions to TRIPS, to allow for public policy measures, akin to GATT:XX. Further, can exceptions under GATT—say to protect public health or the environment—flow through to TRIPS and open up additional flexibilities not present in the actual text? The answer seems to be no. But this Article performs a parallel function in clarifying the scope for public policy measures outside the regular ambit of IP law. As the *EU—Geographical Indications* panel describes it,

[t]hese principles reflect the fact that [TRIPS] does not generally provide for the grant of positive rights to exploit or use certain subject matter, but rather provides for the grant of negative rights to prevent certain acts. This fundamental feature of [IP] protection inherently grants Members freedom to pursue legitimate public policy objectives since many measures to attain those public policy objectives lie outside the scope of [IP] rights and do not require an exception under [TRIPS].

TRIPS:8 helps define the scope and rationale of interventions for public health, for example, and for the complementary interplay between IP and competition policy tools.

These objectives and principles bear the imprint of the negotiating dynamics of TRIPS. Developing country negotiators included them to safeguard their domestic policy interests as TRIPS negotiations moved towards stronger IP standards than they assessed to be in their immediate interests and could constrain the necessary space for domestic policy. A key panel report, *Canada—Pharmaceutical Patents*, acknowledged that these provisions would guide the analysis of specific exceptions to patent rights under TRIPS (although this could not amount to renegotiating the balance of interests established in TRIPS), in the critical context of facilitating access to medicines. Since then, at Ministerial level the Doha Declaration on TRIPS and Public Health referred to the objectives and principles as setting the interpretative context for TRIPS as a legal text (though not citing the articles directly), and the parallel declaration setting the negotiating mandate for Doha explicitly invoked these two articles in giving directions to the TRIPS Council. Thus these two provisions have continued to guide both the political and legal context of international IP law, even though some specific interpretative questions remain open to debate.

Exhaustion of Rights

Article 6 indicates that nothing in TRIPS 'shall be used to address the issue of the exhaustion of [IP] rights'—parallel importation, or whether an IP right can be used to block the importation of otherwise legitimate goods from other countries—whether, and when, an IP right is considered 'exhausted' following a legitimate sale and thus can no longer be used to restrain further sales in other jurisdictions. Continuing controversy and divergent economic interests meant that it could not be settled in the TRIPS negotiations, so that TRIPS is explicitly— almost conspicuously—silent on this issue. This negotiation outcome has generally been taken to imply that a country has considerable liberty to adjust its settings as it chooses—subject to the obligation to ensure that effective enforcement mechanisms are available for truly illegitimate products. This outcome is perhaps ironic, since exhaustion is the most 'trade-related' of all IP issues— whether, and how, an IP right is capable of legitimately restraining international trade in IP-protected goods. Recognizing the policy significance of choices on parallel importation in the field of public health, the Doha Declaration provided that each Member is 'free to establish its own regime for . . . exhaustion [of IP rights] without challenge'—subject, however, to the overarching principles of non-discrimination (national treatment and MFN), recalling the pivotal importance of these principles in the international trade regime.

Part I: Practical Points

- National treatment need not mean identical treatment for foreign and domestic nationals (although that is the usual choice taken); in principle, it means offering 'effective equality of opportunities' to use the national IP system.
- The obligation to extend non-discriminatory treatment is far-reaching, covering a wide sweep of the substantive standards of IP laws as well as how they are administered and enforced, and allowing limitations that are much narrower than in conventional trade law; but it does not include IP rights not covered by TRIPS and need not be extended to non-members of the WTO.
- There is no hierarchy between the GATT/trade law version of national treatment, and the TRIPS/IP law versions of national treatment—they apply in parallel, harmoniously, and panels have used GATT jurisprudence to colour their interpretation of TRIPS.

- The objectives and principles of TRIPS help illuminate the point that domestic policymaking concerning IP law both can and should serve broader public policy goals: the 'objectives' identify those goals, and the 'principles' help map out the policy space for TRIPS-consistent policy interventions.
- National regimes on 'exhaustion' or 'parallel importation' can be tailored to meet domestic economic and policy interests, but are subject to the rules of non-discrimination.

Part II: Standards Concerning the Availability, Scope, and Use of IP Rights

Part I reads something like conventional trade law; Part II is a significant departure, moving beyond general principles to set detailed minimum standards on substantive IP law that are mandatory for WTO Members. Part II was also a landmark in IP treaty making, as it codified major standards that had not until then been defined internationally. For instance, over 100 years after Paris was first negotiated, no international standard had existed on what subject matter was eligible for a patent; and no international rules existed on protection of trade secrets. For those areas of IP it covers, TRIPS systematically defines:

- what material should be eligible to be protected, and for how long;
- what acts by third parties this material should be protected against, or the specific 'rights' that are associated with each form of IP; and
- what exceptions and limitations can constrain the exercise of those rights, or in what circumstances third parties can be given latitude to use the protected material without the permission of the right holder.

TRIPS does not define *who* should hold the rights—something that the *Havana Club* case confirmed—thus leaving a major area of IP law and practice untouched (although entitlement to apply for and to hold IP is still subject to the main principles of non-discrimination). And these standards do not protect IP directly— TRIPS *itself* does not directly protect a single patent, trademark or design. Part II is only a codification of the expectations that trading partners have of one another in protecting IP within their national systems. In some countries, TRIPS standards may directly enter national law in certain circumstances, given the 'direct effect' of international law in those jurisdictions (the legal principle whereby international law becomes binding domestic law, even without implementing legislation, for a country that applies the so-called 'monist' theory of international law). But even in those cases, IP is protected and enforced under national legal systems, not directly as international law between Members. A patent or registered design remains a bundle of rights granted and effective under national law; infringement of an IP right remains a matter to be determined within national legal processes. Copyright piracy and trademark counterfeiting do not breach TRIPS as such; they breach national laws that give effect to TRIPS standards in domestic legal systems.

Paris, Berne, Rome, Washington—and TRIPS

TRIPS is one step—albeit a big one—in the long historical development of international IP law, and Part II of TRIPS—the substantive standards for IP protection—is intertwined with Paris and Berne especially, but also the Rome and the Washington (Integrated Circuits) treaties. TRIPS incorporates almost all the standards of Paris and Berne. When this hybrid character of TRIPS had to be closely scrutinized for the first time—in WTO dispute panels—several teasing legal questions had to be answered:

- Do the actual articles of TRIPS outweigh the provisions of Paris and Berne that it imports by reference, as more recent law on the same point, or is there no hierarchy between them?
- Should TRIPS, and the articles of Paris and Berne it includes, be interpreted in the light of the well-documented diplomatic history of the many conferences that had negotiated and revised Paris and Berne from the 1890s to the 1970s, or should TRIPS be freshly interpreted as trade law, with a clean slate—in other words, was it just the bare text of these treaties that was copied and pasted into TRIPS, or did the diplomatic context and background also make the transition?
- Should later developments (since TRIPS was concluded) in the sphere of WIPO also be taken into account when reading TRIPS?

The linkage between TRIPS and these earlier treaties can be tricky, yet has great significance—we have seen how the AB overruled a panel on whether a whole category of IP (trade names) was imported at all from Paris into TRIPS. Dispute settlement practice has developed—not legally binding precedent, but now generally accepted—on these questions, and this is essential for reading and interpreting the standards of TRIPS Part II:

- the articles of *Paris* and *Berne* within TRIPS have the same status and are considered to have come into effect at the same time as the actual articles of the TRIPS text itself;

(cont.)

- the diplomatic history of *Paris* and *Berne* is used extensively when interpreting not only *Paris* and *Berne* articles within TRIPS, but also related TRIPS articles that employ similar concepts;
- and later developments in WIPO, even subsequent to TRIPS itself, have been checked for consistency with readings of TRIPS.

This evolution is illustrated graphically below in the development of copyright law (Figure 4.2).

Ultimately, while adhering to the fundamental responsibility to read the TRIPS text in a sober, unadventurous manner, so as to promote stability and predictability in the system, dispute panels have also recognized the policy interest in maintaining coherence and avoiding fragmentation of international standards or using dispute settlement to resolve bigger policy differences.

Exceptions to IP protection: the art of the policy balance

Some critics of TRIPS point to an apparent asymmetry: Part II is mandatory in the standards it sets for the availability and scope of IP rights, but only permissive in the exceptions or limitations that apply. So to comply with TRIPS, patents must be available for most forms of invention and the associated rights to take action against infringing acts must be provided, but there is no obligation to grant an exception to allow third parties to conduct private research on the patented invention, even though this is certainly permissible. Does this structure reflect a particular set of values: look after the right holders first, and leave other interests as an optional afterthought? Like so much of the debate about TRIPS, this kind of analysis can prove to be a self-fulfilling prophecy rather than describing an inevitable state of affairs. Exceptions and limitations have long been critical issues in domestic and international standard-setting on IP, and the long diplomatic history of Paris and Berne shows an evolving debate, responding to shifts in technology and public interest concerns. Setting a suitable ceiling on how rights can be enforced is seen as crucial in achieving the objectives of IPR protection, and the balance of interests called for in TRIPS:7. The debate concerns issues of privacy—to what extent can IP enforcement intrude on the personal domain—as well as wider public policy questions, such as limitations on the scope of copyright that provide for educational and archival use of copyright material.

For better or worse, TRIPS negotiators concluded that limitations and exceptions should be settled in detail on the domestic plane and—for the most part—did not make them mandatory. Setting upper limits on IP rights is an important area of policy flexibility under TRIPS for achieving the objectives of TRIPS:7 and making use of the policy space defined by TRIPS:8, and forms an integral part of IP law. Attempts to define allowable exceptions and limitations more explicitly in the text of TRIPS failed in the negotiations. Accordingly, the scope for such measures is expressed in terms of general principles—drawing on pre-existing international law, specifically the 'three step test' which was originally included in Berne:9.2, a provision which defines permissible exceptions to the exclusive right to control reproductions of copyright works. This test was adapted and applied much more broadly, to define allowable exceptions to most categories of IP—the extent to which the Berne language was borrowed and adapted for other fields can be seen in the comparative chart below. The perceived importance of this balancing process, and the measure of uncertainty about the rules, are evident from the fact that these provisions have been the subject of three disputes concerning TRIPS, among the most important cases from a systemic and policy point of view. One consequence of the legal logic of TRIPS is that the domestic policymaker cannot point to specific forms of exceptions defined under TRIPS, but must defend precise policy choices under a broad general rule. This gives policy leeway at the national level, but can require careful legal analysis to defend such choices when they are challenged. The need for greater understanding about the effect of these provisions, too, has meant that—unlike most early TRIPS disputes—these disputes were not settled at the consultation phase, but proceeded to a full panel finding, involving detailed analysis of the legal effect of these provisions. *US–s 110(5) Copyright Act*, concerned TRIPS:13, which defines the allowable limitations and exceptions to copyright; *Canada–Pharmaceutical Patents* concerned TRIPS:30, the analogous provision covering patent rights; and *EU–Geographical Indications* dealt with exceptions to trademark rights under TRIPS:17. The other similar provision, TRIPS:26.2 on exceptions to design rights, has not been raised in a TRIPS dispute.

There has been much scholarly and political debate about the three-step test within copyright law, and its adaptation in areas of industrial property law. Analysts are anxious that the tests may be too unclear, thus chilling policy flexibility, or that, as legal tests, they may be simply too restrictive on public policy choices. But these tests can be powerful tools for domestic policymakers. They contain compelling legal ideas that go to the heart of fairness and equity in the IP system and its public policy settings. And the legal uncertainty that shrouds them is a measure, too, of the flexibility they afford to domestic policymakers. The very nature of these rules means that systematic fairness and balance in domestic policymaking is a strong

Table 4.1 Berne/TRIPS Provisions on Limitations and Exceptions

Field of IP	Berne:9.2 on right of reproduction	TRIPS:13 on copyright	TRIPS:17 on trademarks	TRIPS:26.2 on designs	TRIPS:30 on patents
Nature of limitation or exception	'Possible exceptions'; a matter for legislation . . . to permit reproduction	Limitations or exceptions	Limited exceptions such as fair use of descriptive terms	Limited exceptions	Limited exceptions
Scope of application	In certain special cases	Certain special cases			
Conflict with normal exploitation	Does not conflict with a normal exploitation of the work	Does not conflict with a normal exploitation of the work		Does not unreasonably conflict with the normal exploitation of protected industrial designs	Does not unreasonably conflict with a normal exploitation of the patent
Prejudice to right holder's interests	Does not unreasonably prejudice the legitimate interests of the author	Does not unreasonably prejudice the legitimate interests of the right holder	Takes account of the legitimate interests of the owner of the trademark	Does not unreasonably prejudice the legitimate interests of the owner of the protected design	Does not unreasonably prejudice the legitimate interests of the patent owner
Third party interests			Takes account of the legitimate interests of third parties	Takes account of the legitimate interests of third parties	Takes account of the legitimate interests of third parties

defence against whether the choice of exceptions and limitations is appropriate and legitimate. Put another way, would good faith domestic policymaking aim to create unreasonable conflict with normal commercial use of the IP system and to prejudice legitimate interests unreasonably? Generally, of course not, although in some compelling cases of public interest, further curbs on IP rights are envisaged, and permitted, under TRIPS—most notably the issuance of compulsory licences and government use orders for patented technologies which have been widely discussed in terms of making available essential medicines.

The choice of TRIPS negotiators to draw on this provision of Berne to shape an important public policy mechanism in a wide range of fields of IP opens up a rich vein of law and legal possibilities, once some conceptual issues are resolved. TRIPS:13, with general effect on the full bundle of rights associated with copyright, draws directly on the text of the corresponding provision, Berne:9.2, which only defines exceptions for the right of reproduction. This created a major question of treaty interpretation—what is the relationship between the later, general exception of TRIPS:13, and the more specific exceptions for particular rights already defined in Berne? And did this negotiating choice also have the effect of introducing all of the background law and diplomatic history of Berne—dating back a century—into the much more recent text and context of TRIPS? Further, did the textual links—the use of identical terms—between the exceptions for copyright and for industrial property rights mean, too, that all these areas of IP would be guided by the diplomatic history of Berne? These legal questions are potentially complex, and they were not entirely settled at the time TRIPS was concluded. But subsequent dispute settlement cases—*US s 110(5) Copyright Act, Canada—Pharmaceutical Patents* and *EU—Geographical Indications*—all had to deal with them in order to reach practical outcomes. In practice, the approach that evolved was:

- to recognize that these provisions legally evolved from the negotiating context of Berne, so to take account of the history of Berne when reading the terms;
- when considering such key concepts as 'unreasonable prejudice', 'normal exploitation,' and 'legitimate interests' that define allowable exceptions to different forms of IP right, to ensure general consistency in the way these terms are interpreted, while recognizing the distinct policy contexts of different forms of IP.

These disputes reinforced these core legal ideas and the principles governing public policy and IP in ways that were unforseen prior to TRIPS, but in a manner that now gives invaluable guidance to domestic policymakers. The abstract terms—legitimacy, reasonableness, normality—that are so central in the balancing of interests in IP policymaking now have a richer, more systematic context. Amidst the legal clutter and detailed analysis, these central principles put IP policymaking on a clearer conceptual basis than ever before, establishing a general rule of fairness and equity in balancing legitimate commercial interests with public policy considerations. The fact that this matters in the real world will be seen when we look at these specific disputes in more detail in Chapter 5.

The range and nature of interests involved, and how they are balanced, continue to differ dramatically between these fields of IP—copyright law has not become a branch of patent law, or vice versa—but the cross-fertilization between these fields that TRIPS brought about has enabled a more objective understanding of the key terms used to define how rights and interests are to be balanced in practice. The choice by negotiators not to define allowable exceptions through a positive list, but rather to articulate a set of broader policy principles, ultimately gives domestic policymakers greater flexibility to adapt and redefine exceptions and limitations to track the fast-changing economic, technological and legal context which give them purpose and meaning—provided policymakers have a clear and objective grasp of the essence of these principles. Given that it is a body of international trade law and not a kind of international IP legislation or a model law, TRIPS generally functions as the expression of agreed principles rather than as directly applicable detailed texts that would tend to pre-empt the drafting and refining of the national laws that give practical effect to these policy principles.

Substantive Law of Copyright

The substantive standards that TRIPS sets on copyright have deep roots in existing international law, principally Berne. TRIPS imports and applies almost all the substantive provisions of Berne, creating a separate obligation on WTO Members to comply with its standards, apart from the existing commitments that parties to Berne already owed to each other (164 countries are bound directly by Berne, separately from the obligations of WTO Members). This means that, on paper, there are two parallel, but closely intertwined, copyright regimes. If badly handled, this parallelism might have lead to a splintering of copyright law, and the emergence of conflicting streams of 'trade-related' copyright and 'WIPO' copyright; this risk increased as WIPO developed new copyright norms after TRIPS, while dispute settlement on copyright was pursued in the WTO. For the most part, these concerns have not been realized in practice. Some legal and structural questions remain to be ironed out, but the overall system has generally been strengthened and its essential principles clarified. The interplay between the Berne/WIPO tradition and the more recent TRIPS normsetting is best illustrated in a simplified graphic form (see Figure 4.2).

TRIPS took up the text of Berne, but left behind administrative provisions and the substantive obligations concerning moral rights—the rights to be identified as author and to object to derogatory use of copyright works. The exclusion of moral rights from TRIPS might suggest that these IP rights are not 'trade-related,' although they can be of significant commercial interest to authors. In effect, this was a measure of the different compliance cultures between the Berne Convention

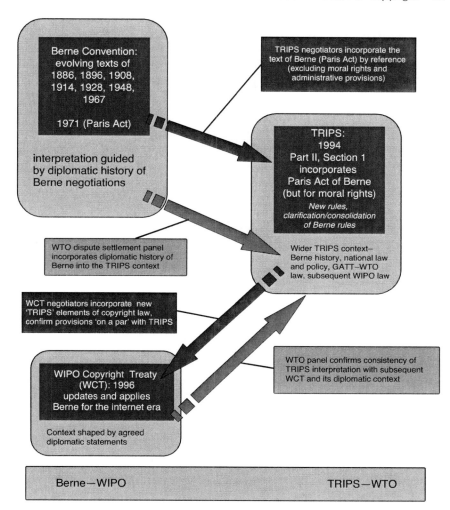

Figure 4.2 Co-Evolution of the Text and Context of International Copyright Law

proper (in which compliance was not closely monitored and enforced) and the expectations of TRIPS—the United States, in particular, was reluctant to accept strong standards, effectively enforced, regarding moral rights, even though it continued to be separately bound to respect these standards as a party to Berne. TRIPS itself makes clear that its provisions cannot be used to diminish existing obligations under Berne.

In building positively on existing Berne standards, TRIPS also clarified copyright issues that had been debated for some time:

- articulating the fundamental principle that copyright does not cover ideas, but only their expression; TRIPS sets a ceiling to copyright protection by stipulating that copyright shall not extend to 'ideas, procedures, methods of operation or mathematical concepts as such'.
- confirming that computer software in both source and object code should be protected by copyright as a literary work, and that compilations of data are also protected by copyright if they constitute 'intellectual creations'.

Substantive Law of Trademarks

Section 2 represented a considerable advance in the harmonization of trade mark law internationally. For the first time, there was a single international definition of a registrable trade mark, of the rights available under a trade mark, and of the nature of infringement, as well as the systematic rule governing public policy limitations and exceptions discussed above. TRIPS therefore represented a significant development on the existing Paris Convention's provisions on trademarks, towards a very general harmonization of substantive aspects of trade mark law. Reflecting the roots of TRIPS in commercial pressure for more effective controls on trade in counterfeit goods, this section extends and clarifies Paris provisions on well-known marks.

But TRIPS still falls well short of the idea of an international registry of trademarks, such as the Madrid system administered by WIPO. As in other areas of IP law, TRIPS simply articulates the general level of protection that WTO Members expect of one another, and does not protect individual items of IP. There is one exception: under Paris:6*ter*, incorporated into TRIPS, countries are required to prevent the unauthorized use and registration as trademarks of 'armorial bearings, flags, and other State emblems . . . official signs and hallmarks indicating control and warranty' which are notified by parties to Paris or WTO Members, or international intergovernmental organizations (protection is not absolute—it need not prejudice rights acquired earlier in good faith, it need not apply to use or registration that does not suggest a connection or mislead the public, and a country has 12 months to object to another's request for protection). Having incorporated this system from Paris into TRIPS, the WTO did not set up a parallel scheme for notifying and protecting these official signs and symbols, but rather agreed with

WIPO to communicate any requests for protection to WIPO for incorporation into the collection that WIPO already maintained. Often overlooked by practitioners, this is an inexpensive form of global protection for official emblems and forms of certification that supplements the regular trademark and geographical indications systems (see the recent example from Tunisia in Figure 4. 3). The name and acronym of the WTO itself are protected under this scheme, as the following extracts from the official communications show,

The International Bureau of the World Intellectual Property Organization (WIPO) presents its compliments to the Minister for Foreign Affairs and has the honor to communicate to him, pursuant to Article 6*ter*(3)(b) of the Paris Convention for the Protection of Industrial Property, as revised at Lisbon on October 31, 1958 (Lisbon Act), and at Stockholm on July 14, 1967 (Stockholm Act), a reproduction of the name, abbreviation, emblem and seal of the World Trade Organization for which protection is requested under the said Article 6*ter*.

It is recalled that the countries bound, under the TRIPS Agreement, to comply with the provisions of Article 6*ter* of the Paris Convention (Stockholm Act of 1967) are obliged to afford protection to armorial bearings, flags and other emblems, abbreviations and names of intergovernmental organizations, whether or not they are bound by Articles 1 to 12 of the Stockholm Act of 1967 of the Paris Convention.

TRIPS:20 is closer in form to conventional GATT trade law—it limits regulatory controls that unjustifiably encumber the use of trademarks in the course of trade, and in particular that impair their function as distinguishing a firm's goods or services from those of other companies. By one view, not universally held, this article contains a suggestion of an entitlement to derive legitimate commercial benefit from a trademark in the marketplace—recalling the link between IP protection and effective market access considered in terms of capacity to exercise

الديـــوان الوطني للصنـــاعات التقليديــة

National Office for Handicraft
Office National de l'Artisanat

Figure 4.3 An Official Sign of Tunisia (registered under the 6*ter* System)

the competitive advantage conferred by a trademark. Indonesia successfully defended a complaint that its national car programme infringed this article—the panel found that constraints on trademark usage for foreign partners in the programme were not official requirements but part of a voluntary arrangement. This article is generally considered to address requirements such as an obligation to sell a product with the trademark or business name of a local licensee prominently alongside an established trademark.

Substantive Law on Geographical Indications

One of the more 'trade-related' areas of IP law (recall the related provisions on 'marks of origin' in the original GATT), GIs have been a source of controversy and trade friction since at least the 19th century—in some cases, concerning the very same terms (think of long-running debates over terms such as 'Budweiser' or 'Champagne'). TRIPS did not fully resolve the contentiousness of GI protection, but did establish a clearer international framework as well as an ongoing agenda for negotiations, which have continued to the present, both bilaterally between trading partners and multilaterally within the WTO. However, TRIPS did not establish a single template for GI protection, and countries have reported their compliance with TRIPS obligations through a host of different means:

- specific laws on GIs, appellations of origin and related terms, either cast in general terms, or regulating one area such as agricultural products or trade in wine
- trademark law, including specific measures on certification and collective marks, and other laws governing certification, hallmarks and other national signs and symbols
- general laws on repression of unfair trade practices and on protection of consumers
- specific laws on labelling of products, health protection, and food safety
- other regulations on product standards and taxation
- the common law on economic wrongs, such as the tort of passing off

To simplify a complicated area of law, the main questions are: What terms or symbols are eligible for protection as GIs? What acts by third parties should they be protected against? And what legitimate exceptions apply, such as use of generic terms and prior trademarks?

(i)   What must be protected?

Under TRIPS, a GI identifies a good as originating in a particular location, 'where a given quality, reputation or other characteristic of the good is essentially attributable to its geographical origin.' The GI does two things—it points to where the good comes from, and it recalls the good's qualities that are associated with that origin. A GI is broader in scope than the earlier concept of 'appellation of origin', present in WIPO's *Lisbon Agreement for the Protection of Appellations of Origin and their International Registration*. For instance, unlike an appellation, a GI need not be a place name, but could in principle be an image or another term. A GI is generally assumed to embrace a wider range of local characteristics than an appellation, for instance in allowing more for general commercial reputation and not just natural or environmental factors, but debate continues on this question.

(ii)   What actions is a GI protected against?

GI protection is a branch of IP law but does not necessarily entail the creation of a distinct item of property. It is expressed in terms of giving 'interested parties' the 'legal means' to prevent certain acts. But just what those excluded acts are and should be has long been debated. TRIPS provides for two broad levels of protection, reflecting two schools of thought on the purpose of GI protection:

- Preventing use of GIs that misleads the public as to the actual geographical origin of the good, or other forms of unfair competition—looking at the product, the consumer assumes from the GI on its label that it comes from the place indicated, when in fact it does not; or
- Preventing the use of GIs to identify a product not from the location in question, even when the public is not misled and the true origin of the product is clear—so the consumer need be in no doubt that the product comes from somewhere else.

The second, 'higher' level of protection is reserved under TRIPS for wine and spirit GIs, although many countries have sought its extension to other goods more associated with developing countries, such as agricultural products and handicrafts. The difference is best understood in terms of the purpose of protection—the general level aims to prevent consumer deception and other dishonest practices; the higher level aims to give the original producers a wider ambit of market access, by precluding competitors from alluding to the reputation of the protected GI and the character of the goods it identifies. In a trade law setting, this difference amounts to different ideas about what kind of trade is illegitimate, and what kind of competitive relationship is appropriate between traders who use GIs to identify and to describe their goods.

(iii) What exceptions are allowed?

TRIPS:24 sets out a range of exceptions that may limit the protection available for GIs: in common with the general logic of TRIPS, these exceptions mostly need not be applied, but represent options available to Members to take account of the general public interest and the interests of third parties when fine-tuning protection. These exceptions are more precise than the three-step logic discussed above for IP rights, but do aim to make possible the same kind of equitable balancing—so even if a GI is protected in its territory, a country need not suppress the continuation of certain good faith or long-lasting use of the GI by other traders, and need not suppress the use of common names for goods or services, or customary terms for grape varieties. The exception is stronger for prior trade mark right and the use of one's personal name: TRIPS provides that its GI provisions 'shall in no way prejudice the right' of anyone to use their name in the course of trade, unless the use is misleading. The complex interplay between GI protection and trademark protection is discussed separately below.

Reflecting the highly 'trade-related' character of GI protection, this section of TRIPS sets up a unique set of processes that envisage negotiating away permissible exceptions, including for individual GIs—covering, for instance, agreements to cease treating a certain term as a generic or descriptive term and to establish exclusive rights over the term as a GI—a process sometimes termed 'clawback'. These negotiations have typically occurred in bilateral settings—so, for example, in bilateral negotiations on wine trade with the EU, several 'new world' wine producers agreed to cease using terms such as champagne, port, and burgundy, in exchange for improved access to the European wine market. This approach represents a kind of 'managed trade' or 'fix outcomes' approach to defining what is legitimate trade relating to GIs, in contrast to the general TRIPS approach of setting broad international rules to be interpreted and applied at the domestic level. TRIPS:23.4, and subsequent declarations by WTO Ministerial Conferences, mandate the negotiation of a multilateral register to facilitate protection of GIs for wine and spirits, potentially a more specific tool than the broader rules-based approach generally taken in TRIPS as a body of trade law. These negotiations have continued inconclusively up to the present—a reminder of the important, but contested, role of GIs in political conceptions of what amounts to fair and unfair trade, and how this distinction should be drawn in practice.

Just Getting Along? Geographical Indications, Trademarks, and Coexistence

GIs and trademarks, and the trade interests behind them, are typically seen in policy debate as representing directly opposing interests, even betokening a cultural divide—North/South, artisan/corporate, Old World/New World. Legally, under TRIPS, a right to use a trademark is an *exception* to GI protection and a right to use a GI is an *exception* to trademark protection. And some of the longest running disputes in this field concern conflicting claims to GI and trademark protection—the *Budweiser* saga being the best known. Confusingly, though, GIs may be protected *as* trademarks, and the very same GIs are protected through both the trademark system and special GI laws. Both forms of protection have their roots in the law that protects the consumer against misleading information on the labelling of products. And in both cases, the law evolves from the basic rationale of protecting consumers against deception towards a kind of 'property' or commercial interest that is considered of value in itself and entitled to protection against various forms of unfair competition, encroachment, usurpation or dilution by rival traders. To take an objective, practical perspective, these two aspects of IP constitute a broader law of 'distinctive signs', within which the relationship between trademarks and GIs needs to be explained systematically. This is not to suggest that there is no conflict or tension between the two sets of standards and the interests behind them, but to understand the structural elements within which conflicts can be managed—a microcosm of the overall TRIPS project, that of providing an objective legal framework to deal with IP disputes that will inevitably arise in trading relations. The panel in *EC—Trademarks and Geographical Indications* explored this territory, clarifying the appropriate form of 'coexistence', which it defined as 'a legal regime under which a GI and a trademark can both be used concurrently to some extent even though the use of one or both of them would otherwise infringe the rights conferred by the other'.

A coexistence regime may be needed because the one sign may 'indicate' very different things, depending on where and how it is used. A geographical term may identify or describe different aspects of different products: a geographical

Madrid Trademark System:
International Registration for
a 'Roquefort' collective mark
301162 (30.11.1962)

(459) ROQUEFORT

Number	459
Date	20.12.1967
Holder	Producers and groups of producers enjoying the appellation of origin in question
Appellation	ROQUEFORT
Publication	N° 2 : 08/1968
Country of Origin	FR
Nice Classification	29
Product	Ewe's milk cheese
Area of Production	Municipality of **Roquefort** sur Soulzon (Aveyron)
Withdrawal	MX - 29.09.2003 (Date of the initial refusal: 14.06.1969)
Legal basis	The judgement of the Civil Court of Saint-Affrique of December 22, 1921; Law of July 26, 1925 guaranteeing the **Roquefort** cheese appellation of origin

Lisbon System for
Appellations of Origin:
International Registration
for 'Roquefort'
459 (20.12.1967)

Figure 4.4 'Roquefort' Appellation and a Roquefort Trademark Protected in the WIPO Lisbon and Madrid Systems

term may serve as a GI as defined in TRIPS:22.1, such as *Roquefort* for cheese; an original geographical allusion or connotation may be superseded by a secondary meaning that a term develops as a distinctive trademark (*Philadelphia* for cream cheese, for instance); or a geographical term may be a descriptive element or a GI within a trade mark (Baileys *Irish* Cream or *Champagne* Laurent-Perrier); it may be a term in common use to describe a product's properties (now a descriptive term, *suede* originally denoted the origin of gloves from Sweden)—see Table 4.2 on the different meanings of the term 'Orange'. GI and trademark law must, in part, recognize the diversity and evolution of actual linguistic usage, but there are also benefits from providing predictability and clarity by defining how a term can be used in commerce, and putting other traders clearly on notice. Rules on GIs and trademarks are, therefore, an important component of the 'legitimate trade' and the fair basis for competition that TRIPS, as an IP and trade agreement seeks to promote. And in certain cases, recognizing 'legitimacy' in trade does entail allowing the scope of trademark rights and GI protection to overlap, or to set a clear

Table 4.2 Multiplicity of Meanings in the Law of GIs and Trademarks

The sign or indication	Legal status	Possible relevance to TRIPS
Orange	Australian GI for wines	TRIPS:22, 23 (GI protection) TRIPS:23.3
Vin de pays de la Principauté d'Orange	French GI for wines	TRIPS:22, 23
Orange County	US GI for wines	TRIPS:22, 23
Lower orange	South African GI for wines	TRIPS:22, 23
Orange™	Trademark for telecommunications	TRIPS:15.1
ORANGE	Trademark for amplifiers and sound equipment	TRIPS:15.1
Vin d'orange	Grape wine, flavoured with orange fruit	TRIPS:24.6
Orange wine	Wine produced from orange fruit	TRIPS:24.6
Orange wine	'White' wine with an orange tint from extended contact with grapeskins	TRIPS:24.6
Orange	Common personal name	TRIPS:24.8

*this table is purely illustrative and does not suggest any term used has a legal status or significance

line between the legitimate scope of each. The *EU—Trademarks and Geographical Indications* Panel had to articulate how these two sets of rules should interact. In essence, the Panel followed a neatly symmetrical approach: where the one term has potential significance both as GI and as a trademark, a positive right to use a GI may be considered a fair use exception to a trademark owner's right to exclude use of that GI, given that use of a GI can be considered a special kind of the legitimate descriptive use that is often allowed as a kind of 'fair use' exception under a trademark right; equally, a right to use a trademark may be a fair use exception to (or not prejudiced by) GI protection, as TRIPS:24(5) provides. So where a GI and a trademark overlap on the same term, TRIPS does not require exclusive use of the term to be vested in either the trademark or the GI: in limited circumstances, a GI could even legitimately be recognized in the face of a prior trademark right—within the scope of the trademark owner's right to *exclude* commercial use of the term, there may be a residual right to *use* a GI, akin to fair use of descriptive terms, as a legitimate interest of third parties, provided the trademark owner's own legitimate interests are preserved.

Substantive Law on Industrial Designs

Often eclipsed in TRIPS analysis by more politically sensitive areas, Section Four on the industrial design protection is a potentially valuable policy tool and practical pathway for emerging economies seeking recognition of their distinctive cultural attributes in the global marketplace. Industrial design protection can combine features of copyright and industrial property systems. National policies can differ considerably in how designs are protected within the broad set of principles articulated by TRIPS. Under TRIPS, protection must be available for 'independently created industrial designs that are new or original', potentially a wide range of designs. But the scope of eligible designs may be limited by Members to safeguard certain well-established public policy interests. In particular, they may exclude designs that 'do not significantly differ from known designs or combinations of known design features' (so as to ensure protected designs are legitimate creations) and that are dictated essentially (not 'exclusively') by technical or functional considerations—so that design protection can focus on visual appearance and not become a kind of exclusive right over the way a product functions. Given the importance of textile production for many emerging economies, and their trade interests in this field, this Section places particular emphasis on the need for inexpensive and uncomplicated protection of textile designs. Apart from the optional exclusion of designs on technical or functional basis, this section also sets out permissible exceptions from the scope of the design right along the model of the three-step test, discussed above. As for other areas of IP, this TRIPS rule is an international first in establishing a systematic basis for public policy limitations on the design right.

Substantive Law on Patents

A handful of articles on patents have undoubtedly been the most controversial element of TRIPS, politically, legally, and symbolically. When 'TRIPS' and 'IP' are invoked in political debate, it often turns out to be a reference to this element of

TRIPS. Over a third of TRIPS disputes concern this section, as do half the reported findings of TRIPS non-compliance. Following the pivotal 'Doha Declaration on TRIPS and Public Health' in 2001, this Section is the only part of the entire Uruguay Round package of trade law that Members have agreed to amend since negotiations concluded in 1994. Even the objective of IP protection set out in TRIPS:7 maps more closely to the principles of patent law than any other field of IP (GI protection, or performers' rights, for instance, do not lend themselves so much to promoting technological innovation, technology dissemination, or the mutual advantage of producers and users of technological knowledge referred to in this article).

Yet this section also has a more modest role, in defining for the first time in a multilateral instrument some of the core concepts of patent law—what tests should apply to determine whether an invention should be patented, what public policy exclusions from patentable subject matter are appropriate, and to what extent should rights under patents be curtailed. TRIPS establishes a common platform for patent law, but does not by any means serve as a single template for national patent law. Some concerns expressed about TRIPS restricting the scope for national policymaking would not survive a close reading of the text. For instance, some of the core patent law issues *not* addressed by TRIPS are:

- The definition or character of an 'invention', novelty, non-obviousness or inventive step, and utility or industrial applicability—more generally, how to draw a line between a true invention and a mere discovery;
- The nature of the prior art base, or the defined body of knowledge against which novelty and obviousness are assessed;
- Whether competing claims to an invention are decided according to the first to file an application or the first to invent;
- Who is considered the actual inventor and who is the legitimate owner of a patent, and the rights and entitlements relating to publicly funded inventions.

TRIPS standards did nonetheless represent a landmark in substantive international patent law, effectively setting aside a number of policy options that countries had previously chosen to apply, and in politically sensitive areas. TRIPS introduced:

- The rule that true inventions in all areas of technology should in principle be patentable, including agricultural chemicals, pharmaceuticals and microorganisms, subject to certain key exceptions.
- A rule against discrimination between local and overseas inventions.
- A minimum patent term of at least 20 years from the filing date.
- More rigorous procedural requirements for the grant of compulsory licences.

- A reversal of the burden of proof in certain circumstances so that a product alleged to have been produced by a patented process is taken to be an infringement unless proven otherwise.
- An obligation to provide some form of protection for new plant varieties.

In several key respects, these standards give effect to a general trade policy objective of establishing an effective and non-discriminatory opportunity for firms to compete in foreign markets. The 'trade-related' aspects of patent law date back to the first version of Paris in 1883, which established two key principles to give foreign firms a better chance to compete on the basis of their patented technology—first, national treatment itself, enabling them to obtain and exercise patents on par with their domestic competitors; and second, a right of priority, which made it practically achievable to secure timely patents in foreign markets, by allowing foreign filings to be effectively back-dated to the first application filed. A long international debate ensued on other trade-related patent questions— such as whether requirements for the patent holder to 'work' the patent (ie to make the patented technology available to the public) may apply when a patented technology is imported and not produced locally. TRIPS established a rule against discrimination on the basis of local or foreign manufacture, raising a question whether this ruled out such 'local working' requirements. The US filed a WTO complaint against Brazil addressing such a measure, although this case was settled without a panel report so it produced no clear guidance on the issue. Some have argued that a bona fide intervention to promote local working may be defensible if it can be made out to be non-discriminatory; others caution against this reading. However, the changing character of industry policy and the internationalization of manufacturing processes, taken together, have generally reduced expectations—firmly entrenched in some patent laws in the early industrial age— that the public benefit from patent exploitation should be measured solely in terms of domestic manufacture. This means that, in general, the importation of the patented technology meets the test of reasonably meeting the domestic market: in a globalized market, stronger emphasis lies on maintaining healthy competition and access to technology, rather than favouring domestic producers. This shift towards more competitive, internationalized exploitation of patents is consistent with the integration of patent law into the multilateral trade law regime.

As for other forms of IP, TRIPS sets clear standards for what is eligible for patent protection; what rights should be available under a patent and for how long; and how those rights should be circumscribed. These standards have been the subject of continuous debate and some dispute settlement, but the net effect is to provide guidance on what level and scope of protection is sufficient to meet the legitimate expectations of trading partners. These standards are most often viewed as a constraint on policymaking, as a reduction of legislative choice, and as enforcing the convergence of national laws—even while promoting trade interests, systemic efficiency, fairness, and predictability. But such general rules can also serve to safeguard regulatory diversity. Provided their laws are compliant with the international standards, countries have, in principle, a free hand to explore options—to exercise flexibility—particularly where areas of public policy are concerned. The domains of flexibility are best categorized as

- Pre-grant: the kind of questions that a patent office is typically involved in when deciding whether or not to grant a patent—the choice of what should in principle be patentable, and what is not (eg higher life forms, morality exceptions, medical treatments), and who is eligible to apply for or obtain a patent on a given invention;
- Post-grant: the kind of questions that confront regulators and judicial officials once a patent is granted and is being exercised in the marketplace, for instance concerning the scope or reach of patent rights (eg exceptions for research, or defining the reach of patent claims); when to intervene in the public interest (eg to issue a compulsory licence or government use order); and whether and how patents should be linked with other areas of regulation (such as the linkages with regulatory approval of pharmaceuticals that some countries apply).

The standards therefore create a broadly defined common platform that defines mutual expectations and provides for essentially compatible patent law systems, while also allowing considerable flexibility at the national level. What is, on the one hand, a minimum obligation—patents must be available on pharmaceuticals, for instance—is also a safeguard for policy choice, free from legal challenge—so, under TRIPS, a country still has certain flexibility in determining what amounts to sufficient inventiveness for an invention to be considered patentable. Of course these are not unbounded flexibilities—the key terms would be interpreted with reference to general practice and their normal linguistic import—but the range of defensible choice need not be construed in very narrow terms.

This section introduces another form of IP almost by default: it requires that plant varieties be protected by patents or by 'an effective *sui generis* system', or by both. Some countries have chosen, therefore, not to use patents for plant varieties. Of course this provision raises the question of what would make a *sui generis* (or specially tailored) system of plant variety protection into one that is 'effective'. Many countries have chosen the existing UPOV system for plant variety protection. As the one recognized international system for plant variety protection, this would doubtless meet the requirement for effectiveness, but there is continuing discussion as to what other *sui generis* systems would also comply with this one-word criterion.

Substantive Law on Integrated Circuit Layout Designs

The standards on layout designs (or 'topographies') of integrated circuits essentially give effect to a modified form of the WIPO Treaty on Intellectual Property in Respect of Integrated Circuits (the Washington Treaty or 'IPIC Treaty'), as this earlier attempt to negotiate international standards of protection did not, as negotiated, meet the needs of its key proponents and never entered into force. TRIPS therefore creates a binding obligation to apply protection 'in accordance with' key articles of Washington, even though the underlying treaty itself is not binding. The provisions were strengthened by TRIPS negotiators to ensure that exclusive rights extended to articles containing an infringing integrated circuit. However, reflecting trade-related concerns of the negotiators, the standards establish a limitation on exclusive rights to make it not merely permissible but mandatory to limit remedies available for traders who innocently trade in infringing integrated circuits, or articles including them: once they are on notice as to the infringement, they can continue to trade in 'stock in hand', and need only pay the right holder a reasonable royalty, based on regular commercial practice. Protection of integrated circuits does not require a registration system and can be implemented through a non-formality system roughly akin to copyright. In those few countries where registration systems apply, the usage has been relatively low: between 2000 and 2008, Canada reported an average of just over three applications a year, by contrast with roughly 40,000 patent applications annually.

Substantive Law on Undisclosed (Confidential) Information

Section 7 articulates multilateral legal standards for protection of undisclosed (confidential) information or trade secrets in this field for the first time, and creates a distinct category of IP protection for data used in regulatory processes. In doing so, it creates a link with the evolution of international IP law under the Paris Convention. Paris:10*bis* creates a general rule for the suppression of unfair competition, defining it in very general terms ('any act contrary to honest practices in industrial and commercial practices') and giving three specific instances of unfair competition—creating confusion with the commercial presence of a competitor; making false allegations about a competitor's products or business activities; and misleading the public about one's goods. TRIPS requires WTO Members to apply this obligation; after the AB's ruling regarding trade names in

Havana Club, it is reasonable to assume that this obligation applies, just as any other field of IP covered by TRIPS.

The TRIPS negotiators then explicitly built upon this base to provide a systemic link with the protection of information. TRIPS provides that *in the course of providing effective protection against unfair competition* (as required by Paris:10*bis*), Members must protect undisclosed information and certain regulatory data presented to government authorities. Scholars puzzle over what this phrase means for the TRIPS standards. Does it mean, for instance, that the nature of protection required under these new provisions should be coloured by the scope and history of the Paris provision on unfair competition; or should those provisions be interpreted in isolation from Paris?

Interpretation does not present a major issue for the protection of trade secrets in general—in codifying standards for the first time, TRIPS actually sets out quite familiar tests: information must be secret, reasonable steps should have been taken to keep it so, and it should have commercial value because of its confidentiality. However, it is often overlooked that this section requires more than simply protecting the information against disclosure—the protection must extend to use, without consent, 'in a manner contrary to honest commercial practices', that term being defined to include breach of contract, breach of confidence and inducement to breach, as well as obtaining undisclosed information in the knowledge (or in gross negligence in failing to know) that it was acquired though such practices; so TRIPS does not create a true property right, but certainly requires a form of protection that 'reaches through,' past an initial breach of confidence. This broader scope of protection may be justified by reference to the idea of 'acts contrary to honest practices' within the general definition of unfair competition. In short, seeking commercial advantage from information that you know (or should know) was gained illicitly is a form of unfair competition, and 'illegitimate trade' in the broader sense of TRIPS.

But more illumination is needed when coming to understand the other form of protection defined in this section. TRIPS:39.3 provides that competitors should not be entitled to unfair commercial advantage from data submitted to a government regulatory authority in relation to approval of pharmaceutical or agricultural chemical products which utilize new chemical entities. In other words, it is not sufficient for such data to be kept confidential—it must also be protected against unfair commercial use by others. This apparently abstruse question has in fact been considered a major bilateral trade issue, and is debated closely—especially over the extent to which it precludes a competitor from using protected data to obtain approval for a competing product. This section is therefore not just about the law of confidentiality, but represents an important new departure in the international law of unfair competition. For the particular industries concerned—pharmaceuticals, agricultural, and veterinary chemicals—it also represents a continuing trade and regulatory issue.

Substantive Law on Anti-Competitive Practices

The abuse of IP rights threatens two objectives of TRIPS as an IP-in-trade agreement: the flow of legitimate trade, and the diffusion of technology. Earlier attempts were made to codify measures against the abuse of IP, from the Havana Charter, the original blueprint of the WTO's precursors, to the 1970s draft UNCTAD Code on Transfer of Technology. Under Havana, countries would have been obliged to counter restrictive business practices affecting international trade 'which restrain competition, limit access to markets, or foster monopolistic control', including 'preventing by agreement the development or application of technology or invention whether patented or unpatented' and 'extending the use of rights under patents, trade marks or copyrights' to matters which fall beyond the legal scope of those rights. TRIPS does not mandate specific standards for action against such abuses, but provides a clear entitlement for steps to redress anti-competitive use of IP, in accordance with the 'balance of interests' objective of Article 7 and the general principles of Article 8. Being permissive only, it does not require remedies against anti-competitive licensing practices. Nonetheless, it is a clear statement in international law on the nature of abuse of IPRs, and it provides specific instances: exclusive grantback conditions, conditions preventing challenges to validity, and coercive package licensing. It does positively oblige WTO Members to cooperate with other Members who are seeking to enforce measures against anti-competitive practices involving firms based on their territory, including by supplying necessary information. The mechanism established is not unlike the provisions on marks of origin in the original GATT—less emphasis on specific rules, more focus on establishing a cooperative mechanism. Equally, a Member can seek consultations in the event that their nationals are involved in an investigation with another Member. Despite considerable debate and continuing concerns about the potential anti-competitive abuse of IP rights, this practical mechanism has rarely if ever been applied in practice.

Part II: Practical Points

- For most forms of IP, TRIPS sets general standards for what should be protected under national law; what rights should be available; and how those rights can be cut back or overridden to attend to public policy needs and legitimate third party interests.

- These standards define the basic expectations of trading partners for effective access to markets based on IP protection; they cannot substitute for actual IP laws and their administration, which determine the ultimate impact and effectiveness of IP protection in practice.
- This means there is significant scope to adapt the general standards of TRIPS according to domestic economic priorities, legal traditions and other considerations; meeting the substantive standards of TRIPS is sufficient, in principle, to ensure confidence against legal challenge and the threat of retaliation by trading partners, but will rarely be enough to amount to good policy or effective legislation, and considerable additional work needs to be done to develop, refine, and review laws to attain the policy objectives of IP articulated in TRIPS.
- TRIPS, Berne and Paris standards are of equal value and status, and one set of articles does not trump or post-date the others; they need to be read coherently together.
- TRIPS establishes an unprecedented coherence in the application of legal terms and concepts that define permissible public policy exceptions and limitations for most forms of IP, based on an original Berne model; this cross-fertilization sheds important light on these concepts and lends some coherence, but these are distinct and diverse fields of public policymaking, ranging across technology, distinctive signs and creative works. An illuminating analogy between these forms of IP does not mean exceptions are defined by a single, restrictive template.

Parts III and IV: Enforcement and Grant of Intellectual Property Rights

Most IP rights are never litigated. But if there is no confidence that IP can be effectively enforced, IP ceases to have practical value in commerce. IP enforcement becomes a trade issue because the routine commercial-scale infringement of a firm's IP can amount to effective denial of market access to the extent that that firm relies on IP to compete. Lack of systematic enforcement may induce the greater resort to secrecy or restrictive technological measures. It may also frustrate the fulfilment of the public policy goals that legislators seek to advance when introducing IP laws. A major impetus for the TRIPS negotiations was the perception that a country could adhere to existing IP treaties and yet not provide adequate remedies to curb trade in infringing goods. As the panel in *China—Intellectual Property Rights* pointed out,

pre-existing international intellectual property agreements contained comparatively few minimum standards on enforcement procedures beyond national treatment and certain optional provisions. One of the major reasons for the conclusion of the TRIPS Agreement was the desire to set out a minimum set of procedures and remedies that judicial, border and other competent authorities must have available to them.

The major developed economies set great store by their continuing capacity to compete internationally through use of the IP system. They argued that infringing trade was illegitimate and a form of unfair competition. IPR enforcement, just as much as substantive IP law, threatened to become a major source of bilateral trade friction, leading to strong interest in establishing an agreed framework of enforcement standards within a trade rules system. Concerns over infringing trade centred on pirated copyright works and counterfeit trademark goods, but lack of effective capacity to enforce other IP rights such as patents could also fuel tensions, as could unreasonably burdensome, discriminatory, procedurally questionable or indiscriminate enforcement procedures.

For this reason, an essential negotiating impetus for TRIPS lay in the call for effective enforcement, a demand that predated the Uruguay Round and found an imprint in the inconclusive GATT work on trade in counterfeit goods dating back to the 1970s. This Part of TRIPS goes to the heart of the rationale for IP as a matter to be handled by trade law; and it far exceeds earlier international law in the depth of detail and breadth of scope of enforcement measures that it prescribes. But as for the rest of TRIPS, it is an error to assume either that the treaty language is simply an expression of the interests of IP right holders, or that it had no antecedents in earlier IP law. The enforcement provisions are drafted with a careful eye on the equitable balancing of interests, and to provide safeguards for legitimate traders, responding to a concern articulated throughout the negotiations that IP enforcement should not encumber or frustrate legitimate trade. The abuse of IP enforcement to disrupt legitimate trading activities is a common concern for many firms, whether IP owners or not, and stimulated the development of a number of safeguards at the national level which in turn shaped the TRIPS language. Once again, the logic of TRIPS pivots on a notion of 'legitimate trade', and TRIPS imposes positive obligations not unduly to hamper trade that does not infringe IP rights, even while recognizing that firms should expect credible and effective means of appropriately enforcing their IP rights. Also, past IP treaties, notably Paris and Berne, did include positive obligations to enforce IP rights, including border measures, and GATT required that IP enforcement measures must not be discriminatory against imported goods (a panel decision confirmed this).

In working with the TRIPS enforcement provisions, we need to be clear on their status and character.

- Two ideas of 'enforcement' arise concerning TRIPS; while they are sometimes confused in debate, they are distinct ideas and must be kept distinct. First, TRIPS is considered more 'enforceable' than past international IP standards because if a country fails to comply, others may bring a complaint under the WTO dispute settlement mechanism (discussed in Chapter 5)—this is a matter of relations between trading partners about their mutual expectations of one another as defined by legal standards. Second, 'enforcement' under TRIPS concerns the standards that are expected of national laws and national authorities in providing a system for specific IP rights to be enforced. If I infringe your trademark, you should be able to enforce your rights effectively under national law; but if, in the course of enforcing IP rights, the legal system routinely fails to meet the minimum standards enshrined in TRIPS, then the matter may rise to government-to-government level, and may result in a TRIPS dispute—findings of non-compliance in a TRIPS dispute settlement can be 'enforced' through international trade relations, although this is yet to happen in practice. So adequate standards of enforcement under domestic law are required by TRIPS, an international obligation among others that can be 'enforced' ultimately by a trading partner denying other trade benefits in retaliation.
- The TRIPS standards do not require specific enforcement outcomes—failure to close down a specific pirate CD plant is not in itself a breach of TRIPS; the obligations are to make suitable legal procedures and remedies available, not to apply them in any particular instance. As the *China—Enforcement* panel observed, its task was 'not to ascertain the existence or the level of trademark counterfeiting and copyright piracy in China in general nor to review the desirability of strict IPR enforcement'. Widespread, overt, endemic IP infringement in an economy may raise serious questions about whether the required standards have indeed been met, but is not *in itself* an infringement of TRIPS, and it is not an obligation under TRIPS to achieve the impossible goal of eradicating literally all infringing activity. For the most part, right holders need to initiate enforcement actions, and the government's main role is to ensure reliable, effective, and balanced enforcement mechanisms for them to use.

Part III therefore sets out general principles that govern the availability of enforcement mechanisms, requiring that:

- procedures not be too burdensome or costly;
- remedies be expeditious and sufficient to deter infringement;
- procedures not become barriers to legitimate trade;

- safeguards be available against abuse;
- proceedings be fair and transparent for right holders and alleged infringers alike, and open to review.

These principles are carried through into detailed provisions concerning civil enforcement procedures, criminal procedures, and specific measures for dealing with infringing goods at the point of importation (border measures). Reflecting the more prevalent forms of infringing trade which prompted the TRIPS negotiations, criminal remedies and border measures are only required in the case of copyright piracy and trademark counterfeiting. For other IPR infringements, only civil remedies need be provided, but countries can choose to apply criminal sanctions and border measures.

In codifying detailed rules on enforcement of IPRs, Section III includes an important proviso (TRIPS:41.5): there is no obligation to establish a distinct judicial system for IPR systems, and TRIPS does not affect 'the capacity of Members to enforce their law in general'. There are no obligations relating to the dedication of resources for IPR enforcement as against general law enforcement. There is also an undertaking that enforcement procedures should be applied so as to 'avoid the creation of barriers to legitimate trade and to provide for safeguards against their abuse'. (TRIPS:41.1)

The rules for civil enforcement procedures cover:

- Procedural fairness and equity (TRIPS:42), including limitations on mandatory personal appearances, entitlement to substantiate claims and present relevant evidence, and protection of confidential information;
- Evidence (TRIPS:43), including obligations on making evidence available to the opposing party, and the court's authority to preliminary and final determinations in the event of a party withholding evidence or impeding a procedure;
- Injunctions (TRIPS:44), particularly the availability of injunctions restraining the entry onto the market of imported infringing goods;
- Damages and recovery of costs (TRIPS:45) and other remedies (TRIPS:46), particularly the disposal or destruction of infringing goods and of materials and implements used to create infringing goods;
- Information on third parties (TRIPS:47), an optional provision allowing for courts to order that infringers provide information on third parties involved in the production or distribution of infringing goods;
- Indemnification of the defendant (TRIPS:48), requiring safeguards for defendants where enforcement procedures are abused, with limited exceptions for public officials.

TRIPS aims not to tilt enforcement procedures towards the complainant, but requires national legal systems to maintain a fair and equitable balance, with guarantees of due process that should provide equal comfort to the defendant and complainant in infringement cases. However, the special character of IP—the intangible nature of IP, and the way it is embedded in traded goods—led TRIPS negotiators to introduce two special enforcement mechanisms geared to infringement of IP in particular: interim court orders, and border measures.

Since evidence of IPR infringement can be easily destroyed, courts in some countries developed a practice of permitting intrusive inspections by the lawyers of one side to secure evidence of infringement before a case was fully heard on its merits—but subject to stringent safeguards. TRIPS negotiators took an unprecedented step in bringing such a specific judicial procedure within the scope of obligations under international trade law: governments are required to ensure that courts have the authority to permit provisional measures 'to preserve relevant evidence in regard to the alleged infringement', including giving orders *inaudita altera parte* (without giving the alleged infringer a chance to be heard) 'where there is a demonstrable risk of evidence being destroyed'. The obvious risk that such orders may prejudice the defendant's legitimate interests means that authorities must have the authority to order 'appropriate compensation for any injury caused by these measures'. Similar provisional measures are required especially 'to prevent the entry into the channels of commerce ... including imported goods immediately after customs clearance'. These orders must also be available *inaudita altera parte* where appropriate, in particular where any delay is likely to cause irreparable harm to the right holder. The same safeguards against abuse are required. But allowing even preliminary court orders without giving both sides a chance to be heard posed difficulties in some legal traditions—the US initiated TRIPS disputes against both Denmark and Sweden, which were only settled when they passed laws to provide for such orders in civil procedures.

Controls on the import of infringing goods exemplify the common roots of IP and trade law, being measures to restrict trade that is agreed as being illegitimate. Paris and Berne already required some, rather limited, border measures to guard against imports, and earlier IP-related work under GATT also focused on combating trade in counterfeit goods. So the idea that countries should seize infringing goods at the border was already part of the international legal landscape. But, impelled as it was by the perception that current obligations were ineffectual, TRIPS introduced more systematic measures to control the infringing imports. These measures are mandatory only for the two predominant categories of infringing trade:

- Pirated copyright goods, or

     copies made without the consent of the right holder in the country of production and which are made directly or indirectly from an article where the making of that copy would have constituted an infringement of a copyright or a related right under the law of the country of importation.

- Counterfeit trademark goods, or

any goods, including packaging, bearing without authorization a trademark which is identical to the trademark validly registered in respect of such goods, or which cannot be distinguished in its essential aspects from such a trademark, and which thereby infringes the rights of the owner of the trademark in question under the law of the country of importation.

Imports that appear to fall into either category can be kept out of the domestic market for a brief period, while the right holder initiates a court action or similar legal proceedings. This 'suspension' from entry into the market—which is not a definitive seizure or impoundment of the goods—can be triggered directly by customs officials, or on application by the right holder supported by prima facie evidence of infringement and a detailed description of the goods. But the goods must be released into the domestic market if the right holder does not take such legal action (unless, of course, the goods fall foul of another legal requirement, such as controls on narcotics or pornographic material). If the court hearing leads to a finding of infringement, the remedies available include the destruction or disposal of the infringing goods.

Because TRIPS is designed to safeguard legitimate trade from the impact of IP infringement, procedural safeguards are built in to balance the interests of the importer or consignee:

- the authorities can seek a security or equivalent assurance to protect the defendant's interests and to deter abuse of the process;
- if legal proceedings are not been commenced within ten days of the suspension (extendable by another ten), then the goods are normally to be released; and
- the applicant for such measures can be required to pay compensation for any injury caused to legitimate traders by wrongful use of the procedure.

Because of the relative ease of trading in infringing copyright and trademarked goods, conditions for release from customs of goods which are alleged to infringe other forms of IPRs (such as patents and industrial designs) are less rigorous.

TRIPS allows for WTO Members to apply border measures for other forms of IP infringement, and for controls on the export of infringing goods, but does not mandate them. The authorities can be permitted to inform the right holder of detailed information about the importer, consignee and the suspended goods, to facilitate further enforcement. Customs officials can also be empowered to take *ex officio* action to suspend the release of prima facie infringing goods on their own initiative (ie prior to any intervention by the right holder), although the right holder still has to bring forward a complaint to finalize the matter. The reach of border control measures need not cover non-commercial goods contained in travellers' personal luggage or sent in small consignments.

Criminal procedures

Uniquely in international IP agreements with wide membership, TRIPS also specifically requires criminal remedies, a matter normally reserved for domestic law and policy. These standards have now been closely analysed by the *China— Intellectual Property Rights* Panel, which acknowledged 'the sensitive nature of criminal matters and attendant concerns regarding sovereignty'. In contrast to border measures, which are directed at certain kinds of goods (the conventional ambit of trade law), criminal remedies aim at a particular kind of behaviour on the part of individuals. When infringement amounts to wilful trademark coun- terfeiting or copyright piracy on a commercial scale, TRIPS requires that criminal remedies must be available—including imprisonment, fines or both of these— and they must be a sufficient deterrent, so that token fines may not be enough. The remedies must also cover, when appropriate, the seizure, forfeiture and destruction of infringing goods and the means used to create them. The Panel clarified that there are no exceptions to these obligations, which require that criminal remedies should cover *all* acts of wilful trademark counterfeiting or copyright piracy on a commercial scale. But the Panel noted four limitations—the obligations only cover trademarks and copyright; they apply only to counterfeit- ing and piracy, not all forms of infringement; infringement must be 'wilful'— 'focussing on the infringer's intent'; and infringement should be on a commercial scale. What raises a level of infringement up to the threshold of 'commercial scale' was a pivotal issue in the *China-IPRs* dispute—which in part concerned whether certain minimum thresholds in Chinese criminal law were low enough to meet this standard. The Panel found it was a factual question, focused on the country itself, dependent on the magnitude or extent of typical or usual commer- cial activity with respect to a given product in a given market; ultimately, the threshold is linked to profit-making activities.

Acquisition and maintenance of IPRS and related inter-partes procedures

Effective and fair administration of IPRs is an important element of a balanced IP system. To put it another way, if the process of obtaining the grant of an IP right is burdensome, arbitrary or protracted, this can effectively deny the expected commercial benefits of IP protection, even if the laws on the books meet expectations. Equally, if decisions on the grant of IP rights are inconsistent or non-transparent, and if no recourse is available to a full consideration of a case on its merits, the public interest also suffers, along with the interests of third parties such as opponents to registration. Even from a strictly commercial perspective, market access relating to the IP system may also entail the capacity effectively to oppose ill-founded IP rights claimed by others, as much as securing legitimate IP rights for oneself. TRIPS broke new ground in international IP law in codifying the procedural standards that countries could rightly expect of one another in the acquisition and maintenance of IP rights. Part IV of TRIPS expresses an expectation of reasonable promptness in the registration of IP such as patents, trademarks, and registered designs, so that the capacity of right holders to derive commercial benefit is not too greatly limited by procedural complexities and delays. But it also requires that decisions taken on the grant or refusal of IPR should be subject to an independent review process—either by a separate court, or a 'quasi-judicial' authority such as an appeal board. And the general standards of procedural fairness that TRIPS requires for enforcement are also applied to decisions on whether to grant or refuse an IP right.

Parts III and IV: Practical Points

- Expectations of effective access to IP protection in foreign markets extend under TRIPS beyond the legal availability of IP rights under national law: they extend to the processes for granting and enforcing those rights. Even GATT, prior to TRIPS, required that IP be enforced without undue discrimination.
- These expectations are, for the most part, expressed as general principles, leaving scope for detailed interpretation at the national level. In essence, there should be reasonable confidence that it is possible to take effective action against any infringement of IP covered by TRIPS, through remedies that are timely and that deter future infringements.
- TRIPS standards do not aim to impose enforcement mechanisms weighted towards right holders; they require open, non-discriminatory, predictable and procedurally sound enforcement in a way that should equally benefit right holders and other traders, and serve the general public interest. Thus enforcement procedures must avoid creating barriers to legitimate trade and should safeguard against abuse.

- For most IP enforcement, the right holder has the responsibility of initiating any enforcement action, and the core obligation on the government is to ensure that effective, legally well-founded mechanisms are put in place so that right holders can take the necessary action. But TRIPS provides scope for government-initiated (*ex officio*) enforcement action, while not specifically requiring it, and ensuring procedural safeguards.
- TRIPS also defines what countries can legitimately expect of one another in the form of reasonably prompt and fair procedures for deciding on the grant of IP rights, and in providing scope for higher review of decisions on grant.
- The core principles of non-discrimination—national treatment and MFN—apply in this area as well; even pre-TRIPS GATT law confirmed that enforcement of patents could not treat imported products less favourably than products of domestic origin.

Part V: Dispute Prevention and Settlement

Transparency and dispute prevention

This Part of TRIPS pairs two sets of obligations: provisions on dispute settlement which have often been strongly emphasized but are rarely used, and provisions on transparency which have been largely overlooked but are used extensively. But there is a fundamental linkage between these two sets of obligations: lack of transparency about national laws and regulations has in itself been a source of bilateral trade friction, and can foster disputation; conversely, TRIPS promotes systematic transparency in order to forestall disputes.

National systems for granting, administering and enforcing IPRs are generally complex and difficult to interpret. Lack of authoritative information about national IP systems, and difficulty in interpreting national systems, can, in itself, lead to misunderstandings or doubts about the effect of IP laws. It is also a potential constraint on the flow of trade and investment. At worst, lack of understanding about the operation of national systems could fuel bilateral trade tension.

The original GATT, in 1947, established a general principle of transparency for 'laws, regulations, judicial decisions and administrative rulings of general application'. Paris and Berne both require laws and legal texts to be communicated to WIPO. And if, for many firms, capacity to compete legitimately in foreign markets depends on using the IP system, this creates a legitimate demand for information about what material is protected against what criteria, about the scope of rights and their limitations, and about how rights and other IP-related interests can be defended through the national legal system. Transparency in itself is therefore an element of effective market access.

TRIPS builds on past requirements for transparency in both trade law and IP law and constructs a transparency mechanism of unprecedented reach and systematic procedure, covering the 'availability, scope, acquisition, enforcement and prevention of the abuse of IP rights', notably falling under the title 'dispute prevention'. It requires Members to notify all their relevant laws and regulations,

---

Republic Act No. 8293—The Intellectual Property Code of the Philippines

Trademarks Regulations—IPO Office Order No. 17 (1998)—Amendment; IPO Office Order No. 08 (2000)—Amendment

Rules and Regulations on Voluntary Licensing

IPO Rules and Regulations on Settlement of Disputes (Involving Technology Transfer Payments and the Terms of a License Involving the Author's Right to Public Performance or Other Communication of his Work)

Rules and Regulations on Inter Partes Proceedings (Petitions for Cancellation of a Mark, Patent, Utility Model, Industrial Design, Opposition to Registration of a Mark, and Compulsory Licensing)

Rules and Regulations on Administrative Complaints (for Violations of Laws Involving Intellectual Property Rights)

Revised Rules and Regulations on Settlement of Disputes (Involving Technology Transfer Payments and the Terms of a License Involving the Authors Right to Public Performance or Other Communication of His Work)

Rules and Regulations on Utility Models and Industrial Design—IPO Office Order No. 09 (2000)

Rules and Regulations on Inventions

Rules and Regulations Establishing the Fee Structure of the Intellectual Property Office

Copyright Safeguards and Regulations

Intellectual Property Office Uniform Rules on Appeal

Layout-Design Regulation

Philippine Rules on PCT

Amendment to the Philippine Rules on PCT Applications,

Amendment to the IPO Fee Structure,

Philippine Republic Act No. 95022 also known as the 'Universally Accessible Cheaper and Quality Medicines Act of 2008', and of Joint DOH-DTI-IPO-BFAD Administrative Order No. 2008-01 or the Implementing Rules and Regulations of R.A. 9502

The 'main dedicated IP laws and regulations' notified by the Philippines to the TRIPS Council since 2001 from the document series IP/N/1/PHL . . . (see Table 4.5). These were augmented by over 40 'other laws and regulations' which included *the Constitution of the Republic of the Philippines, the Civil and Penal Codes,* and *the Rules of Civil and Criminal Procedure,* as well as specific measures such as *the Inventors and Invention Incentives Act* and an *Executive Order Creating the Inter-Agency Committee on Intellectual Property Rights.*

Figure 4.5 Laws of the Philippines Notified to the TRIPS Council

and to provide details of important judicial decisions on request. TRIPS also requires Members to supply further information in response to written requests. This provision fosters a greater understanding of national IP systems, thereby promoting greater confidence in their effective operation and facilitating trade and investment between Members.

The TRIPS Council built on these provisions by organizing a structured, progressive review of each Member's national IP laws, yielding an impressive body of information about their IP systems. Few other international agreements have so much detailed, uniform, official documentation of actual implementation. But this information is strikingly little used, despite the strong commercial, political, and academic interest in IP laws and systems. From a legal point of view, this material is a unique record of TRIPS implementation, potentially useful as an informal guide to clarifying the perceived nature of TRIPS obligations, as it is provided under TRIPS:63 for the specific purpose of assisting the TRIPS Council 'in its review of the operation of [TRIPS]'.

Laws should be notified 'without delay' (normally 30 days) after the relevant provisions of TRIPS come into effect for a Member. Subsequent new laws must also be notified. This notification process has produced a specific series of WTO documents, containing the texts of national legislation and some explanatory material—this information now covers more than 120 distinct jurisdictions. The focus of notification is the 'main dedicated intellectual property laws and regulations', defined as,

the main laws and regulations on the availability, scope and acquisition of each of the categories of intellectual property covered by the TRIPS Agreement, together with such other main laws and regulations as are dedicated to intellectual property, such as those on border enforcement.

Notification also covers 'other' laws and regulations which are not dedicated to the field of IP, but nonetheless pertain to the IP system, such as laws and regulations on enforcement and the prevention of abusive practices. Main dedicated laws are notified in an official WTO language (French, Spanish or English) to enhance access. The 'other' laws and regulations need only be notified in a national language.

A special procedure was adopted for notification in relation to enforcement: many TRIPS requirements for civil, criminal, and border control enforcement measures are not met through specific legislation, but through judicial and administrative arrangements, and general civil and criminal codes and practice. The notification requirements are therefore also met by responding to a checklist of questions concerning enforcement procedures and remedies—the collated answers now cover just short of 100 jurisdictions.

Following notification of their laws and enforcement mechanisms, each Member undergoes a review of their national IP systems within the TRIPS Council, through an exchange of questions and answers. This peer-review process led to thousands of questions and answers being put to WTO Members, which elucidated extensive details about the character of IP law and regulations, how they are interpreted and applied in practice, the role of other laws and measures such as criminal and civil codes, and the legal basis for many measures. The WTO also conducts other reviews, beyond the TRIPS Council, which yield extensive practical information regarding IP protection at the national level (the regular Trade Policy Review, and the provisions of bilateral and regional trade agreements bearing on IP).

Box 4.2 Some of the questions posed during the TRIPS Council review of Australia's IP enforcement regime (IP/Q4/AUS/1)

- Please explain the procedure and the legal basis pursuant to which Australian law provides for the payment of adequate remuneration in case of Government use of intellectual property [TRIPS:44.2]
- Is it correct to say that intellectual property infringement cases often end in the interim interlocutory stage? If yes, what seem to be the reasons? Is this desirable in the interest of justice?
- Does any intellectual property enforcement agency have the legal power to seize and forfeit suspected infringing articles, whether or not a charge has been laid? If not, why?
- Please explain who shall pay the cost of detentions based on [TRIPS:51] or destruction stipulated in [TRIPS:59].
- Please explain any provisions in the enforcement system in Australia that ensure expeditious remedies. In addition, please explain what provisions are available to prevent deliberate delays by the parties to a proceeding and indicate the circumstances in which such provisions will be applied.
- In civil proceedings, are there any proof facilitation provisions which could create legal presumptions of intellectual property subsistence and ownership and thus could excuse the right owner from appearing in court and to testify these issues? If not, why?

Since TRIPS came into force, several additional notification and review processes have been established, leading to a unique body of information on national measures not only to protect IP in areas of policy sensitivity (such as biotech patenting), but also to promote technology transfer to least developed countries and to provide technical assistance on TRIPS, as well as contact points on IP enforcement and technical cooperation. Table 4. 3 summarizes the scope of the notifications and review processes, which a practitioner of international or comparative IP law can scarce afford to overlook.

Table 4.3 Transparency in Practice—Overview of Notifications under TRIPS

Provision	Content of notifications	Documents*
TRIPS:63.2	**Main dedicated IP laws**	IP/N/1/[ISO country code]/*
	Copyright and Related Rights	P/N/1/[cc]/C/*
	Trademarks	IP/N/1/[cc]/T/*
	Geographical Indications	IP/N/1/[cc]/G/*
	Industrial Designs	IP/N/1/[cc]/D/*
	Patents (including Plant Variety Protection)	IP/N/1/[cc]/P/*
	Integrated Circuits	IP/N/1/[cc]/L/*
	Undisclosed Information	IP/N/1/[cc]/U/*
	Industrial Property (General)	IP/N/1/[cc]/I/*
	Enforcement	IP/N/1/[cc]/E/*
	Other (eg Unfair Competition)	IP/N/1/[cc]/O/*
	Checklist on enforcement measures	IP/N/6/[cc]/
TRIPS:69	Enforcement contact points	IP/N/3/
TRIPS:67	Contact points for technical cooperation	IP/N/7/[cc]/
Doha 'paragraph 6' decision	Importing country's notification	IP/N/9/[cc]/
Doha 'paragraph 6' decision	Exporting country's notification	IP/N/10/[cc]/
	TRIPS Council review of laws	
	Copyright and related rights	IP/Q/[cc]/
	Trademarks, GIs, designs	IP/Q2/[cc]/
	Patents, integrated circuits, undisclosed information	IP/Q3/[cc]/
	Enforcement, acquisition, maintenance of IP	IP/Q4/ [cc]/
TRIPS:24.2	**Checklist on Protection of Geographical Indications**	IP/C/W/117/

Table 4.3 (*cont.*)

Provision	Content of notifications	Documents*
TRIPS:27.3(b)	*Patent protection of plant and animal inventions; Plant variety protection*	*IP/C/W/125*
TRIPS:67	*Technical cooperation activities by developed country Members*	*IP/C/W/539, 517, 476, 455, 426, 408, 377, 306, 203, 154, 109, 77, 34***
TRIPS:66.2	*Incentives for technology transfer to LDCs*	*IP/C/W/536, 519, 497, 480, 452, 431, 412, 388, 132***
Trade Policy Review Mechanism	*Trade Policy review materials:* *** *Reports by Governments* *Reports by the WTO Secretariat* *Minutes of the Trade Policy Review Body* *Questions and answers by WTO Members*	*WT/TPR/G/** *WT/TPR/S/** *WT/TPR/M/** *WT/TPR/M/**
GATT:XXIV, Enabling Clause GATS:V	*Texts, Abstracts, Presentations and Reports on bilateral and regional trade agreements****	*<http://rtais.wto.org/>*

* All documents available at <http://docsonline.wto.org>, searching under these document symbols; the three-character ISO code is used, eg PHL for 'Philippines' (in the position given here as [cc]). For instance, to obtain all enforcement checklists, search for the document symbol 'IP/N/6/'; and to obtain the checklist for the Ukraine, search for 'IP/N/6/UKR/'.
Many of these documents are published with the suffixes 'Rev' (revision) or 'Add' (addendum).
** one document number allocated for each annual set of reports.
*** Not focused on TRIPS and IP, but frequently containing information on IP laws and policies.

Dispute settlement

Part V also articulates the linkage between TRIPS and the general dispute settlement mechanism established for the package of WTO Agreements. TRIPS: 64 states that GATT:XXII and XXIII and the DSU apply to consultations and the settlement of disputes under TRIPS. But TRIPS itself gives no special guidance as to how disputes should be settled, neither as to substance nor as to procedure. So any dispute concerning TRIPS is dealt with in the same manner and according to the same procedures as any other dispute concerning WTO Agreements covered by the DSU; and several 'TRIPS' disputes have indeed been bundled with complaints under other WTO Agreements.

There is one exception, a question that exemplifies continuing uncertainty over the proper status of IP standards within the multilateral trade law system. Under WTO law in general, the cause of action for disputes is not, in principle, simple failure to comply with treaty obligations. A complaint should concern the nullification or impairment of expected benefits under an agreement treaty. Nullification or impairment can result from (i) non-compliance with treaty obligations; (ii) measures that are treaty-consistent; and (iii) 'the existence of any other situation'. So-called 'non-violation' (ii) and 'situation' (iii) complaints are rare enough in conventional trade law disputes, and are treated circumspectly; how to apply them to TRIPS is a matter for continuing debate. TRIPS negotiators precluded their application to TRIPS disputes for an initial period of five years, and set the TRIPS Council a mandate to consider recommendations for scope and modalities for such disputes. No recommendations have been agreed, and successive Ministerial Conferences have declared continued moratoria on such disputes. So for the time being, complaints under TRIPS can only be brought on the basis that a trading partner has failed to abide by TRIPS obligations.

Dispute settlement under TRIPS, a matter of great practical import, is dealt with separately in Chapter 5

Part V: Practical Points

- The transparency function of TRIPS aims to ease tensions and prevent disputes between trading nations, by making IP laws and their operation easier to understand.
- But it also produces much information of practical use to the practitioner, analyst, legislator and policymaker, covering the great majority of the world's legal jurisdictions and spanning all legal traditions and states of development, and providing information in well-established standard formats allowing ease of comparison.
- Enforcement information is provided through a standard checklist which circulates practical information that can be difficult to secure by other means.
- The TRIPS Council review process is a unique body of authoritative information provided by governments on their IP systems covering areas of particular interest to trading partners.

Part VI: Transitional Arrangements

Part VII: Institutional Arrangements: Final Provisions

More than 15 years after TRIPS entered into force, it may seem timely to disregard 'transitional arrangements'. But Part VI includes measures of continuing importance. TRIPS:66.1 provided that least developed countries (LDCs—see Box 4.3) need not apply TRIPS provisions until ten years after it entered into force, that is until 2005. This grace period has since been extended to 2013 and may in principle be further prolonged (the TRIPS Council is required to extend this grace period 'upon duly motivated request'); so for the time being LDCs need not comply with TRIPS provisions, other than observing the essential rules of non-discrimination and avoiding measures resulting in 'a lesser degree of consistency' with TRIPS.

TRIPS:66.2 requires incentives 'for the purpose of promoting and encouraging technology transfer to [LDCs] in order to enable them to create a sound and viable technological base'. This provision has grown in importance as LDCs look to appropriate technology transfer to help them achieve their social and economic goals. Against a background of concern that this obligation be effectively implemented, the Doha Ministerial Conference agreed that the TRIPS Council would 'put in place a mechanism for ensuring the monitoring and full implementation of the obligations'. In 2003, the TRIPS Council agreed that developed country Members 'shall submit annually reports on actions taken or planned in pursuance of their commitments under Article 66.2.' These submissions are reviewed annually, giving Members an opportunity to ask questions about the notifications, and to 'discuss the effectiveness of the incentives provided in promoting and encouraging technology transfer.'

TRIPS:67 requires industrialized countries to assist developing countries in implementing TRIPS, reflecting concerns that TRIPS could only be carried out through a cooperative process, as the then Minister for Trade of Indonesia put it at the Marrakesh Conference that adopted TRIPS:

Among the new obligations which we consider as a major concession is the agreement on intellectual property. In order for us to implement the agreement fully, we require technical assistance from our developed trading partners. As we make our adjustment, what we need most is technical cooperation and not legal harassment.

Numerous national programmes have sought to give effect to this obligation, and are reported to the TRIPS Council, along with reports from several active

Box 4.3 Least developed country members of the WTO

The UN recognizes 48 countries as 'least developed'; the following 31 are WTO Members, with limited obligations under TRIPS until at least 2013: Angola; Bangladesh; Benin; Burkina Faso; Burundi; Cambodia; Central African Republic; Chad; Democratic Republic of the Congo; Djibouti; Gambia; Guinea; Guinea Bissau; Haiti; Lesotho; Madagascar; Malawi; Mali; Mauritania; Mozambique; Myanmar; Nepal; Niger; Rwanda; Senegal; Sierra Leone; Solomon Islands; Tanzania; Togo; Uganda; Zambia.

intergovernmental organizations and national contact points for technical cooperation.

Part VII defines the role of the TRIPS Council within the WTO as the key body for administering the TRIPS Agreement (all WTO Members are entitled to take part in the Council's work). It holds regular sessions for its general work, and special sessions for Doha Round negotiations on the GI Register. TRIPS:69 requires WTO Members to 'cooperate with each other with a view to eliminating international trade in goods infringing intellectual property rights'. It establishes a network of contact points in their administrations for the exchange of information on infringing trade, a potentially valuable tool that has mostly been overlooked in practice. Recognizing that effective enforcement against international infringing trade cannot be achieved in isolation within national borders, TRIPS:69 requires Members to 'promote the exchange of information and cooperation between customs authorities with regard to trade in counterfeit trademark goods and pirated copyright goods'.

This Part clarifies the status of IPRs already in existence when TRIPS came into effect—what treatment must be given to already protected subject matter. This is not a trivial or narrow technical matter, as it turned out: this provision was the subject of a dispute between the US and Canada. When giving effect to TRIPS, Canada did not change its rules regarding the duration of patents filed before 1 October 1989 to give them the 20-year term that TRIPS requires; the US claimed that existing patents should run for the full 20-year term. The AB found that existing rights had to be treated consistently with TRIPS, even if they were created prior to TRIPS coming into effect. The retrospective effect of TRIPS is very limited, and it does not govern acts which occurred before it entered into force, but it does cover rights that still exist as a result of decisions taken prior to its entry into force. So past infringing acts need not be controlled (provided infringement has ceased by the time TRIPS enters into force), but the rights available and their duration should comply with TRIPS, even if the IP was granted before TRIPS entered effect (so the rights available under an old trademark registration should comply with TRIPS standards). This was the critical distinction confirmed by the Appellate Body in the *Canada—Patent Term* case: the act of granting protection to a certain element of IP, and the right to take legal action that flows from that act.

This Part also provided for a unique measure, a so-called 'mailbox' arrangement for certain critical fields of patented technology. One point of sensitivity in TRIPS negotiations was the extension of patent protection to subject matter that some countries had expressly excluded from patent protection, namely pharmaceutical and agricultural chemical products, reflecting longstanding policy sensitivity concerning patents on this subject matter. Under the Part VI transitional arrangements, TRIPS:65.4 gave developing countries another five years—beyond the general five-year grace period they enjoyed—to extend the scope of patent protection to areas of technology not earlier covered by their patent laws; this meant pharmaceuticals and agricultural chemicals did not have to be patented before January 2005. As a *quid pro quo*, TRIPS:70.8 and 70.9 provided a unique kind of interim protection—a 'mailbox' allowing applications for patents in these two fields to be filed from the date TRIPS entered into force, even though patents did not have to be granted until the final grace period ends; while these applications waited in the mailbox, Members had to provide exclusive marketing rights for a limited period.

This form of IP protection was temporary and transitional in character, but its significance to trade interests yielded an important early dispute settlement case. Both the EU and the US challenged the arrangements made by India to implement this measure; the case turned on whether interim administrative arrangements under Indian law (that fell short of specific legislation) provided sufficient legal certainty to meet TRIPS obligations. On appeal to the AB, the US challenge yielded an important early decision on WTO law, dealing with such fundamental questions as the very cause of action for a TRIPS dispute, the expectations that one Member can require of another under TRIPS, and the relationship between domestic law and international legal standards, reining in a potentially more expansive reading by the Panel. The AB clarified that under TRIPS, a Member's 'legitimate expectations' of another Member were 'reflected in the language of the treaty itself'. In essence, while a Member was free to choose its means of giving effect to any TRIPS obligation, the means chosen had to provide sufficient predictability and legal certainty—an administrative order that appeared to contradict the legislation in force could not provide this.

The TRIPS review agenda

This Part also required the TRIPS Council to review the 'implementation' of TRIPS once the initial five-year grace period for developing countries had expired—that is, in the year 2000—and to review TRIPS again every two years after that 'having regard to the experience gained in its implementation'. The Council is also empowered to undertake reviews in the light of other developments that 'might warrant modifications or amendments' to TRIPS. Hence, TRIPS was not drafted as a static legal document, but has a 'built-in' review agenda which foresaw a dynamic and interactive approach to TRIPS standards at the collective level of the TRIPS Council, taking account both of actual experience in implementing TRIPS and developments that could justify its amendment. This 'Article 71' review process has not evolved as a comprehensive review of TRIPS. Instead, the review mandate has been applied mostly to pursue an interest that barely registered during the original TRIPS negotiations, but has since emerged as a major field of IP law and policy: traditional knowledge and genetic resources. In 1999, Cuba, Honduras, Paraguay, and Venezuela proposed that this review address 'protection of the intellectual property rights of the traditional knowledge of local and indigenous communities'. Ministers at Doha in 2001 referred to this review as one basis for instructing the TRIPS Council to work on the relationship between TRIPS and the Convention on Biological Diversity and the protection of traditional knowledge and folklore.

Apart from the overall 'Article 71' reviews, TRIPS required 'built-in' reviews in specific areas where policy differences could not be fully reconciled in the original negotiations, and which are indeed debated no less vigorously today:

- the protection of plant and animal inventions, through patents and distinct plant variety protection (Article 27.3(b))
- protection of geographical indications (Article 24.2)
- an international system for notifying and registering geographical indications for wines and spirits (Article 23.4)
- the scope and modalities that should apply to non-violation and situation disputes under TRIPS (Article 64.3)

These 'built-in' reviews, mandated in effect by the Uruguay Round deal, have yielded much valuable documentation over many years, but have not reached any substantive outcome, let alone a revision of the treaty text—despite now enduring longer than the Round itself. A debate has ensued as to what the term 'review' means—does it imply a potential revision of the text itself, suggesting a more dynamic legal text, or does it simply entail an information flow about the implementation of TRIPS at a national level?

Two issues later emerged, for which the Uruguay Round negotiators made no provision, but which precipitated 'reviews' of TRIPS in different senses of that word:

- Following the establishment of a WTO Work Programme on Electronic Commerce in 1998, the TRIPS Council also considered the application of TRIPS rules to electronic commerce (including protection of copyright and trademarks in the digital environment); this led to some valuable analysis by the Secretariat and some useful discussion papers, but no specific decisions or clarifications have been made regarding the interpretation or application of TRIPS standards in the online environment.
- By far the most momentous 'review' of TRIPS, indeed dominating the political landscape of TRIPS in the years from 2001, concerned access to medicines. The Doha Ministerial Conference itself issued a stand-alone Declaration on TRIPS and Public Health, which in its paragraph 6 mandated the TRIPS Council to develop an 'expedient solution' for the difficulties faced by countries with

limited production capacities in using compulsory licence as a means of leveraging access to medicines; this process has led to agreement to amend TRIPS by adding an Article 31*bis* and an Annex—this amendment has not yet entered into force, but it is already effectively operational through an earlier agreement on a waiver of the relevant provisions.

Part VII excludes a Member from entering reservations under TRIPS (unless the other Members give consent); and it provides for security exceptions, so that nothing in TRIPS shall be construed, among other things, to 'prevent a Member from taking any action which it considers necessary for the protection of its essential security interests', relating to nuclear materials, military materiel, and acts taken 'in time of war or other emergency in international relations'. The exception also extends to action taken in pursuance of obligations under the United Nations Charter for the maintenance of international peace and security.

Parts VI and VII: Practical Points

- TRIPS was not conceived as a fixed or inert text, but includes built-in review processes; these have not delivered any changes to its text, however. The one change agreed to the text was not foreseen in the original text: a significant amendment to facilitate access to medicines for countries with limited manufacturing capacity. But the built-in reviews have also yielded valuable, uniquely detailed and comprehensive surveys, and analysis of practice and policy positions in sensitive and controversial areas, which are valuable resources for practitioners.
- The transition measures have not been empty formalities, but touch on the concrete interests of existing right holders, leading to several disputes. They also address the specific context of least developed countries, whose concerns have come increasingly into focus in recent years as attention has turned to measures to promote technology transfer to these countries and better to define and respond to their needs.
- TRIPS foresees cooperation between Members as essential both for effective implementation of TRIPS by developing countries, and for curtailing the trade in infringing goods, and indeed establishes cooperation as a positive obligation in both cases. A network of contact points has been set up and published to facilitate this cooperation.

5

Trade Rules or Trade Wars? Settling TRIPS Disputes

> The legitimate expectations of the parties to a treaty are reflected in the language of the treaty itself.
>
> *Appellate Body, India—Patents*

> WTO rules are reliable, comprehensible and enforceable. WTO rules are not so rigid or so inflexible as not to leave room for reasoned judgements in confronting the endless and everchanging ebb and flow of real facts in real cases in the real world. They will serve the multilateral trading system best if they are interpreted with that in mind. In that way, we will achieve the 'security and predictability' sought for the multilateral trading system by the Members of the WTO through the establishment of the dispute settlement system.
>
> *Appellate Body Report, Japan—Alcoholic Beverages*

TRIPS Dispute Settlement in Context

Its critics view the WTO as a vigorous agent of enforced economic change and neoliberal reform, using the power of its legal instruments to impose its will on sovereign nations, rooting out illicit national regulations, and punishing miscreants. TRIPS is seen at the sharp edge of the WTO's compliance agenda, emerging as it did at the bidding of major developed economies against the resistance of developing countries.

By this account, the prospect of 'WTO sanctions' for 'non-compliance' changed the very character of international relations on IP. The mechanisms for enforcing compliance with TRIPS—the 'teeth' of TRIPS—have, in this view, supplanted an earlier, more permissive and forgiving international regime. The way TRIPS within the WTO system defines, manages, and settles disputes, as well as its linkage with broader trade interests, does indeed set it apart from other international IP treaties. But TRIPS was also negotiated in order to provide a multilateral safe haven from the unilateral assertion of economic interests through trade sanctions—what was termed 'aggressive unilateralism' in the late 1980s—superseding the earlier possibility for unbounded exercise of economic muscle to exert influence. Working within a more stable and predictable rule of law in international relations on IP means not only that it is possible to speak of objective international standards for what IP protection is 'adequate', but also that it is feasible to consider the legitimate scope and impact of 'sanctions' or economic retaliation for non-compliance with those standards.

General customary international law accepts the legitimacy of taking countermeasures (suspending benefits under a treaty in response to another country's breach of their obligations) to induce a country to comply with international obligations. The WTO system provides a specific, transparent and objective mechanism for managing such countermeasures when it comes to disputes about the covered multilateral trade agreements, including TRIPS. 'WTO sanctions' are more accurately seen as a system for setting limits to retaliation, and managing retaliation, rather than as creating a separate category of more aggressive international sanctions that lie beyond the scope of the general background of international law. Technically, a retaliatory trade sanction is termed a 'suspension of concessions or other obligations'. Specific market access benefits under the WTO agreements may be temporarily suspended to encourage withdrawal of a noncompliant measure. Retaliation is a bilateral response, lacking the character of a fine or a penalty; and there is no retrospective element, such as compensation or reparation for past damages. This more modest view of trade sanctions under TRIPS may once have seemed naïve or defensive (see 'Defending TRIPS', Chapter 2); but now seems justified in the light of 15 years' actual experience with settlement of WTO disputes.

The explicit recognition of possible sanctions under WTO dispute settlement does nonetheless concentrate the minds of legislators and policymakers on compliance with treaty obligations, more so than for earlier IP conventions (including those, like Paris and Berne, built into TRIPS). The concern to comply with TRIPS—and to be seen to be complying—was a major stimulus for active legislative programmes, especially as many developing countries worked to bring laws into line with TRIPS within the agreed transition periods (mostly by 2000). But it is important to recognize that government legislative choices are not determined, for the most part, by the fear of direct economic reprisals, but rather from a wider legal and political interest in adhering to agreed standards. And one rationale for agreeing to cover IP standards within a multilateral dispute settlement system was to safeguard scope for legitimate legislative choices at the domestic level.

For a practitioner, the essential impact of the inclusion of IP into the WTO dispute settlement system has been to create a more stringent and more 'judicial', yet more objective and transparent, standard for assessing and defending the adequacy of national IP systems than the ad hoc, and more anarchic, system that prevailed before. The potential, ultimate consequences of non-compliance are significant, even if they are almost never felt in practice. But equally important is the political and legal 'freedom to operate' for national systems that results from the linkage of the dispute settlement system with the substantive standards of TRIPS—if one can confidently assert or defend one's choice of legislation as being TRIPS-consistent, the objective legitimacy of those choices is strengthened, and the prospect of direct economic retaliation is significantly reduced (even if indirect political and economic pressure may still be felt).

If a threat of retaliatory 'trade sanctions' was what mattered the most, then you would expect actual government choices to depend more on a pragmatic risk assessment of the likely consequences of losing a dispute, rather than on the intent to comply with the standards of TRIPS as such. Yet even when governments introduce controversial measures, they will typically claim that they are TRIPS consistent. It would be truly exceptional to hear the argument that they have considered the likely impact of trade sanctions and decided to proceed with non-compliant legislation anyway, on the basis that the benefits still outweigh the costs. On the whole, governments prefer to maintain consistency with international standards, rather than conceding that it is only the prospect of sanctions that motivates them to comply with TRIPS. The only case so far of anything resembling 'sanctions' for TRIPS non-compliance—actually, mutually agreed arbitration on compensation between two powerful developed economies—did not, apparently, create a strong incentive for immediate observance of TRIPS standards, as the measures remain in force a decade after they were formally found not to comply.

TRIPS disputes and trade sanctions in practice

The rate of formal disputation under TRIPS is lower than many expected when the text was signed in 1994. Apprehensions over a salvo of disputes aimed at developing countries for non-compliance have eased. The WTO has 153 Members, all bound to some extent by TRIPS; over 120 of these (all but the LDC Members) have very extensive obligations under TRIPS covering a wide range of IP law and its enforcement, of great import for several key economic sectors; but there has been an average of two TRIPS disputes per year; many TRIPS disputes were settled or effectively withdrawn before a panel finding; of the 12 disputes that led to actual legal determinations on TRIPS compliance, only three found a developing country to be non-compliant (India, in two parallel disputes on the same point, and China in one dispute). See Table 1.2 in Chapter 1 for a summary of disputes.

Since TRIPS came into force in 1995:

- most TRIPS-related disputes were levelled against developed countries;
- the WTO has not authorized any 'sanctions' for non-compliance with TRIPS;
- one country has agreed to pay arbitrated compensation for non-compliance with TRIPS: this was a major developed economy;
- three developing countries used TRIPS in cross-retaliation to try to leverage legitimate market access in other economic sectors;
- two developing countries have brought TRIPS complaints against a major developed economy to safeguard shipments of generic medicines;
- the only country, so far, to defend with full success a complaint of TRIPS non-compliance was a developing country, Indonesia.

It may be deflating both for the critics and the proponents of TRIPS and the WTO, but a realistic look at the actual experience of dispute settlement shows more modest outcomes than the early expectations voiced on both sides of an energetic debate. Crucially, non-compliance with TRIPS produces no automatic response. To use a rough analogy, no parking inspectors are out policing adherence to the rules and issuing tickets for any infractions—it is as though, should you park your car illegally, it would be up to other motorists to pursue a claim that you have breached parking regulations and that this caused a nuisance to them. A low level of disputation does not, therefore, mean that every Member is otherwise 100 per cent compliant with their TRIPS obligations in every detail. Nor should the significance and influence of the compliance and sanctions regime be measured by a head-count of actual disputes. But it is a reminder that there is a practical and political threshold to initiating and pursuing a dispute, and that there are other less directly contentious means of pursuing trade interests connected with IP.

A practitioner needs to take a realist, pragmatic assessment of the true character and context of dispute settlement, and what can trigger an actual dispute. After all, what are the 'teeth' of TRIPS, and how is their imprint felt in practice? Scholars debate over the essential legal and political character of the WTO as a regime—is it essentially a bundle of bilateral deals between States, which are managed in a multilateral forum, or do countries have a distinct, stand-alone obligation to comply with multilateral standards, a responsibility to the WTO itself, as it were? Both these theoretical possibilities are argued with some force in an important theoretical debate. But, in practice, finding and enforcing compliance with TRIPS does require the deliberate initiative of one country to take action against another. It does not flow from any multilateral action and still less on an initiative of the WTO *as such*.

A finding of non-compliance with TRIPS, and certainly any form of permissible 'sanction', can only result if a bilateral dispute is launched and carried through the DSU procedure at least to the point of a panel finding. In turn, that means a national government has to be seriously concerned about the state of IP protection in a trading partner, be sufficiently convinced that it has a legal case under TRIPS, and be prepared to take a conspicuous step with potential ramifications for trade relations. The complainant should also be willing to accept the wider policy implications of having its legal arguments prevail in a particular case. Although each case is technically decided independently and does not create binding precedent, in practice each panel report and AB finding contributes to an authoritative understanding of how TRIPS is read and applied. Hence the findings in any case may in time affect the domestic choices of the complainant as much as the respondent in that case.

Since disputes arise in the context of bilateral trading relations in the real world, political and practical constraints naturally apply. In short, there are considerable pragmatic filters, otherwise, many more disputes would be triggered, as many countries are technically non-compliant in some way with TRIPS, and have acknowledged as much in the course of TRIPS Council reviews (normally, though, mentioning that work is under way to bring the laws into compliance). Say a developing country Member is yet to enact a law protecting integrated circuit layout designs, as it should under TRIPS, perhaps because of its limited capacity to draft, pass and implement such a technical law. There would be no direct consequences under the WTO, and no formal finding of non-compliance without a dispute being initiated by a Member which was sufficiently motivated to do so. Yet defending and managing such a dispute would likely divert the same resources that country had available to bring such a law into effect. The ultimate result from the dispute settlement procedure is likely to be a recommendation that such a law should be brought into effect within a reasonable period—an outcome that may ironically be interrupted by the dispute settlement process itself. On the other hand, informal consultations about the need for such a law to be passed may have the effect of pushing a bill up the legislative timetable.

January 2000 was the legal deadline for many developing countries to comply with most substantive TRIPS provisions. Many countries made a massive effort to bring their laws into line in time, but officials were relieved to find, when the deadline passed, that there were no automatic 'sanctions', nor even any formal determinations of non-compliance. In practice, compliance was more to do with establishing a formal and objective framework for organizing trade relations on IP matters, with dispute settlement taking its place within a far broader context of bilateral dealings and WTO transparency measures.

Thus a real dispute arises as a direct practical concern in a trading relationship when one country perceives solid benefits in pursuing that course of action. The WTO will provide a stable, transparent, rules-based means of managing the dispute in a manner that is actually and is perceived to be procedurally fair and balanced. The system, therefore, has the effect of keeping bilateral disputation in perspective and giving it a more objective and proportionate character. Whatever the formal legal construct one gives to the WTO regime, in practice it is a means of managing bilateral disputes over IP protection in a more ordered and predictable manner.

The nature of sanctions should be kept in perspective. The WTO does not order sanctions, but rather sets limits to them. In the rare occasions that a dispute leads to retaliation by a trading partner, the essential role of the WTO is to contain and focus the options for retaliation. The formal ruling sets a cap on any retaliation and clarifies the economic sector where sanctions may apply. Such rulings are rare; still rarer is the step of actual retaliation. The WTO has never yet authorized such retaliation in response to non-compliance with TRIPS. The sole 'sanction' awarded under TRIPS was an arbitral award on compensation: the US and the European Communities agreed to seek arbitration on the compensation payable when US copyright law was found to be non-compliant with TRIPS and thus to impair legitimate European interests. Further, as already noted, the non-compliant measure remained in place ten years after the original finding. Ongoing efforts at resolving this dispute aimed not at legal compliance with TRIPS as an end in itself, but to reach the 'mutually satisfactory resolution' that the DSU itself requires; and ultimately, we learn from experience, there remains a role for the long established process of trade diplomacy to achieve a final settlement of a difficult dispute—the function of the ruling is to facilitate this and give it a more objective grounding.

Is compliance with TRIPS, then, only a matter of resolving disputes to mutual—bilateral—satisfaction? From a practical perspective, the idea is to manage bilateral trade friction on IP matters within a multilateral framework. The legitimate expectations that WTO Members can demand of each other are defined, measured, and enforced, according to agreed multilateral standards. Yet Members are legally bound to comply in good faith with the multilateral standards of TRIPS, in line with the principle of *pacta sunt servanda*. WTO Members therefore wrestle with two ideas of TRIPS compliance—the first, that it should be complied with as an end in itself; a second, more pragmatic approach (particularly on sensitive issues, whereby domestic policy choices may be influenced by a practical risk assessment of TRIPS implications) which may accept a remote possibility of a TRIPS challenge. This second idea of TRIPS 'compliance' shades into the wider, pragmatic management of bilateral trading relations and is not an isolated, formal procedure.

Peer pressure and TRIPS compliance

Failure to comply TRIPS triggers no immediate response, let alone trade sanctions; it is likely that there are many technical violations of TRIPS of greater or lesser significance that simply never come to light in the multilateral trade arena. But WTO Members do feel a general expectation that their laws and policies will be TRIPS-consistent, and not merely because of the potential threat of a dispute. Contributing to this climate of compliance is a set of transparency and peer-review mechanisms, explored in more detail in Chapter 4. Several fall under the heading of 'dispute prevention', recalling that transparency is seen as one ingredient of easing trade tensions; all help to promote understanding of IP laws and their public policy context, while building an expectation of adherence to the agreed standards, even when current areas of non-compliance are acknowledged:

- TRIPS:63.2—notification of IP and other laws, and enforcement measures
- TRIPS Council—review of laws and related measures
- TRIPS:67—Technical cooperation reports
- TRIPS:66.2—Notifications of incentives for technology transfer to LDCs
- Trade Policy Review Mechanism—reports covering IP law and policy
- GATT:XXIV—Reviews including IP elements of bilateral and regional trade agreements.

The Function of TRIPS Dispute Settlement

When TRIPS negotiators set IP standards within the context of multilateral trade dispute settlement, they aimed to address three perceived shortcomings in the international IP regime:

(i)   when a trading partner claimed a country's IP laws and regulatory perfor-mance were inadequate, and amounted to unfair competition in the form of widespread IP infringement, there was no objective framework for defining which expectations were legitimate and which were excessive;
(ii) there was no practical, neutral means available to assess claims of non-compliance with any agreed standards; and
(iii) no ceiling was in place to ensure that responses to frustrated expectations, and any trade sanctions, were proportionate and measured.

The negotiators were more successful in setting substantive standards for IP protection and enforcement than determining precisely how to resolve bilateral disputes especially about IP. They considered creating a distinct mechanism tailored only for IP disputes, but ultimately agreed to include TRIPS as 'just another' covered trade agreement under the DSU, even though the interests at stake and the legal logic of IP disputes differ from conventional trade disputes.

The Cause of Action

When determining the legal character of any dispute settlement system, a core element is the cause of action: what is the factual basis for a well-founded complaint? So, for TRIPS, what is the state of affairs that means a Member (a 'complainant') can legitimately commence a dispute against another Member (the 'respondent'), when it is dissatisfied about the approach to IP protection? Surprisingly, it is not a claim that a country has violated its TRIPS obligations *as such*. TRIPS disputes share the same cause of action as mainstream multilateral trade law: 'the provisions of Articles XXII and XXIII of GATT 1994 as elaborated and applied by the [DSU]'. GATT:XXIII effectively specifies that a complainant 'should consider that any benefit accruing to it directly or indirectly under [TRIPS] is being nullified or impaired or that the attainment of any objective of [TRIPS] is being impeded'. Due to the continuing moratorium on other causes of action, this state of affairs should be 'the result of . . . the failure of [the respondent] to carry out its obligations under [TRIPS]'—in other words, a violation of TRIPS.

In principle, therefore, a complainant is alleging that a *benefit* expected under TRIPS is being nullified or impaired, or an objective of TRIPS is being impeded, *as a result of* another Member's failure to carry out its obligations under TRIPS. Theoretically, then, it should be possible for a complaint to fail, even if the respondent is found not to comply with TRIPS, when the non-compliance does not nullify or impair any benefit expected by the complainant (and it did not impede the objectives of TRIPS). But this theoretical distinction barely applies in practice. The DSU clarifies that '[i]n cases where there is an infringement of the obligations assumed under a covered agreement, the action is considered prima facie to constitute a case of nullification or impairment.' It stipulates that,

. . . there is normally a presumption that a breach of the rules has an adverse impact on other Members parties to that covered agreement, and in such cases, it shall be up to the Member against whom the complaint has been brought to rebut the charge.

Rebutting this presumption is very difficult, and dispute settlement generally proceeds on the working assumption that breaching TRIPS obligations does in itself nullify or impair expected benefits. For instance, in a complaint brought about an EU Regulation on GI protection, the Panel noted that '[i]n cases where there is an infringement of the obligations assumed under a covered agreement, the action is considered prima facie to constitute a case of nullification or impairment' and concluded that 'to the extent that the Regulation as such is inconsistent with the covered agreements, it has nullified or impaired benefits accruing . . . under these agreements'.

The idea has also developed that WTO Members have an inherent, *systemic* interest in seeing compliance with the rules, not merely in remedying specific trade damage: in language endorsed by the AB, one panel remarked:

. . . with the increased interdependence of the global economy . . . Members have a greater stake in enforcing WTO rules than in the past when any deviation from the negotiated balance of rights and obligations is more likely than ever to affect them, directly or indirectly.

This comment arose when the EU questioned the legal standing of the US to challenge the European regime on bananas, when the US did not itself export the product to the EU.

The nature of the cause of action—the idea that disputes are meant to remedy a denial of expected benefits, not just check on formal legal compliance—gains significance when considering the implications of non-compliance. TRIPS and the DSU give no guidance on how to define the nature of 'expected benefits' or how to assess the extent of nullification and impairment of those benefits. Yet these considerations are critical: the DSU sets a ceiling for any retaliation for a successful complaint, 'equivalent to the level of the nullification or impairment' under TRIPS.

Thus, if it were the fear of sanctions that really determined government choices, assessment of the amount of nullification and impairment would be a decisive issue.

The first panel to look closely at TRIPS (*India—Patents*) wrestled with the cause of action for the complaint. It developed the idea that TRIPS compliance boiled down to meeting a trading partner's 'legitimate expectations' concerning IP protection, a concept drawn from the wider law of GATT. On appeal, the AB reined in the scope of TRIPS complaints by ruling that 'legitimate expectations of the parties to a treaty are reflected in the language of the treaty itself'. Extending the GATT concept of 'legitimate expectations' to demand a general sense of reassurance in the enforceability of patent rights was too broad an invocation of the general background trade law. In other words, it is a sufficient defence of a measure to show that it complies with TRIPS—dispute settlement could not explore broader ideas of disappointed expectations beyond what the treaty explicitly provides for. Greater predictability in trading relations through the rule of law is an undoubted public good, but this cuts both ways: meeting reasonable expectations of a predictable level of IP protection serves the mutual interests of trading partners; however, objective legal standards are needed to define what expectations are legitimate, so that disputes are not mired in wrangling over more subjective ideas of what expectations are reasonable.

Uncertainty over the cause of action for TRIPS disputes flows in part from the fact that TRIPS is logically opposite to 'mainstream' trade agreements. GATT sets a ceiling as to how far a government can intervene—one can regulate trade up to a certain legitimate level, but need not. TRIPS sets a floor—one must establish IP protection at least up to the agreed minimum level, but can go beyond it. Under GATT, expectations of market access may be frustrated by additional regulatory measures. For example, the market opening provided by a tariff cut may be negated by a new subsidy scheme or other domestic regulation. But what are the 'legitimate expectations' of market access under TRIPS, and what does it mean to frustrate them? If a country's laws are compliant with TRIPS, but firms encounter other obstacles to extracting expected benefits from their IP, should this state of affairs provide the basis for a dispute? This question—basically about the scope of the cause of action—was not resolved during the Uruguay Round and remains unsettled today. It was, for example, the sole question about TRIPS that was considered by trade ministers at the 2009 WTO Ministerial Conference.

GATT and the DSU provide for three causes of action for conventional trade disputes:

(i)   violation complaints (the overwhelming majority of all disputes, in which the claim is that expected benefits are denied or treaty objectives are thwarted because of measures that fail to comply with WTO obligations);

(ii) non-violation complaints (where laws are compliant with the agreement, but a government measure still nullifies or impairs expected benefits); and

(iii) situation complaints (where any other situation causes nullification and impairment).

Most disputes concern violation of WTO obligations, and the latter two causes of action are relatively rare—as one panel observed, they 'should be approached with caution and should remain an exceptional remedy'. As another panel has put it, 'The reason for this caution is straightforward. Members negotiate the rules that they agree to follow and only exceptionally would expect to be challenged for actions not in contravention of those rules.'

This caution is still more pronounced when considering IP disputes. Indeed, because of uncertainty about the proper scope of disputes about IP and trade, and political apprehension about the legal implications of a potentially wide scope of complaints, TRIPS:64(2) provisionally excluded non-violation and situation disputes, setting an initial five-year moratorium, up to the end of 1999. Meanwhile, during this period, the TRIPS Council was required to develop recommendations for scope and modalities of such disputes under TRIPS. Despite extensive debate, these recommendations were not concluded during that period. The moratorium has since been extended by repeated decisions of Ministerial Conferences. The TRIPS Council is yet to develop the expected recommendations—the matter remains on its agenda, with little sign of recent progress.

Most Members resist the idea of allowing *any* non-violation disputes under TRIPS—they worry that expanding the scope of possible disputes about IP into uncharted territory would introduce uncertainty and unpredictability to the trading system, just the opposite of the core objective of the DSU. They put the view that TRIPS is not a true 'market access' agreement, making it more difficult to consider what market access benefits a country can legitimately claim relating to IP protection. But some argue that TRIPS disputes should be considered no differently from mainstream trade disputes—if legitimately expected benefits from TRIPS are nullified or impaired, there should be some recourse, even if laws are formally compliant with TRIPS; they argue that TRIPS is a market access agreement, bringing with it legitimate expectations of using IP to secure a fair chance to compete in foreign markets. This is not a technical legalistic debate; it reveals basic divergences as to the nature of TRIPS as a regime—is it a market access agreement at all? What are the expected benefits from TRIPS that a country can legitimately claim, beyond formal compliance with its provisions? What indeed are the objectives of TRIPS and what does it mean to thwart them? And it keeps open the question, squarely addressed but not entirely resolved in the Uruguay Round negotiations—if it is agreed that IP is part of a package deal on trade law, and countries can bring to the table concerns about the impact of inadequate IP protection on their trade interests, what is the essential character of such a complaint when it takes on a legal character, and not dealt with on the political or commercial plane?

Remedies

One fundamental objective of TRIPS within the WTO system is to manage IP-related trade disputes multilaterally. Ultimately, it serves as a refuge from immoderate trade disputation that may serve short-term political interests of dominant economies, but would erode the international economic and political environment. Small economies would get little reaction if they threatened unilateral sanctions against the EU or the US to exert bilateral trade leverage. The major economies could, on the other hand, use the prospect of denial of access to their markets to bring about dramatic changes in domestic regulation in smaller trading partners.

TRIPS came into being in part as a reaction to 'aggressive unilateralism'. The major economies made it clear in the 1980s that continuing access to their markets would be conditional on meeting certain unilateral expectations about the protection of IP rights. In turn, this spurred demand for a predictable and clear basis for resolving different expectations over adequate IP protection. Thirteen developing countries tabled a TRIPS negotiating proposal including a provision on 'non-recourse to unilateral measures': 'Parties shall refrain in relation to each other from threatening or having recourse to unilaterally decided economic measures of any kind aimed at ensuring the enforcement of intellectual property rights'. This concern finds more muted expression in DSU:23, which requires Members seeking the 'redress of a violation of obligations or other nullification or impairment of benefits under the covered agreements' to have 'recourse to, and abide by, the rules and procedures of [the DSU]'.

This means that trade sanctions ('suspension of concessions') can only be applied at the time and to the level determined by the multilateral system. This sustains the central logic of the WTO system. Trade sanctions are a last resort, rather than a political weapon, can only be imposed after all possible alternatives have been explored, and can only be imposed at a level proportionate to the independently determined damage caused by the measure originally complained of. Rescind the DSU or remove TRIPS from the WTO system, and the essential effect would be to return anarchy to the management of disputes over

IP in trade—it would not abolish *disputes*—and the prospect of trade retaliation would cease to be objective, bounded, and closely monitored in a multilateral forum.

The formation of the WTO as a multilateral system for monitoring and enforcing compliance with international obligations did not, however, bring an end to national mechanisms for unilaterally monitoring the adequacy of IP protection in trading partners. The most conspicuous of these has been the US 'Special 301' process, but other economies maintain similar systems as well. The EU challenged the Special 301 process in a WTO case that clarified the proper context of such unilateral measures: only the WTO, through DSU procedures, not individual WTO Members, can determine whether a measure is inconsistent with WTO obligations. A national system that made a unilateral finding of non-compliance and used that as the basis for retaliation would itself breach WTO obligations, under the DSU itself. In this case, while the legislation left open the possibility of such non-compliant unilateral action, a Statement of Administrative Action ('SAA') under US domestic law and a statement to the Panel itself both confirmed that domestic procedures would comply with WTO obligations. Without those moderating factors, the Special 301 mechanism may have been non-compliant with the WTO obligation to use the multilateral channel. And of course such unilateral measures are available against non-Members of the WTO—removing such a prospect is one rationale for seeking to join the organization.

TRIPS itself gives no guidance on the practicalities of settling disputes. TRIPS:64 effectively 'outsources' the question to the GATT and especially the DSU. In turn, the DSU codifies and extends the GATT jurisprudence and procedure built up since 1947. It recognizes that the dispute settlement system is,

a central element in providing security and predictability to the multilateral trading system . . . [and] serves to preserve the rights and obligations under the covered agreements.

The essential characteristics of dispute settlement under TRIPS, as a 'covered agreement' under the DSU, can be summarized as follows:

- Disputes are bilateral in origin—one country raises a complaint about another's IP protection—and are not initiated by the WTO or its Secretariat. Private firms have no standing and cannot lodge a complaint (although naturally governments do often take up specific commercial interests when pursuing a complaint).
- The essence of a complaint is that a trading partner has nullified or impaired expected benefits under TRIPS or otherwise impeded TRIPS objectives through failing to comply with its provisions.

- Disputes are between WTO Members concerning IP protection at a systemic level, and do not *directly* concern individual IPRs under national law; dispute settlement is not in effect an avenue of appeal of administrative or judicial decisions whether to grant or enforce IPRs within domestic processes.
- The DSU strengthens multilateralism in dispute settlement: a WTO Member cannot seek redress for 'a violation of obligations or other nullification or impairment of benefits' under TRIPS, other than through the procedures set out in the DSU. They cannot make their own determination that TRIPS has been violated, and can only impose trade sanctions ('suspension of concessions') at the time and to the level determined by the multilateral system.
- The formal objective is settlement of disputes, rather than punishing non-compliance: the aim is 'to secure a positive solution to a dispute.' And 'a solution mutually acceptable to both parties . . . is clearly to be preferred.' While making a formal legal complaint may generally have political overtones, and usually reflects a degree of trade friction, the DSU provides that the use of dispute settlement procedures 'should not be intended or considered as contentious acts.'
- The DSU provides that the dispute settlement system is 'a central element in providing security and predictability to the multilateral trading system.' In ensuring this predictability, Members agree that dispute settlement 'serves to preserve the rights and obligations under the covered Agreements.'
- So dispute settlement has to *clarify* the provisions of TRIPS 'in accordance with customary rules of interpretation of public international law.' It cannot extend or rewrite the provisions as already agreed between Members. It is therefore for good legal and policy reasons that dispute settlement panels and the AB are careful not to go beyond this role of clarifying TRIPS provisions, even though they are criticized for going too far ('judicial adventurism') or not going far enough ('literalism' or 'conservatism') by those who preferred different outcomes.
- The essential aim of the dispute settlement mechanism is to secure a positive solution to a dispute. Preference is given to a 'solution mutually acceptable' to the disputing parties which is consistent with the WTO Agreements. Disputing parties must go through consultations before moving towards a formal finding on non-compliance, and can always reach a mutually agreed settlement at any time in dispute proceedings; the DSU provides several avenues for good offices, conciliation and mediation—reflecting the roots of this system in the more 'diplomatic', less judicial approach to settling disputes that marked the early years of GATT and still flavours the greater part of even contentious trade relations on IP matters.

- If no mutually agreed solution can be found, the first objective is the withdrawal of measures that are inconsistent with TRIPS. But if the immediate withdrawal of the measure is not practicable, then the system provides for compensation 'as a temporary measure'. The last resort is the possibility of trade sanctions (or 'suspension of concessions or other obligations' in the more polite trade jargon), subject to multilateral authorization. This expectation has been borne out in practice—such sanctions have been extremely rare (of over 400 disputes, only a tiny handful have led to actual retaliatory measures, none concerning compliance with TRIPS).
- The logic of the WTO system is that trade sanctions cease to be a political or economic weapon, and can only be imposed at a level proportionate to the independently determined damage caused by the measure originally complained of.

Dispute Settlement Procedure

The DSU establishes the principal stages of dispute settlement as:

- Mandatory good-faith consultations (with the possible involvement of third parties with a trade interest).
- Establishment of a panel to consider the case and to deliver recommendations for resolution of the dispute.
- Possible appeal on points of law to Appellate Body.
- Implementation of panel/AB's recommendation (with arbitrator's decision on a 'reasonable period of time' for implementation).
- Optional compensation in the event of failure to implement within the time determined.
- Retaliation in the form of suspension of concessions, to a degree determined by arbitration.

Of TRIPS disputes, *US—Section 110(5) Copyright Act* has gone furthest through these procedures (although it was not appealed to the Appellate Body, unlike several other TRIPS disputes). It is one of a very small number of WTO cases which dealt directly with possible 'sanctions'—in this case, an arbitrated level of compensation for the nullification and impairment of benefits (compensation is a voluntary and temporary measure, considered an interim step before full compliance with TRIPS). To illustrate how the DSU works in practice, Table 5.1 sets out the procedural steps followed in the US Copyright case, and identifies the relevant DSU provisions.

Table 5.1 Procedural Steps Followed in the *US—Section 110(5) Copyright Act* Case

Procedures	DSU Article
The European Commission resolves to take action against certain provisions of the US Copyright Act, on the basis of a complaint initiated by the Irish Music Rights Organisation (IMRO)	
The EC formally requests consultations. WT/DS/160/1	DSU:4 (TRIPS:64.1)
Australia, Canada and Switzerland request third party rights to take part in the consultations, citing substantial trade interests. WT/DS160/2—Australia, WT/DS160/3—Canada, WT/DS160/4—Switzerland	DSU:4.11
Consultations are held but fail to resolve the dispute	
The EC requests the establishment of a panel .WT/DS160/5	DSU:6 and 7
Upon the *second* request by the EC, the panel is established by the DSU (WT/DSB/M/62). The panel has standard terms of reference: 'To examine in light of the relevant provisions of the covered agreements . . . the matter referred to the DSB . . . and to make such findings as will assist the DSB in making the recommendations or in giving the rulings provided for in those agreements'.	DSU:6
The panel is *constituted* (ie individual members appointed) by the Director General, following failure of parties to agree on panel members. WT/DS160/6	DSU:8.7
Australia, Brazil, Canada, Japan, and Switzerland reserve rights to participate in the panel proceedings as third parties.	
The panel receives written submissions from the two parties and from the third parties, holds an oral hearing, seeks information from the two principal parties and from WIPO, receives second written submissions (rebuttals) and holds second oral hearing.	DSU:12 DSU:13
The panel notifies its need for extended time to consider the case beyond the six months provided for in the DSU. WT/DS160/7	DSU:12.8–12.9
The panel issues an interim report (with factual findings and summary of argumentation) only to the two principal parties for their comment.	DSU:15.1
The panel's final report is issued, its findings expressed in the form of a recommendation for consideration by the Dispute Settlement Body. WT/DS160/R	DSU:15.2 DSU:19
The report is circulated to WTO Members, is considered and adopted by the DSB in the absence of a consensus not to adopt it. WT/DS160/8	DSU:16
The US notifies the DSB of its intention to implement the report's recommendations and elects not to appeal on points of law to the Appellate Body. WT/DS160/9	DSU:21.3

Procedures	DSU Article
Parties discuss but do not reach mutually satisfactory solution as to the 'reasonable period of time' for implementation of the recommendations. The US proposes 15 months, which the EC considers too long.	
The EC requests binding arbitration on the 'reasonable period of time.' WT/DS160/10	DSU:21.3 (c)
The EC and US request the Director General to appoint an agreed arbitrator, making allowance for the expiry of the due date for this appointment. WT/DS160/11	DSU:21.3 (c)
The arbitrator rules that the reasonable period of time is 12 months from the DSU's adoption of the report. WT/DS160/12	DSU:21.3 (c)
The arbitration is circulated to WTO Members. WT/DS160/13	DSU:21.3 (c)
The US requests an extension of six further months or the adjournment of the current session of the US Congress (whichever is earlier) to implement the report's recommendations, and this is granted by the DSU. WT/DS160/1	DSU:21.3
The parties mutually agree that compensation should be paid as a temporary measure, and enter into arbitration to determine the level of nullification or impairment of benefits to the EC. They request that the original panel serve as arbitrators in this proceeding. They communicate agreed procedures for the determination (excluding third parties). WT/DS160/15	DSU:25.2
The arbitration panel is constituted according to the procedures agreed by the parties. WT/DS160/16	DSU:25.2
The arbitration panel communicates its findings that the level of nullification and impairment is € 1,219,900 per annum. WT/DS160/17/ WT/DS160/ARB25/1	DSU:25.2
US provides successive status reports to the DSB on its steps to implement the recommendations and rulings of the DSB, reporting on interaction between the Administration and Congress. WT/DS160/18, WT/DS160/18/Add1 to WT/DS160/18/Add16	DSU:21.6
The EC requests DSB authorization to suspend concessions on the grounds that that the US failed to bring its measures into conformity with TRIPS within the established 'reasonable period of time.'	DSU:22.2
EC requests the DSB to authorize suspension of its obligations under TRIPS 'to permit the levying of a special fee from US nationals in connection with border measures concerning copyright goods' up to the level of nullification determined by the arbitrator. WT/DS160/19	DSU:22.4
US objects to the proposed level of suspension of obligations and procedures followed, and requests arbitration. WT/DS160/20	DSU:22.6
The matter is referred to arbitration and the arbitration panel is constituted. WT/DS160/21 and WT/DS160/21/Corr.1	DSU:22.6
The arbitration is suspended at the request of the two parties. WT/DS160/22	

Table 5.1 (*cont.*)

Procedures	DSU Article
The US presents a status report to the DSB advising that it is engaged in discussions with the EC to find a positive and mutually acceptable solution. The EC expresses concern about delayed implementation. Australia, a third party, expresses concern at the delay and requests that compensation be applied in a non-discriminatory way.	
The parties notify a mutually satisfactory temporary arrangement, involving payment to a fund for supporting performers' rights societies, running until December 2004. WT/DS160/23	DSU:22
US provides successive status reports to the DSB, in the context of the expiry of the temporary arrangement. WT/DS160/24	DSU:21.6
A typical update is as follows,'The US Administration is working with the US Congress on this matter. We will continue these consultations and continue to confer with the European Communities in order to reach a mutually satisfactory resolution of this matter.'	
Australia, a third party in the original dispute, proposes reforms to the dispute settlement process in the light of its exclusion (as a third party) from the compensation negotiated between the two parties: TN/DS/W/8/ TN/DS/W/34TN/DS/W/49	

IP Law and Policy in TRIPS Disputes

We now look at the substantive side of TRIPS dispute settlement—how the treaty standards are interpreted in ways that set boundaries for national options in areas of policy interest. Rather than analyse all the TRIPS issues addressed in dispute settlement, we focus on several interlocking findings in an area of perennial interest to policymakers—how to set exceptions and limitations to IP rights to serve public policy goals. Table 4.1 shows how TRIPS rules in this area use similar concepts; and the Appendix contrasts how dispute settlement panels have interpreted and applied these concepts in practice.

For all countries, effective policymaking in the field of IP entails setting a careful balance between private incentives and rewards for innovation and creativity, and the broader public interest in the availability of new technologies and cultural and educational materials—the very balance articulated in TRIPS:7 as the objective of IP protection. For developing countries, concerned with access to technology and educational materials, establishing the optimal balance of interests is a matter of particular concern, but the issue goes to the core of practical policy-making on IP in any country. One critical aspect of this balance is to set legitimate bounds to exceptions or limitations to IP rights—for instance, to enable generic production of patented pharmaceuticals in an epidemic, to enable educational institutions to reproduce reasonable portions of copyright texts, and to enable fair use by traders of descriptive terms covered by trademark protection.

Three key WTO disputes produced landmark findings on the allowable scope of exceptions to IPRs under TRIPS: *Canada—Pharmaceutical Patents* and *US—Section 110(5) of the Copyright Act*, both complaints brought by the EU; and *EC—Trademarks and Geographical Indications*, two parallel complaints brought by Australia and the United States. These disputes went to the heart of the balance of rights and obligations in TRIPS: what it means, in practice, to give effect to this equitable balancing between rights of creators and rights of access, between private rights and the public interest. The outcomes of these cases generated some critical reactions; but in each case the panels gave legally sober, restrained and essentially fair readings of the critical standards that were under review. No case was appealed to the AB, which itself is sometimes cited as evidence of a 'mutually acceptable' outcome that reflects a good policy balance. The panels had to break new ground in considering two important clusters of issues:

- the appropriate nature and scope of IP rights, the balance of interests under TRIPS, and the scope of legitimate public policy exceptions; and
- the legal relationship between TRIPS and other treaties, especially Berne, and their diplomatic history.

These disputes were not academic exercises; they were impelled by concrete trade interests that were impaired by the measures at issue. Songwriters and composers claimed that they were being denied potential earnings in the US market (a complaint initially launched within internal EU processes by the Irish Music Rights Organisation). European research-based pharmaceutical companies claimed that they were denied fair commercial returns in Canadian markets, as their patent rights were curtailed just when they reached the point when legitimate commercial benefits were at their peak. Traders in agricultural commodities and food were concerned that they confronted obstacles in getting adequate protection for their GIs, and that the GI system may diminish the value of their trademarks.

In an instructive symmetry, the patent and the copyright cases both considered a narrow exception and a broader exception of more debatable policy validity; in both cases, the narrower exception was upheld and the broader exception was found non-compliant with TRIPS; and in both cases, a stronger element of sectoral interest can be identified in the wider exception, while the narrower exception was effectively supported as sound public policy.

In *Canada—Pharmaceutical Patents*, the EU challenged two exceptions to the exclusive rights of patent holders contained in Canada's Patent Act:

- a regulatory approval exception (or 'Bolar' exception, also found in several other countries) which enables generic manufacturers to seek marketing approval during the patent term, for sale of the generic product after expiry of the patent; and
- a stockpiling exception—allowing generic manufacturers to manufacture and stockpile products during the last six months of the patent term in unlimited quantities. Products could be made in substantial quantities in preparation for sale, but would not actually be sold during the life of the patent.

The EC and Canada agreed that the exceptions fell within the scope of exclusive patent rights under TRIPS:28, so the question turned on whether the exceptions could be justified under the three-step test set out in TRIPS:30. The Panel found that the regulatory approval exception passed each of the three 'steps' in the test: it was limited (due to its distinct purpose of allowing steps necessary for regulatory approval only), it did not conflict with normal exploitation of the patent (since patents were not normally used to constrain regulatory processes, but to limit regular commercial activity), and it did not prejudice legitimate interests (since there was no agreement at the policy level that patent holders had legitimate interests in gaining a de facto extension of market exclusivity due to the regulatory process). But the stockpiling exception failed the test, since the exception could not be said to be 'limited' within the meaning of the first step of the test. There was effectively no 'limit' to the extent that a generic producer could make patented products infringing the patent holder's right to prevent others from making or using the patented invention.

In *US—Section 110 Copyright Act*, the EC alleged that US copyright law breached TRIPS and Berne, in particular Berne:11(1) (giving copyright holders an exclusive right to authorize public performance) and Berne:11*bis*(1) (a similar right to authorize public communication of works by loudspeaker or similar instrument). Section 110(5) of the Copyright Act permitted certain commercial establishments (such as bars, restaurants, and shops) publicly to play music that was broadcast on radio and television, without authorization and without royalties under two exceptions:

- a 'business' exemption, allowing free use of broadcast music, provided an establishment's floor area fell within a certain limit. It also allowed amplification of music broadcasts by establishments above this square footage limit, subject to certain limitations on equipment.
- a 'homestyle' exemption, allowing small restaurants and retail outlets to use broadcast music provided that they only use 'homestyle' equipment (the kind of equipment commonly used in private homes).

The panel found that the business exception allowed the extensive commercial exploitation of music for commercial purposes and considered this to breach the three-step test, on the basis that it unreasonably prejudiced the legitimate interests of right holders. The exemption covered the majority of eating and drinking establishments in the US and nearly half of all retail establishments. The Panel found that the far narrower homestyle exception was permissible, since there was limited impact on right holders' legitimate interests.

The copyright and patent disputes covered contentious policy issues that had been addressed, but not fully resolved, in the TRIPS negotiations. Negotiators eschewed specific lists of exceptions in favour of general tests of the legitimacy of exceptions—tests which ultimately concern the way domestic legislative processes deal with diverse interests. Thus the two cases shed light on the difficult interface between standard-setting through negotiations and through dispute settlement. In both of these cases, the dispute was partly due to a failure in the original TRIPS negotiations to clarify the agreed range of exceptions to IPRs. For patents, a list of specific exceptions was not adopted, and the very general language of Article 30 was used, with language borrowed from the Berne Convention despite the differences in the nature of exploitation of patent rights and copyright. Canada had proposed, in the TRIPS negotiations, that exceptions to patent rights be allowed for,

. . . acts done privately and on a non-commercial scale provided that they do not significantly prejudice the economic interests of the owner of the patents; and making or using for solely experimental purposes or scientific research in relation to this technology in respect of which the patent was granted, or a competing technology.

The copyright dispute involved clarifying the status of earlier Berne legal materials (including a 'minor exceptions' doctrine) and touched on the relationship between general TRIPS measures (such as TRIPS:13) and more precise Berne provisions (Berne:11*bis*). For example, Canada and New Zealand proposed in the negotiations that Berne be applied effectively as it stood within TRIPS.

These cases demonstrate how dispute settlement jurisprudence builds on the outcome of trade negotiations on such critical points, a likely continuing trend given the absence of any clear acceptance of a need for a wide-ranging renegotiation mandate for TRIPS that would revisit these issues.

Bilaterally, and within the WTO, negotiations and policy debate continue over GIs. *EC—Trademarks and Geographical Indications* is similar to the last two cases in that it considers legitimate exceptions to IP rights—in this case, exceptions to trademark rights. But it also highlights more directly the dynamic interplay between trade negotiations and dispute settlement as two aspects of a complex political process: dispute settlement as trade negotiations by other means, and the multilateral trade system as a forum for addressing bilateral differences. Against a backdrop of a complex bilateral and multilateral trade controversies over how to protect GIs, both the US and Australia raised parallel complaints against the EU *Council Regulation No 2081/92 of 14 July 1992 on the Protection of Geographical Indications and Designations of Origin for Agricultural Products and Foodstuffs,* and related measures. They claimed that it failed to provide national treatment, and did not properly protect pre-existing trade-marks similar or identical to GIs.

The national treatment issue was raised under TRIPS (concerning treatment of foreign *nationals*) and GATT (which requires national treatment for like *prod-ucts*). The panel found against the EU on the national treatment claims. To register a GI from a country outside the EU, that country had to have GI protection equiva-lent to the EU's system, and to offer reciprocal protection for EU GIs. Applications for registration, and objections to them, had to be examined by a Member govern-ment before being formally transmitted to the EU. This created an extra step for foreign nationals that EU nationals did not face; even though the discrimination was technically against foreign *GIs* and not foreign *nationals*, the panel considered this to be a case of de facto discrimination—it is mostly foreign nationals who would benefit from foreign GIs, and European nationals who would benefit from EU GIs. The panel was not persuaded that 'formally identical' treatment accorded to foreign nationals and EU nationals was a defence against breach of the national treatment principle. Trade rules on IP protection required 'effective equality of opportunities,' in using the IP system to ensure a position in the market.

The EU regulation allowed GIs to be registered even if they conflicted with a prior trademark (provided the GIs were otherwise eligible to be registered). In the shared language of TRIPS on exceptions and limitations, protecting a later GI this way would conflict with 'normal exploitation' of a trademark right, and would prejudice a 'legitimate interest' in exercising that right in the marketplace. But the panel looked closely at the specific provision on exceptions to trademark rights— TRIPS:17—and found it a lighter test than those laid out for patents and copyright.

There was, for instance, no reference to a 'normal exploitation' of the trademark, let alone any obligation to avoid unreasonable conflict. And exceptions only need to be 'limited' and to 'take account' of the legitimate interests of trademark owner, with no reference to unreasonable prejudice.

To the panel, this softer language suggested greater latitude for impacting on the legitimate interests of the trademark owner than for other IP rights— in essence, a more permissive approach to coexistence of conflicting rights. TRIPS:17 precisely allowed exceptions to an exclusive right to prevent uses of a mark that would result in a likelihood of confusion. So some measure of like-lihood of confusion could be a permissible consequence of an exception. So, in principle, a law may permit GIs to be registered, even in the face of conflict with prior trademark rights. But the panel cautioned that this did not allow unquali-fied coexistence of GIs with prior trademarks—after all, the exception to trade-mark rights must be a 'limited'—in other words, a narrow exception, permitting only a small diminution of rights conferred by a trademark. The findings of the panel shifted the focus from a zero sum approach over competing exclusive rights, to clarifying rules for their coexistence instead. The case therefore offers lessons for broader resolution of trade differences over distinctive signs in a borderless global marketplace when good faith conflicts over the linguistic import and legal status of commercial signs are likely to proliferate.

In each of these three cases on exceptions, the panel undertook a close literal reading of the legal text. This approach has found its critics, who are looking for a stronger imprint of policy interests in the interpretative techniques chosen by the Panels. But there are compelling systemic and policy reasons for this more restrained approach, and a consistent choice not to explore 'richer' or more abstract readings of the text. The AB has rejected attempts to read into the texts content that is not there, recalling that dispute settlement is intended to be governed by the agreed rules, rather than undertaking an excursion into policy-making. Two practical points govern this choice: first, WTO dispute settlement procedures aim at mutually satisfactory resolution of disputes, rather than a more abstract legal task; and, second, dispute settlement should not set policy direc-tions, which remain in the hands of the WTO Members themselves.

Practical Insights from Other TRIPS Cases

This chapter has concentrated on the disputes relating to limitations and excep-tions, given their significance for IP law and policy at that most critical point, where private interests and public policy meet head-on. Other TRIPS dispute settlement cases have yielded valuable guidance for policymakers; several of these insights are summarized briefly here.

India—Patents I: What are TRIPS disputes about?

As the first TRIPS case considered by the AB, this case was pivotal in considering how to bridge between domestic legal systems and the requirements of TRIPS as an international treaty, and what it meant to settle disputes about IP protection within the WTO system. Given the longstanding sensitivities over patent protection for pharmaceuticals and agricultural chemicals, TRIPS gave developing countries a longer transition period to protect this material. In exchange, it required them to establish an interim system so that applicants could secure early filing dates for patents in these fields—so-called mailbox applications. The case turned on whether India's system for receiving these applications had sufficient legal basis in domestic law to meet the legitimate expectations of its trading partners. The system was, at the time of the dispute, based not on legislation, but on an 'administrative order', which the US (and the EU, in a parallel complaint) felt was too legally contestable to provide sufficient confidence in the availability of the protection expected for mailbox applications.

As it concerned a transitional measure, the details of the case have little lon-ger term interest. But the AB clarified two key, systemic issues. The first, the very basis of TRIPS disputes, was discussed earlier in this chapter—the AB affirmed that as the expectations of Members regarding IP protection were limited to the text of TRIPS, there was no need and no basis to introduce additional legal theories as to legitimate expectations. The second concerned how WTO panels and the AB should take account of laws at the national level when assessing TRIPS compliance. TRIPS:1.1 confirms that Members are free to determine how best to meet their TRIPS obligations within their own legal systems. This entitle-ment is a fundamentally important flexibility. However, the flexibility is not absolute: the AB held that national laws should provide a 'sound legal basis' for meeting TRIPS obligations. But how to determine what is a sound legal basis, without interpreting domestic law? The AB distinguished between interpreting Indian law 'as such', and 'examining Indian law solely for the purpose of deter-mining whether India had met its [TRIPS] obligations'. A panel had to review national law, otherwise 'only India can assess whether Indian law is consistent with India's obligations under the WTO Agreement'. So domestic laws give evidence of relevant facts, but also as evidence of compliance or non-compliance with

WTO obligations. In this case, the AB was not convinced the system would survive a legal challenge under Indian law.

Indonesia—Autos: National treatment for trademark owners

Among the first claims of TRIPS non-compliance to go to a panel for decision, this remains the only case where such a claim was defended with complete success (several non-TRIPS claims were upheld, however). To benefit from a national car programme, cars had to be sold under an Indonesian trademark belonging to an Indonesian company. The panel held the national treatment obligation of TRIPS relating to trademarks did not prevent,

... the grant of tariff, subsidy or other measures of support to the national companies on the grounds that this would render the maintenance of trademark rights by foreign companies wishing to export to that market relatively more difficult.

The US, as complainant, had not established that denial of these benefits amounted to an unreasonable burden on foreign trademark owners (TRIPS:20). Ineligibility under the programme was not a 'requirement' imposed on foreign trademark holders, in the sense of TRIPS:20.

US—Section 211 Appropriations Act ('Havana Club'): What TRIPS does and does not cover

The EU challenged a US law that restricted dealings with trademarks associated with businesses that were seized following the revolution in Cuba, including the valuable 'Havana Club' trade mark for rum. The AB confirmed that the rules in TRIPS regarding what should be considered registrable as a trademark concerned the properties of the mark itself, and did not address who should be considered the owner or person eligible to apply for a mark. TRIPS is therefore largely silent on this substantial part of IP law (concerning who is entitled to apply for an IP right, or who is otherwise eligible for benefits from protection), provided the law complies with basic TRIPS–WTO principles of non-discrimination.

The AB also overturned a panel finding that proposed a narrow reading of how Paris is incorporated within TRIPS, rejecting the panel's view that TRIPS obligations did not cover an entire category of IP, trade names. Trade names are included in Paris, but are not explicitly listed in the categories of IP covered by Part II of TRIPS. This case was a helpful reminder of the difficulties that would arise from trying to establish a legal hierarchy between 'pure' TRIPS provisions, and those incorporated in TRIPS from the Berne and Paris Conventions.

Canada—Patent Term: On reading the text of TRIPS

TRIPS:33 requires Members to make available terms of at least 20 years from the filing date of a patent application. The AB confirmed that this obligation applied to patents already in existence when TRIPS came into force, not just newly granted patents. This outcome implied that other TRIPS obligations (such as on exceptions and compulsory licensing) would also apply to existing patents (and other forms of IP). This case is of continuing interest because it exemplifies the customary reluctance of the AB to introduce more elaborate constructions of TRIPS provisions than are contained in a more direct literal reading of the text. In general, the AB points to the strong policy rationale for these literal and more concrete reading of the TRIPS texts, as one element of the stability and predictability that TRIPS coverage by the DSU are meant to bring into the international trading system. This is not intended as narrow legalism, but sound legal and institutional policy.

Canada argued that its administrative procedures enabled patent applicants to obtain a 20-year term in practice (for instance, by arranging for delays in patent grant). For the AB, the TRIPS:33 obligation to make 20 years 'available' meant 'available as a matter of legal right and certainty, a readily discernible and specific right, clearly seen as such by an applicant when filing a patent application', and not, as the AB put it, 'only to those who are somehow able to meander successfully through a maze of administrative procedures'. Canada also argued that one could interpret TRIPS:33 to allow a patent term which is shorter than 20 years from the filing date, but is effectively 'equivalent' to such a patent term, taking account of TRIPS:62.2 which envisages some curtailment of the period of protection due to processing delays and 'a reasonable period of time' to grant patents. In a characteristic move, the AB rejected this construction and found out that 'the obligation in Article 33 is straightforward and mandatory: to provide, as a specific right, a term of protection that does not end before the expiry of a period of 20 years counted from the filing date'.

US—Section 301 Trade Act: Strengthening multilateralism

This case went to the heart of the WTO as a multilateral system of law for settlement of disputes concerning TRIPS, and delivered a strong reminder of the importance of that system in safeguarding the security and predictability of the international trading system. In doing so, it touched on a fundamental impetus for the incorporation of TRIPS into the multilateral system—what the Panel called the 'exclusive dispute resolution clause' (DSU:23.1): 'Members have to have recourse to the DSU dispute settlement system to the exclusion of any other system, in particular a system of unilateral enforcement of WTO rights and obligations.'

The US Trade Act had been the essential tool of the US Trade Representative (USTR) in pushing for stronger IP protection, through the unilateral threat of retaliatory trade sanctions, in the period leading up to the establishment of the WTO. The EU claimed that this law was now at odds with the DSB:23 provision on Strengthening of the Multilateral System. The EU argued it required the USTR to determine, unilaterally, whether another country denied rights or benefits to the US under a WTO agreement, whether or not the DSB had adopted a report on the matter; further, it required the USTR to take action under Section 301 of that Act in the case of a failure to implement DSB recommendations. The panel's findings are outlined above (p 141).

China—Intellectual Property Rights: Clarifying legitimate expectations on enforcement

The first case to consider in detail TRIPS standards on enforcement took place against longstanding political divergences as to what countries can expect of one another's systems when it comes to enforcing, and not merely granting, IP rights. As the panel in this case said, 'one of the major reasons for the conclusion of [TRIPS] was the desire to set out a minimum set of procedures and remedies that judicial, border and other competent authorities must have available to them'. The outcome, in the form of a panel report that neither party chose to appeal, usefully clarified the scope of legitimate expectations in this area and made some valuable distinctions for policymakers.

Overall, the case clarified what was already present in the text of TRIPS: the enforcement obligations essentially extend to having adequate and effective remedies available that are sufficient to deter infringement, and do not stipulate particular enforcement outcomes. For instance, the panel indicated that TRIPS:46 contained 'a guide to action by authorities' and did not 'dictate the precise terms of orders in specific cases'. The TRIPS:59 obligation that competent authorities 'shall have the authority' to order certain remedies (such as destruction of infringing goods) left Members free to provide also for other remedies not stipulated there. But the choice taken for disposal of the goods must avoid harm to the right holder.

The recognition and protection of copyright, as a private right, should be distinguished from censorship on the grounds of public interest; the sovereign right to prevent the circulation of works on public policy grounds does not relieve a country of the obligation to protect copyright—so copyright should still be available for a work even if it is not approved for publication. Equally, the existence of copyright in a work does not interfere with the entitlement of governments to review and censor the content of the work.

TRIPS requires that criminal remedies be available for 'wilful trademark counterfeiting or copyright piracy on a commercial scale'. TRIPS defines 'counterfeiting' and 'piracy'. But what threshold of activity amounts to a 'commercial scale'? The panel analysed this key phrase at great length, recognizing that it had to be an objective measure, but should also take account of differences between economies and between commercial sectors. It concluded that the phrase meant counterfeiting or piracy 'at the magnitude or extent of typical or usual commercial activity with respect to a given product in a given market'. So the benchmark was the typical or usual commercial activity for the product in question, a matter that was linked ultimately to profitability.

The panel also rejected bilateral agreements and earlier multilateral model laws as authoritative guides to interpreting the multilateral text of TRIPS. Free trade agreements entered into by the United States and other materials cited lacked 'the breadth to constitute a common, consistent, discernible pattern of acts or pronouncements . . . and does not imply agreement on the interpretation of [TRIPS:61]'.

Cross-Retaliation Cases: TRIPS and Market Access under Other Agreements

Developing country negotiators resisted building TRIPS into the uniform dispute settlement system of the DSU. The scenario they feared was this: if developed countries pursued a TRIPS complaint, they would be able to retaliate by denying market access for exports in other key areas, such as agricultural products or textiles, which could cause greater damage for a developing economy than if the retaliation was confined to IP. When it comes to seeking approval for retaliation, the DSU:22.3 expects Members first to seek to suspend concessions or other obligations in the same sector; then to consider other sectors under the same agreement; then to turn to another covered agreement (so-called 'cross-retaliation'). The permissible scope for retaliation can be broadened at each step if the narrower scope is 'not practicable or effective'—so cross-retaliation is not an automatic right, but depends on showing that the narrower options are not appropriate.

Where such cross-retaliation is the only practicable and effective option, therefore, it means that a country not complying with TRIPS could be faced with denial of market access in relation to goods, services or agricultural products, up to a level equivalent to the nullification and impairment caused by the breach of TRIPS obligations. But the same logic applies in the reverse direction: failure to meet other WTO obligations to allow market access can lead to suspension of TRIPS provisions for the benefit of that country. So, if a country fails to carry out a ruling to remove a non-compliant trade barrier for agricultural products, its nationals may face denial of certain forms of IP protection.

In practice, the original scenario is yet to eventuate—no retaliation has been sought or approved for TRIPS violations—yet three developing Members have requested cross-retaliation under TRIPS to leverage market access in other sectors. Ecuador, Antigua and Barbuda, and Brazil have each been granted the right to suspend TRIPS obligations to respond to non-compliant trade barriers against bananas, online gambling, and cotton. In Brazil's case, since it had a large and diverse economy, other options (punitive tariffs) were considered practicable and effective, but only up to a certain level of nullification and impairment. If the effect of the cotton subsidies exceeded that level, then the arbitrator found justification for cross-retaliation by suspending IP protection under TRIPS.

Such cross-retaliation—like all suspension of concessions in WTO dispute settlement—is considered temporary and second-best only to the withdrawal of the measures that were found to be non-compliant. The essential purpose of cross-retaliation is not to cause punitive damage, but to create an economic and political incentive for the other Member to bring its laws into line with its WTO obligations. DSU:22.8 stipulates that the retaliatory measures shall only be applied until the original non-compliant measure is removed or the dispute is otherwise resolved. To date, no country has actually carried out TRIPS cross-retaliation, but the simple prospect of such retaliation may help leverage a satisfactory solution to the dispute, without the approved suspension of IP protection actually coming into practical effect.

Practical Points

- Actual participation in dispute settlement over TRIPS remains a rarity: since 1995, only six out of 153 WTO Members have defended their IP systems before a panel or the AB. The WTO has never, so far, approved any retaliatory measures ('sanctions') for a TRIPS violation.
- Few cases have been launched against developing countries on the basis of claimed non-compliance with TRIPS; this partly reflects the fact that—unlike

most areas of trade law where disputes often seek the withdrawal of noncompliant regulatory interventions—complying with TRIPS entails building up a major body of legislation and developing the capacity to administer and enforce it. In many circumstances, a formal dispute would not accelerate or facilitate that complex process, and may instead politicize and divert efforts from the implementation process.

- Even without immediate sanctions, the prospect of dispute settlement creates a more stringent culture of compliance which does influence legislative choices, sometimes dramatically. Governments tend to seek to comply with TRIPS out of a desire to signal compliance with international standards, not merely to avoid retaliation.
- Dispute settlement cases so far have produced a clear and consistent body of case law which provides practical guidance for policymakers:
  - The legitimate expectations WTO Members can claim from one another in the protection of IP are defined by the actual text of TRIPS: there is no other, more abstract standard;
  - Members have considerable latitude in determining how best to implement TRIPS standards in their national legal systems, but panels and the AB can still make an assessment as to whether those choices do provide a sound legal basis for the expected level of IP protection;
  - WTO dispute settlement tribunals tend to prefer literal readings of TRIPS text, rather than reading in broader legal ideas or elaborate constructions of the text;
  - This does not preclude the role of public policy and other areas of international law, and the rules on exceptions and limitations provide an avenue for public policy considerations;
  - Building on the heritage of GATT, non-discrimination is a critical concern in ensuring legitimate access to IP systems—this includes de facto discrimination as well as express discrimination;
  - Failure to respect the multilateral character of dispute settlement regarding TRIPS may itself create a breach of WTO rules;
  - The prospect of cross-retaliation creates a pragmatic incentive to comply with TRIPS, but it has also opened up a possibility to use TRIPS to leverage market access in other areas.

6

TRIPS and Global Issues: Navigating IP and Public Policy

... actual or potential conflicts exist between the implementation of the TRIPS Agreement and the realization of economic, social and cultural rights in relation to, inter alia, impediments to the transfer of technology to developing countries, the consequences for the enjoyment of the right to food of plant variety rights and the patenting of genetically modified organisms, 'bio-piracy' and the reduction of communities' (especially indigenous communities') control over their own genetic and natural resources and cultural values, and restrictions on access to patented pharmaceuticals and the implications for the enjoyment of the right to health ...

Sub-Commission on the Promotion and Protection of Human Rights, resolution 2000/7

We recognize the gravity of the public health problems afflicting many developing and least-developed countries, especially those resulting from HIV/AIDS, tuberculosis, malaria and other epidemics.

We stress the need for the [TRIPS Agreement] to be part of the wider national and international action to address these problems.

Doha Declaration on TRIPS and Public Health, 2001

TRIPS arises in a host of public policy debates, in part due to its immediate impact as a legal instrument, but also because it serves as a conspicuous symbol of the globalization of IP protection. The attention that TRIPS attracts gives it a perceived significance well beyond its true legal reach as a treaty. TRIPS and IP are now embedded in a range of vigorous, sprawling debates, dealing with the law, policy and underlying systems of values that affect our health, environment, wellbeing, and human rights. Each debate has generated a massive literature; only a simple landscape is offered here, since one brief chapter cannot cover the full spectrum of legal questions and policy positions raised in these debates.

Navigating through these issues requires a clear practical grasp of each of the following aspects of TRIPS and public policy, and of how they interact:

- Policy: the policy objectives, values and ethical basis of TRIPS as a set of IP standards within the WTO system of trade law;
- Law: questions of legal interpretation—the relationship between TRIPS and broader public international law, such as human rights or environmental law—and how public policy considerations relate to TRIPS law;
- Institutions: international organizations, government representatives and agencies, activists, and other actors who convene or take part in analysis, and debate about TRIPS and policy issues;
- Practice: options for applying TRIPS standards to serve broader public policy goals, and learning from the range of choices already made at the national level.

The advent of TRIPS itself helped precipitate the wider attention to IP issues that is evident in a number of today's public policy debates—its implementation accelerated the development of stronger IP laws in many countries, increased transparency in national laws and regulations, and sharpened the focus on IP issues among a much wider community of interests. Early debates over TRIPS concerned the implications of IP law intruding into the traditional domain of trade law. For trade lawyers, this move was akin to the extension of trade law to other areas of 'behind the border' regulation and policy (the 'trade and . . .' debate). Later, TRIPS debates took on a far more diverse character as the Agreement entered a swirl of controversies about the impact of IP on other areas of public policy and international law ('TRIPS and . . .' debates).

From the 'Trade and . . .' question . . .

'Trade and . . .' debates explore the scope and legitimacy of trade law: how to reconcile a relatively technical field of law within a more diverse and complex policy and legal context. How can and should the trade law system, and the WTO as an institution, deal with the environment, human rights, labour standards, health, culture and other areas of public policy? Two views predominate. Either trade law should stick to its last, and concentrate on ensuring that legitimate trade can continue in a non-discriminatory way, and keep out of the 'behind the border' issues of domestic regulation and policy, and wider areas of international law, which would confuse the trade law system and deny its vital purpose of ensuring a degree of predictability and stability. Or trade law should not be divorced from the wider domain of public policy and regulation—it cannot turn a blind eye to environmental impact or the essential rights of workers; by this view, it would lack essential legitimacy if it operated in isolation from the broader context of law and policy.

Often assumed to be at odds with one another, these two points of view need not be in fundamental tension. Overall, trade law keeps focus on maintaining a stable and legitimate trading environment through the transparent and predictable rule of law, while respecting the wider context of public policy; and a balanced trade law system should aim at fairness, transparency, and the social and economic benefits, even the human flourishing, that other areas of international law and policy also aim to bring about.

TRIPS is a tough 'trade and . . .' debate in itself. Indeed, some practitioners of trade law and trade policy looked askance at TRIPS as a 'trade and . . .' agreement in the WTO, and an unwelcome distortion of the scope, reach and rationale of trade law. By this view, TRIPS was not really about trade, but clumsily yoked the well-defined area of international trade law to a cluster of 'behind-the-border' issues, questions which were properly the subject of domestic regulation and international standards administered by other institutions (in this case, WIPO).

By setting standards for domestic regulation, would TRIPS open the gateway to new linkages, to a new generation of 'trade and . . .' agreements—on trade and environment, trade and labour, trade and human rights, and more? If *trade law* could now dictate how a country should regulate pharmaceuticals, software and music, what would stop it setting standards for the environment or for the workplace? Or was the protection of IP different, a legitimate claim on the part of countries seeking reasonable access to one another's markets, a proper recognition of the knowledge content of trade? For its negotiators, then, TRIPS was characterized by the revolutionary step of bringing substantive IP standards into the heart of international trade law—TRIPS seemed to be redefining the essential idea of what trade law should be about. But, certainly, it precipitated a shift in international IP law and policy, dramatically broadening the base of international law, policy and institutions dealing with IP.

. . . to debating 'TRIPS and . . .'

After gaining legal effect in 1995, TRIPS has developed a new political life. 'IP and trade' has become a systematic part of the international legal landscape; indeed, we have seen the growth of trade *in* IP. Today, policymakers, analysts, diplomats wrangle over how the IP system can and should be reconciled with wider areas of international law—'TRIPS and . . .' debates concern human rights, health, the environment, food security, indigenous rights. TRIPS is drawn into some of the most formidable public policy issues of today, reaching well beyond the conventional scope of either IP law or trade law. When considering human rights, climate change, and the conservation of biodiversity, access to medicines and health innovation, recognition of indigenous knowledge systems, access to knowledge and internet governance, agricultural biotechnology and food security, and bioethics, experts in those fields typically view TRIPS in a critical or sceptical vein and rarely as part of the solution. Given this wider salience, the practice of TRIPS can now entail working through these policy linkages, in both international and domestic debate, at least as much as it concerns managing trade disputes about IP protection and reconciling IP standards with trade policy.

It can be difficult to find a stable foothold for TRIPS in this complicated, shifting set of debates. TRIPS has been disparaged both for privileging 'trade' or narrow economic interests over other social interests in IP policy formulation, and for confusing or corrupting the very conception of 'trade' that a balanced trade law system should cover. By accelerating and framing the introduction of higher standards for IP protection in many countries, especially in developing countries, TRIPS provoked debate and political responses, thus taking on a symbolic character often more potent than its strict legal effect.

Amidst a dense, wide-ranging set of debates about the impact of trade law and the WTO system on vital areas of public policy, TRIPS is cited again and again as 'Exhibit A'—as the most telling example of the intrusion on national regulatory sovereignty in the name of narrow trade interests. The mid-90s saw massive protests over the expected impact of TRIPS on access to seeds, with reports of over half a million Indian farmers taking to the streets in protest even before the TRIPS text was concluded. When the 2007 film *Battle in Seattle* gave an account of the activism at the tempestuous Seattle Ministerial Conference, the impact of TRIPS on access to medicines was singled out as the sole substantive WTO issue.

By and large, TRIPS adopted standards that were no radical departure from mainstream IP laws in many developed countries in the late 1980s. With some very important exceptions (notably pharmaceuticals patents, test data protection, and the rigour of IP enforcement), its standards were on the whole not fundamentally at odds with the legal mechanisms that some developing countries already had on the books. The forms of IP protection recognized in TRIPS, and the principles underlying them, had mostly resulted from well over a century of progressive legal evolution (again, there are some important exceptions, such as protection of test data). TRIPS expressed standards that were intended to advance the public welfare on a range of fronts, and equally had significant public interest safeguards built into them. They were not a simple imprint of sectorial interests. And the evolution of IP law has been healthily contentious throughout its history, as the dynamic rebalancing of interests takes place in a process of continual testing and recalibration of the essential principles of the system.

So why, apparently, a sudden, dramatic shift to the centre of attention? In the space of a decade or so, could TRIPS single-handedly have transformed an obscure area of commercial law into a set of major policy controversies? The implementation of TRIPS has sparked perhaps the most vigorous and contentious—certainly the most global in reach—of the sceptical reviews of the policy legitimacy, effectiveness, and fairness of the various strands of the IP system that have periodically recurred over its history.

Several factors have driven this trend:

- Greater geographical reach: TRIPS forced the pace of legal evolution in many developing countries, and drew them into levels of IP protection they may not have pursued spontaneously, while reducing public policy flexibility as a natural consequence of agreeing to binding international rules.

- Technological and social changes: objectively, the impact of the IP system grew, as its effects reached further into the daily life and welfare of a broader cross-section of society, and touches on areas as diverse as digital music files, GM crops, flu vaccines, folklore, and labelling dairy produce.

- Political reaction: implementation of TRIPS precipitated the defensive assertion of interests seen to be under threat, and some adopted the working assumption that granting TRIPS-consistent IP rights was a zero-sum encroachment on the public domain or even an intrusive constraint on public policy and regulatory sovereignty.

- Structural asymmetry: TRIPS defines the standards that amount to an agreed level of sufficient protection of IP. It did not, for the most part, positively mandate other mechanisms that are integral to the effective and balanced functioning of the IP system, such as competition safeguards including remedies for abuse of IP rights, clear and well-established exceptions to IP rights, transparency and technical proficiency in the administration and grant of rights (including substantive examination of IP applications and effective opposition proceedings), and even the availability of a a body of skilled private practitioners of IP law. All these elements are eminently possible and permissible under TRIPS, and indeed could be considered almost to be expected within its framework, but are not for the most part required as positive obligations. The 'balancing' of rights and obligations, mediating between rights and exceptions, is highly desirable but for the most part optional or discretionary, meaning a deliberate investment of legislative, regulatory and administrative resources may be needed to give it effect.

TRIPS in the Practice of Public Policy

Even its negotiators may not have anticipated the full extent of its future role in public policy debate. But TRIPS came 'hard wired' to serve that function. TRIPS:7 contains the most concise and authoritative statement of the public policy role and context of the IP system in any binding international legal instrument. And the text and context of TRIPS contains many other important elements that help define the productive interaction between IP standards and broader public policy issues, for instance:

- enshrining, in TRIPS:8, the concept of domestic legal space to allow for governments to address vital areas of public policy need;
- addressing, for the first time in international IP law, ideas of fairness, transparency, procedural equity and balance in how IP is administered and enforced;
- acknowledging that effective enforcement of IP requires positive cooperation between countries;
- creating specific obligations for technology transfer to LDCs;
- articulating the scope for measures to address licensing practices that thwart fair and beneficial competition and prevent technology transfer;
- creating systematic tests for exceptions and limitations, based on broad principles of fairness and balanced, adapted to the context of each cluster of IP law.

The public policy context of TRIPS was set in sharper focus in 2001. Concerns about potential impact on access to medicines culminated in the negotiation of the Doha Declaration on TRIPS and Public Health. Trade ministers reached the point when, in effect, the *political* understanding of TRIPS had to be better aligned with its actual character as a legal instrument; on the whole (with one important exception), they concluded that its revision or renegotiation as a legal text was unnecessary, but a clear signal was needed about how TRIPS should be read and applied. Accordingly, while directly addressing one critical issue—that of health—the Declaration illustrates how TRIPS interplays with public policy issues more generally. For instance, it:

- identified the need for TRIPS 'to be part of the wider national and international action' to address health problems;
- emphasized both innovation and public access to the fruits of innovation;
- confirmed that TRIPS 'does not and should not' prevent Members from taking appropriate, TRIPS-consistent measures to address priority policy interests;
- articulated the concept of 'flexibility', already embedded in the provisions of TRIPS;
- linked the technical task of treaty interpretation with attaining the public policy objectives recognized by TRIPS;
- shed light on specific policy interventions, including remedies such as compulsory licences, and choices on exhaustion of rights; and
- stressed the distinct needs and interests of LDCs.

TRIPS and Global Public Goods

> It is not beyond the power of political volition to tip the scales towards a more secure peace, greater economic well-being, social justice and environmental sustainability. But no country can achieve these global public goods on its own, and neither can the global marketplace. Thus our efforts must now focus on global public goods.
>
> *Kofi Annan, UN Secretary-General*

The concept of a 'global public good' has entered policy discussions in many areas that involve TRIPS, referring to such goods as a clean environment, health, dissemination of knowledge, and global security, including the peaceful and just settlement of disputes. A 'public good' is, in principle a technical economic concept, referring to goods that are not used up when anyone benefits from them ('non-rivalrous') and that no-one can be prevented from enjoying ('non-excludable'). The IP system itself is intended to be one means of producing public goods. For example, making inventions temporarily excludable through the grant of patent rights is intended to generate useful technologies that pass, ultimately, into the public domain and are then non-excludable knowledge goods.

Global public goods are those that are available worldwide—for instance, all can benefit from the peaceful resolution of international disputes, the safeguarding of common resources such as the environment, the dissemination of knowledge, and the availability of new medicines. The idea of 'global public goods' also conveys wider implications for those challenges where common global efforts

WORLD TRADE

ORGANIZATION

WT/MIN(01)/DEC/2
20 November 2001

(01-5860)

MINISTERIAL CONFERENCE
Fourth Session
Doha, 9 - 14 November 2001

DECLARATION ON THE TRIPS AGREEMENT AND PUBLIC HEALTH

Adopted on 14 November 2001

1.   We recognize the gravity of the public health problems afflicting many developing and least-developed countries, especially those resulting from HIV/AIDS, tuberculosis, malaria and other epidemics.

2.   We stress the need for the WTO Agreement on Trade-Related Aspects of Intellectual Property Rights (TRIPS Agreement) to be part of the wider national and international action to address these problems.

Figure 6.1 Reconciling TRIPS and Public Policy: Opening Paragraphs of the Doha Declaration

are needed for effective solutions. Already in 1946, the Constitution of the World Health Organization declared that the 'achievement of any State in the promotion and protection of health is of value to all'.

Working systematically with TRIPS in dealing with international policy issues means reconciling two ideas of 'global public good' that can at first seem incompatible:

(i)   The systemic benefits of clarity, objectivity, and transparency in the international law that is mutually agreed to apply to resolving IP disputes: predictable, rules-based management of the IP dimension of trade relations—as the TRIPS preamble states, 'reducing tensions' through commitments to resolve disputes on IP 'through multilateral procedures'—contributing to the global public goods of peaceful, orderly management of disputes, and of clarity and predictability in the international knowledge economy;

(ii)   The policy dimension: the idea that the legal standards of TRIPS are not arbitrarily set, but amount to a common articulation of how to balance legitimate innovator and creator rights with public interests in a mutually beneficial way that transcends zero-sum tradeoffs, in line with TRIPS:7. Ideally, TRIPS implementation should foster new technologies and cultural works and other widely enjoyed public welfare outcomes, but also engender confidence in the legitimacy and fairness of the international legal system—in short, delivering the global public goods of new knowledge, new technologies, sounder consumer information, made available equitably.

Rigour and clarity of legal standards may come at the expense of policy flexibility, scope for national sovereignty over regulation, and welfare-maximizing domestic policies. But these goals are not in fundamental conflict, and with some care can be harnessed together. The Doha Declaration did this—as a political statement on how TRIPS can form part of a wider effort on public health, it linked the formal exercise of treaty interpretation with the public policy objectives articulated in TRIPS:

In applying the customary rules of interpretation of public international law, each [TRIPS] provision . . . shall be read in the light of the object and purpose of [TRIPS] as expressed, in particular, in its objectives and principles.

Core Principles: Law and Policy

Embedded within TRIPS are certain core principles that can guide the consideration of TRIPS at this broadest level of debate over public goods, policy objectives, and ethical values:

- a utilitarian judgement that well-functioning and well-governed IP mechanisms, founded on sound public policy and balancing exclusive rights and the general public interest, will on the whole produce a diverse range of public goods more effectively and more systematically than if no such system was in place;
- this kind of balanced system is to the *mutual* advantage of public and private interests, with the expectation that the resultant benefits will not be zero-sum, but offer overall advantage;
- an ethic of fairness, equity and non-discrimination, both in terms of procedural requirements within domestic administration and legal enforcement, and in terms of international dispute settlement;
- an expectation that objective rules-based settlement of international disputes will enhance the security and predictability of the trading system, in turn enhancing welfare outcomes, and will also safeguard national sovereignty and policy flexibility in areas of pressing domestic concern.

These principles can be useful in clarifying and supporting public policy debates, and recall the strong vein of public interest and concern for equity and balance that runs through the law and policy of IP. But such general principles do not have direct application when interpreting TRIPS as a legal text. Situating TRIPS within its policy context does, however, pose some formal legal questions:

- How can or should the wider field of international law—say human rights law, or multilateral environmental agreements—influence the more technical reading of TRIPS as a legal text, when it performs its most consequential function, that of providing an objective benchmark to settle disputes? The AB said that WTO law was not to be 'read in clinical isolation from public international law', thinking especially of the international rules of treaty interpretation. Might TRIPS obligations play out differently in practice if they were given a specifically 'human rights' or 'environmental' reading? What would this mean for practical dispute settlement? Or are there ways of reading TRIPS text that treat it unadventurously, soberly, as 'black letter law' while still respecting the wider set of interests, principles and hard legal obligations that make up the complex field of public international law?
- Do TRIPS standards and principles conflict with other international legal instruments or can they provide support for their policy objectives? What interventions are needed to strengthen coherence? For instance, WTO Members have long debated whether TRIPS conflicts with the Convention on Biological Diversity (CBD), and how it can be harnessed or adjusted better to promote the CBD's objectives—views range from arguing that there is no conflict, or that TRIPS needs to be implemented with an eye to promoting coherence, to specific proposals to amend the TRIPS text with the intent of reducing conflict and build harmony between the two instruments;
- Should the obligations of other legal instruments—say, human rights conventions or a new climate change deal—not merely influence the reading of TRIPS

146   United Nations — Treaty Series • Nations Unies — Recueil des Traités   1993

Have agreed as follows:

Article 1. Objectives

The objectives of this Convention, to be pursued in accordance with its relevant provisions, are the conservation of biological diversity, the sustainable use of its components and the fair and equitable sharing of the benefits arising out of the utilization of genetic resources, including by appropriate access to genetic resources and by appropriate transfer of relevant technologies, taking into account all rights over those resources and to technologies, and by appropriate funding.

Figure 6.2 The Objectives of the 1993 Convention on Biological Diversity

or remain consistent with it, but actually 'trump' or supersede TRIPS altogether, as some have argued? If so, what would be the practical effect of such a move when countries sought to resolve their differences through the WTO dispute settlement system?

And in Practice

Public goods such as sustaining biodiversity, avoiding calamitous climate change, or distributing essential medicines are not achieved through theoretical legal debate or even by the formulation of binding international law. They are ultimately practical concerns, a consequence of the accumulated impact of numerous discrete choices and practical steps. For instance, the actual impact of the patent system is felt not from the mere presence or absence of a formal system of assessing, granting, and enforcing patents, still less the international rules that influence such a system, but from how specific legal rights are used and regulated in practice. If tangible welfare gains for public health are to be yielded from the patent system, they will emerge from an accumulation of individual practical choices, not just from the relatively abstract process of shaping the legislative framework within which rights are defined, administered, and deployed. Equally, any tangible harm felt in the real world would also result from specific choices about how certain individual IP rights are exercised in practice, and not *directly* from the passage of stronger or weaker patent legislation, nor from the interpretation or application of TRIPS standards. The actual impact of an IP right depends on how it is excercised, where, by whom, and to what end. Observing whether or not a certain technology is patented offers little insight into how the technology is effectively put to work and whether, and to whom, its benefits are practically available. Taking the example of medical R&D, Figure 6.3 illustrates how product development is rarely reduced to a simple either/or choice between highly exclusive IP rights or the public domain; practical product development and medicine dissemination pathways typically entail optimizing a range of variables, including the degree of leverage maintained over key technologies, the mix of public inputs and private interests, and the extent to which commercial incentives are deployed.

This broader perspective recalls that actual outcomes in areas of greatest policy concern cannot depend solely on how the applicable international rules are formulated or reconciled, but ultimately on how IP rights are deployed in practice and on decisions by regulators and administrators on the grant and enforcement of rights. The balance of interests also includes the application of regulatory

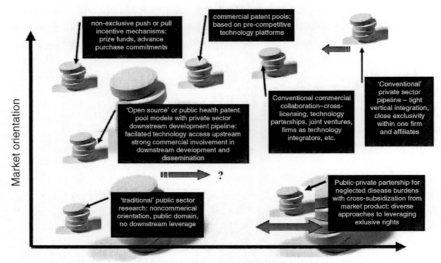

Figure 6.3 IP Management Options in Medical R&D

interventions such as measures to deter or remedy the abuse of IP rights. TRIPS:40 recognizes that some licensing practices can have adverse effects on trade and may impede the transfer and dissemination of technology, and confirms that Members are entitled to take action to prevent these practices. TRIPS also requires equitable and procedural safeguards against abuses of IP enforcement measures that interfere with legitimate trade.

For the policymaker, this perspective means broadening the scope of discussion to cover not only the desirable scope and eligibility of the IP rights that can and should be granted—and how to define legal limitations and exceptions to these rights—but also how to encourage or require certain preferred practices in the exercise of rights and how to deter or penalize certain damaging forms of abuse.

TRIPS provisions on the public policy role of IP rights resonate with an historic law often cited as one of the origins of Anglo-American patent law—the English Statute of Monopolies of 1623—which took aim against burdensome monopolies based on 'misinformacions and untrue pretences of publique good', but identified true patents of invention as a legitimate entitlement—recognizing patents of 21 years for 'any manner of new manufacture' for 'the first and true inventor or inventors' provided that they are not exercised so as to be 'contrary to the lawe nor mischeivous to the state by raisinge of prices of commodities home or hurt of trade or generally inconvenient'. This early statute, dating back

Figure 6.4 The English Statute of Monopolies 1623

to well before the industrial age, recalls the idea of 'balance of rights and obligations' of TRIPS:7, the complementarity between the promotion of fair competition and exclusive IP rights and the role for such pro-competition measures as foreseen in TRIPS:40, and the policy rationale for carving out the patent of invention as a specific, time-bound exception from the general rule against monopolies.

Towards Reconciliation

Reconciling TRIPS and public policy therefore requires considering the impact of IP at several levels, in a systematic manner:

- The values and interests identified and promoted in international laws and policy processes, and the involvement and active participation of interested parties in the formulation and implementation of international laws and standards.
  - For instance, how does TRIPS give scope for the right to health, and what expectations does it create for improved transfer of technology in vital areas?
- The legal rights and obligations of countries under specific legal instruments, and how those instruments are and should be interpreted and implemented.

- For instance, what does TRIPS require in the patenting of green technology, how should clinical trial data be protected, and what words or symbols must be protected as geographical indications?
- The public policy and legislative options ('flexibilities') available to countries within the international legal framework, and the interests and political processes that lead governments and legislatures to exercise these options in different ways.
    - For instance, what kind of medical innovations can be excluded from patent protection, and what exceptions are allowed for educational copying of journal articles or textbooks?
- How individual IP rights granted or recognized under national laws are exercised, by who, and subject to what legal safeguards, policy guidelines, and practical incentives.
    - For instance, who holds the most important portfolios of green technology, in what countries are the patents in force and where is the technology in the public domain? What policies govern how publicly funded IP should be exercised? And what actions amount to anticompetitive or abusive licensing practices that are contrary to the law?

The interests, values and policy considerations at each of these levels, and how we integrate these layers of analysis, can differ enormously for countries in different states of economic development, for different industry sectors, and for diverse fields of law and regulation. Sound policy in one area—say, promoting innovation in medicines for neglected diseases—will not translate easily across to another field—promoting a low carbon economy, or ensuring cultural diversity. But a study of legal and policy issues in one area can illuminate possibilities in other fields, provided we keep in mind the objective differences, and avoid forced analogies between diverse fields. What follows is neither a complete analysis nor an authoritative account of the law or policy in any one area, but a brief comparative sketch of topical issues, to assist the practitioner in navigating a set of fascinating but often perplexing policy debates.

TRIPS and Human Rights

Because of the central role and broad sweep of human rights law, the human rights dimension is pivotal to finding the appropriate role and place for TRIPS with the system of public international law. IP law, in all its guises, is not fundamentally at odds with human rights, including—including especially—at the level of basic principle. The theoretical justification for the IP system is usually set out according to one of two broad schools of thought:

- a natural rights rationale—the idea that there is an inherent entitlement to protection or recognition of one's intellectual productions; to use the language of TRIPS's three-step tests, a right holder's interests in IP protection are *legitimate* as a matter of essential fairness; and
- a utilitarian basis—IP laws are justified in pragmatic terms, as practical regulatory interventions consciously implemented to deliver public welfare outcomes, or public goods; the right holder's interests in IP protection are legitimized by reference to concrete policy objectives, such as the development and diffusion of beneficial technologies, and not as ends in themselves; these objectives constitute public goods that are consistent with human rights considerations.

In stating the objective of IP protection, TRIPS:7 mentions utilitarian outcomes, such as 'promotion of technological innovation' and 'social and economic welfare'; but it also invokes ideas of equity and fairness. It would read too much into TRIPS to assign it to one theoretical camp or the other, although it does have an undoubted utilitarian emphasis. By contrast, human rights are generally held to be absolutely justified in themselves—they are to be respected in their own right, and are not instrumental means of achieving other, higher policy objectives.

Human rights experts have typically been sceptical or critical of TRIPS: they see the IP 'rights' it recognizes and protects as operating as a lower level in the legal hierarchy than human rights, as being more contingent and temporary, with limited inherent worth or justification, and as conflicting with human rights in practice or even in principle. The international law of human rights does recognize a 'right to protection of the moral and material interests resulting from any scientific, literary or artistic production of which one is the author'; this human right is ideally promoted by the rights flowing from tenure of IP. But some human rights commentaries have stressed that it should not be conflated or identified with IP rights as such; moreover, they argue that even this human right is not absolute, but is subject to 'limitations in the public interest', setting it within a utilitarian context.

When navigating the broader legal and policy environment, therefore, a TRIPS practitioner may encounter a negative or at best cautious view on the part of the human rights community, exemplified in the Resolution of the Sub-Commission on the Promotion and Protection of Human Rights quoted at the head of this chapter. Some, more critical viewpoints effectively view IP mechanisms as privileges to industry interests, directly at odds with a human rights outlook. Their critics cite TRIPS and the IP system as potentially problematic for several specific human rights:

- the right to health, especially inasmuch as this involves access to essential medicines, but also research on neglected diseases;
- the right to food, in particular the debate over the impact on farmers and consumers of patents on seeds and basic food crops;
- the right to benefit from scientific progress and its applications, and the right to development. One view is that the patent system especially throws up barriers to the enjoyment of such advances, although in principle it is designed exactly to promote and disseminate practical benefits from scientific progress;
- the right to take part in cultural life and the right to education: their critics consider copyright rules encumbering access to and dissemination of educational materials, and the use, sharing and adaptation ('remixing') of cultural works. This debate found an imprint in the Appendix to Berne, which provides special arrangements for compulsory licences in developing countries including for teaching, scholarship and research. Again, in principle, a balanced copyright system would preclude unreasonable constraints but in the human rights context concerns are voiced that it is weighted on the side of the copyright holder.
- the rights of indigenous peoples, in view of defensive concerns that TRIPS-consistent patent systems may misappropriate traditional knowledge and genetic resources, and in the light of calls for the positive protection of collective rights over traditional knowledge, on which TRIPS is largely silent;
- the right to benefit from the moral and material interests relating to one's own intellectual creations: while the IP system should in principle be tailor made to advance this human right in particular, a critical view argues that it is at best inadequate and at worst in tension with it.

The human rights debate therefore touches on wider public policy issues involving TRIPS, and offers a framework for thinking through how to reconcile TRIPS, a reasonably precise legal instrument, with the ever more diverse and complex policy and political context that surrounds it. If you accept reconciliation as a worthwhile goal, three broad avenues present themselves:

- structuring a response around a zero-sum assumption that basic legal principles and the values behind them are inherently at odds and that reconciliation may entail dealing with intrinsic conflicts;
- taking a defensive approach and safeguarding against negative impacts resulting from national implementation of TRIPS standards;
- constructing a mutually beneficial, positive-sum relationship between TRIPS and the principles of human rights law.

The last of these avenues is potentially the most productive, because of a general preference in international law (recognized, as we have seen, at a practical level in TRIPS dispute settlement) for coherence, consistency and avoidance of intrinsic conflict between international legal instruments. Further, TRIPS itself and the Doha Declaration both explicitly articulate, to an unprecedented degree in international IP law, exactly the same concerns that drive the human rights debates.

Taking a lead from the human rights debates, several cross-cutting themes arise when analysing the role of TRIPS law in public policy:

- What material should be 'protected'? Few question the legitimacy of limited and balanced rights over genuine innovation and creativity, but are the rules of TRIPS properly applied so as to recognize true advances in technology and the creative domains, while weeding out claims of questionable merit?
- Whose innovation should be recognized, and for whose benefit? Do the TRIPS rules privilege one, more individualistic or 'atomistic' form of innovation and creativity, the solitary inventor or the lone artist, over cumulative, collective processes? Does the 'trade' dimension of TRIPS favour innovation led by the market, rather than innovation to meet human needs, such as neglected diseases? Or are these misleading, zero-sum false dichotomies?
- What should be the content of the public domain? Some material should remain free for all to use—whether it concerns a language, song, image, knowledge or chemical compound—but what are the necessary ingredients of the public domain; how should they be safeguarded to ensure continued access; and how should these settings differ according to a country's cultural and economic status?
- What are the limits to exclusivity? If an IP right is essentially a right to exclude, often within a commercial context, how far can and should the right reach into private or non-commercial activities? How should the various 'interests' cited in TRIPS three-step tests be weighed and balanced? And when should an IP right lose its exclusivity, and just become a right to be paid a reasonable royalty?
- Access to technology and technology transfer. If technology can indeed serve as a solution to social, environmental and developmental problems, what does it mean to have a system for technology diffusion that is at once fair and equitable, and efficient and effective in addressing those problems? How do particular rights and interests in sectors such as health, biodiversity, and climate change affect our sense of what is a fair, balanced, and useful system for enabling access to needed technology?

- What role for the market? IP and competition policy share common roots, dating back to the historical origins of patent law, and are truly complementary—competition without innovation is static, and innovation is itself a form of competition. But, as TRIPS recognizes, heavy-handed and abusive exercise of IP rights can stifle competition and suppress legitimate trade and technology transfer, imposing a net cost on society. What does it mean to get the right balance between beneficial competition, and legitimate property rights over useful innovation and the distinctive characteristics of businesses?
- What kind of trade is 'legitimate'? Embedded in TRIPS is a conception of 'legitimate trade'—an essential logic that trade which free-rides on recognized IP rights is, in a certain sense, 'unfair', and that governments should commit to setting up the necessary regulatory means to suppress that trade; but TRIPS also recognizes that protection of IP should not impede other forms of legitimate trade. This concept of 'legitimate trade' is at once a relatively precise legal concept, and a potential avenue for recognizing much broader policy interests than the specific elements of IP law.

The Universal Declaration on Human Rights recognizes rights to participate in cultural life, to enjoy the arts, and to share in scientific progress and its benefits, and equally for authors of scientific, literary and artistic productions to benefit from the resulting moral and material interests; the International Covenant on Economic, Social and Cultural Rights elaborates and legally reinforces these rights. An authoritative *General Comment* on the Covenant points out that an author's rights to material and moral interests should not be *equated* with specific IP rights over this subject matter—IP rights being generally more temporary, contingent and utilitarian in character than human rights—even though IP rights can help serve as tools to secure these more fundamental rights. Further, commentary stipulates that the right to moral and material interests is not absolute but is subject to limitations and must be balanced with other economic, social, and cultural rights. Indeed, human rights law strikes a balance between author or innovator rights and other human rights (regarding culture, education, and benefits from the application of scientific progress, among others) analogously to the way in which public policy questions concerning TRIPS are resolved. Table 6.1 illustrates this analogy.

Human rights concerns are not new in IP lawmaking. For instance, the 1928 Rome Conference revised the Berne Convention, in part to deal with the impact on copyright of new broadcasting technologies. The diplomatic records of the conference disclose a protracted debate about how to reconcile the rights of the authors of creative works with the public interest in participating in cultural life—an exact mirror of human rights discussions today on balancing authors' rights against rights to take part in culture and education (see Table 6.1). The outcome was Berne:11*bis*, a provision considered in the WTO dispute *US—Copyright Act*.

UNION INTERNATIONALE

POUR

LA PROTECTION DES OEUVRES LITTÉRAIRES ET ARTISTIQUES

ACTES DE LA CONFÉRENCE

RÉUNIE A ROME

DU 7 MAI AU 2 JUIN 1928

Figure 6.5 Diplomatic Record of the Rome Conference: Also a Human Rights Debate?

Table 6.1 Linking Human Rights with IP Policy Ideas

The human rights perspective	Policy 'balance' within TRIPS
Governments to integrate into their national and local legislations and policies, provisions . . . that protect the social function of intellectual property. *Sub-Commission on Human Rights, Resolution 2000/7, Intellectual Property Rights and Human Rights*	IP protection [should be] . . . conducive to social and economic welfare—TRIPS:7
Given . . . differences between a human rights approach and [TRIPS], much still depends on how [TRIPS] is actually implemented. [TRIPS] offers significant operational flexibility and the High Commissioner urges WTO member States to use this operational flexibility in ways that would be fully compatible with the promotion and protection of human rights. *The Impact of [TRIPS] on human rights, Report of the High Commissioner for Human Rights, 2001*	TRIPS:1.1—Members shall be free to determine the appropriate method of implementing [TRIPS] provisions . . . within their own legal system and practice. TRIPS:8.1—Members may, in formulating or amending their laws and regulations, adopt measures necessary to protect public health and nutrition, and to promote the public interest in sectors of vital importance to their socio-economic and technological development [consistently with TRIPS].
Rights to moral and material benefits from scientific, literary or artistic productions recognized alongside rights to cultural life, education, benefits from scientific progress, and health.	Mutual advantage of producers and users of technological knowledge . . . and a balance of rights and obligations—TRIPS:7

Table 6.1 *(cont.)*

The human rights perspective	Policy 'balance' within TRIPS

States, in implementing systems for IP protection, are encouraged to consider the most appropriate mechanisms that will promote, on the one hand, the right of everyone to take part in cultural life and to enjoy the benefits of scientific progress and its applications and, on the other hand, the right of everyone to benefit from the protection of the moral and material interests resulting from any scientific, literary or artistic production of which he or she is the author . . . the High Commissioner encourages States to monitor the implementation of [TRIPS] to ensure that its minimum standards are achieving this balance between the interests of the general public and those of the authors.

The Impact of [TRIPS] on human rights, Report of the High Commissioner for Human Rights, June 2001

The human rights perspective	Policy 'balance' within TRIPS
The High Commissioner . . . encourages the [WTO Doha Ministerial Meeting] to consider establishing closer links between the promotion and protection of human rights and [TRIPS]. *Report of the High Commissioner for Human Rights, June 2001*	We agree that [TRIPS] does not and should not prevent Members from taking measures to protect public health. Accordingly, while reiterating our commitment to [TRIPS], we affirm that the Agreement can and should be interpreted and implemented in a manner supportive of WTO Members' right to protect public health and, in particular, to promote access to medicines for all. *Doha Declaration on the TRIPS Agreement and Public Health, November 2001*
The right to the protection of the moral and material interests resulting from one's scientific, literary and artistic productions is subject to limitations and must be balanced with the other rights recognized in the Covenant. *General comment 17 on ICESR Art 15 1(c)*	. . . a balance of rights and obligations. . . . limited exceptions to the exclusive rights conferred by a patent . . . taking account of the legitimate interests of third parties. Art 7, Arts 13, 30
Limitations must be determined by law in a manner compatible with these rights, must pursue a legitimate aim, and must be strictly necessary for promotion of general welfare in a democratic society . . . proportionate . . . least restrictive measures must be adopted. . . compatible with the very nature of the rights protected under Art 15 1(c). *General comment 17 on ICESR* *Art 15 1(c)*	. . . limitations or exceptions [to copyright confined] to exclusive rights confined to certain special cases which do not conflict with a normal exploitation of the work and do not unreasonably prejudice the legitimate interests of the right holder. TRIPS:13

The human rights perspective	Policy 'balance' within TRIPS
Limitations may . . . require compensatory measures, such as adequate remuneration, for the use of scientific, literary or artistic productions in the public interest. . . . *General comment 17 on ICESR* *Art 15 1(c)*	. . . the right holder shall be paid adequate remuneration in the circumstances of each case, TRIPS:31 . . . right to obtain equitable remuneration which, in the absence of agreement, shall be fixed by competent authority. Berne:11*bis*, 13

Public Health

IP and public health is a fundamental policy concern in itself—this issue domi- nated the immediate domain of the TRIPS Agreement in a decade from the year 2001. The health debate is also an important model for considering how to reconcile TRIPS with other public policy interests. In a nutshell, the debate concerns balancing 'access' (getting medicines to those who need them) with 'innovation' (ensuring a sound foundation and the necessary resources for the development of needed new medicines). The debate some- times sets these objectives at odds with each other, in a zero-sum analysis, but can also more positively look at how to promote both objectives in a harmonious manner.

The Issues

- Harnessing private sector resources to create new medical innovations that benefit the public, and closing the gap between the focus of medical innova- tion and the actual health needs of people worldwide, especially the poor;
- Leveraging public and philanthropic investment in medical research and development to yield public health outcomes;
- Cutting the cost of medicines and other barriers to access, including through use of TRIPS flexibilities;
- Mapping the scope and trends of health innovation through patent information;
- Transparency about the actual scope and reach of patents, and greater preci- sion in the scope of patents granted so that they correspond to genuinely useful new inventions;
- Creating incentives to produce clinical trial data on the safety and efficacy of new medicines, while avoiding obstacles to the effective use of these data.

TRIPS provisions

- TRIPS:6—options include international exhaustion to reduce prices through competition, or national exhaustion to strengthen domestic capacity.
- TRIPS:7—sets out a policy framework for innovation and access to technologies.
- TRIPS:8—clarifies the scope for domestic policy measures to promote public health.
- TRIPS:27—pharmaceutical products are patentable. No discrimination as to technological field and place of invention. Optional exceptions for certain medical inventions, and on certain morality and health grounds.
- TRIPS:29—patent applicants must disclose their inventions to enable others to carry them out.
- TRIPS:30—scope for limited exceptions to patent rights, including enabling generic producers to secure regulatory approval before patent expiry.
- TRIPS:31—wider exceptions including for commercial scale production under compulsory licence or government use order, subject to procedural and equitable safeguards.
- TRIPS:39—certain clinical trial data should be protected against unfair commercial use.
- TRIPS:44.2 remedies for infringing government use may be limited to payment of remuneration only.
- Doha Declaration: TRIPS must be part of the action to address health problems. It does not and should not prevent measures to protect public health, and can be interpreted and implemented to support public health and promote access to medicines for all; reaffirming the right to use flexibilities for this purpose, including through the rules of treaty interpretation, the grant of compulsory licences with freedom to determine their grounds, and the option of establishing a regime on exhaustion without challenge.
- TRIPS Protocol (TRIPS 31*bis*): additional flexibility for countries with limited pharmaceutical manufacturing facilities to use compulsory licensing for access to medicines.

Areas of divergence and of reinforcement

The Doha Declaration was plain: TRIPS is meant to be part of the solution, not to present an obstacle for public health. The idea is to recognize true medical innovation and enable it to be managed effectively, while not creating unreasonable barriers to access. Policy debate and practical initiatives on TRIPS and public health have concentrated on the patenting of pharmaceuticals, although there are several other areas of interaction between TRIPS and public health. In bringing pharmaceutical products into the scope of patentable subject matter, TRIPS reversed the policy preferences of a number of countries which had chosen not to permit patents in this area: this outcome was a key objective for TRIPS proponents, and thus a major concession on the part of developing country negotiators. They sought to balance this measure with several safeguards—longer phase-in periods for product patents (TRIPS:65.4), and the general principles of TRIPS:7 and TRIPS:8. Yet this delayed introduction was counterbalanced by an obligation immediately to receive applications for such patents (the mailbox provision, TRIPS:70.8) and to extend exclusive marketing rights until a patent is granted or refused (TRIPS:70.9). As a measure of its perceived value, even this transitional provision was quickly contested— India and Pakistan fielded some of the earliest TRIPS disputes on the adequacy of their interim arrangements (the US complaint against India was taken to the AB).

Enabling a genuine new and inventive pharmaceutical to be patentable is not meant to get in the way of public health—it is meant to promote it, by structuring and facilitating the necessary innovation and development processes required to deliver a safe new drug to the public. The Doha Declaration summarizes centuries of debate and evolution of the patent system in two succinct sentences: IP protection is 'important for the development of new medicines'—the innovation aspect—but there are 'concerns about its effects on prices'—the access dimension. The essence of patent law applied to public health is ensuring that innovation and access are not zero-sum—so that promoting innovation does not unduly obstruct access, and measures to promote access do not deter vital innovation of new products. Articulating this ideal balance is unobjectionable, but achieving it in practice is a complex and demanding task for national authorities, against a constantly evolving backdrop of new technologies and new health challenges. Divergences in how to achieve this outcome at the national level cover both *pre-grant* issues—the questions a patent office must consider before granting or refusing a patent on a claimed medical invention—and *post-grant* issues—the kind of legal safeguards, exceptions and regulatory interventions that can apply to patents on pharmaceuticals once they have been granted and are exercised in the marketplace. A key pre-grant issue concerns whether patents should be available for inventive new medical uses of known pharmaceutical compounds. The most debated post-grant measure is the compulsory licensing of pharmaceutical patents—the Doha Declaration clarified the rights of WTO Members concerning the use of this legal mechanism, but in a continuing policy debate, its potential role in achieving price reductions for medicines is set against the possible negative impact on the development of new medicines if exclusive patent rights were routinely or systematically converted to a right to receive remuneration.

Strategies and options

Since TRIPS is not a model law, it is up to national lawmakers to determine how general international principles should be applied in practice. But equally TRIPS establishes an agreed baseline both for the foundations for a balanced and effective national system, in which innovation and access to the fruits of innovation are leveraged in a positive sum way, and for clarifying the legitimate expectations that countries can claim in terms of benefits from one another's IP systems but also the scope for regulatory autonomy—the policy space within which the legitimate choices of individual countries can be immune from legal challenge. The distinction between broad international rules and the detailed choices applied in national legislation leaves significant—but not unlimited—latitude to determine what medical innovations should be patented, and what kinds of intervention can be undertaken to promote access to patented medicines.

For many countries, the territoriality of patent rights means that patents can present little direct impediment to access to medicines, because relatively few pharmaceutical patents are applied for in the majority of developing countries. There is no automaticity about patent availability—an application has to be made in each country or region where protection is sought. If no patent is sought or granted in a country, then the subject matter in principle enters the public domain. This 'freedom to operate' is of course of limited value if the country concerned lacks the industrial capacity itself to produce needed medicines or if patents in other economies impede the possibilities for importation of needed drugs. Avenues are, however, available to leverage access to affordable medicines in this situation—including the 'paragraph 6' mechanism mandated by Doha. Even where a patent is granted and remains in force in a country, the detailed technological information contained in a patent document is intended to be widely disseminated and learned from, so as to contribute to further research and innovation.

Further, much of the impact of a patent—positive or negative—on the public interest and on public health in particular will depend not on its bare legal existence or absence in a country, but how it is exercised and used, including the approach taken to licensing. Thus the same patent—literally the same piece of paper—could in practice be used to help structure a public sector mechanism to promote non-profit research on neglected diseases or to flout competition policy through abusive licensing practices. TRIPS provides for safeguards against abusive licensing, and affords scope to override patent holders in allowing government use or compulsory licensing of patented technologies in the wider public interest. Other incentives can be used to encourage openness in licensing (such as cheaper fees for patent holders who offer 'licences of right' on reasonable terms to any interested party). A range of other mechanisms may be used to address the problem of neglected diseases and constraints on humanitarian access to essential medicines.

Table 6.2 Charting the Policy Space: An Overview of Options and Actors

Who exercises the options?	Pre-grant (prior to issue of a patent)		Post-grant (after a patent is issued)	
	Options	Examples	Options	Examples
Legislatures	Scope of patentable subject matter	Exclusions for higher life forms, methods of medical treatment, morality grounds	Legal scope of patent rights	Research and regulatory use exceptions
			Legislative measures for public policy regulation of or limitations on exercise of patent right	Laws on obligations to 'work' a patent; on compulsory licensing or government use orders; on competition law sanctions on abusive practices
Administrators, patent offices, regulators, courts	Case-by-case application of legal rules; development of detailed guidelines for applying the law	Assessing the patentability of claimed inventions such as through considering the inventiveness or utility of a gene sequences invention	Specific regulatory interventions to protect the public interest	Government use order for non-commercial public use; compulsory license to rectify the effects of anticompetitive actions
Individual firms and institutions	Decision whether or not to seek patent protection for a particular invention	Patenting strategies of publicly funded research institutions	Exercise of patent rights	Choice to pursue tailored licensing strategies (including humanitarian use clauses, open source etc); tiered pricing structures for cheaper medicines in the developing world

The paragraph 6 mechanism: amending TRIPS for access to medicines

A compulsory licence under a pharmaceutical patent may be of little use to a country that lacks its own drug production capacity and that must therefore import its medicines, because a potential producer in a foreign country may be constrained by patents in force there. TRIPS:31(f) limits compulsory licensing to serve predominantly the *domestic* market in that country, so a compulsory licence would not be available to enable a firm to focus on a foreign country's requirements. Paragraph 6 of the Doha Declaration on TRIPS and Public Health instructed the TRIPS Council to find a solution to this limitation. The result was agreement on, first, a waiver (the 'August 30, 2003 decision') and then a formal amendment to TRIPS (the Protocol Amending the TRIPS Agreement, introducing a new Article 31*bis* and an Annex to the TRIPS text). The waiver will be operational until the agreed amendment enters into legal force—this occurs when two-thirds of WTO Members have formally notified acceptance of it.

In very simple terms, how does it work? An eligible importing country (lacking its own manufacturing capacity) can notify its needs for medicines to the TRIPS Council. Another country, one that is capable of meeting those needs from *its* domestic manufacturing capacity, can issue a compulsory licence to enable the necessary production and export to the country in need (obviously it only needs to issue such a licence if the needed medicine is actually covered by a patent there). While the need to be met is in the *importing* country, the 'paragraph 6' mechanism creates a new legal option for the country that would produce and export the medicines. The importing country may issue a compulsory licence too, if it needs to (ie if the medicine is covered by patents there), but this was already an option under TRIPS. The system provides for transparency notifications, safeguards against diversion of products from their intended target, and removal of any obligation on the receiving country to pay compensation (in the event that it issues a compulsory licence as well). The system applies to 'any patented product, or product manufactured through a patented process, of the pharmaceutical sector needed to address the public health problems as recognized in paragraph 1 of the Declaration on the TRIPS Agreement and Public Health, including active ingredients necessary for manufacture and diagnostic kits needed for use.

This amendment creates a new legal avenue for access to medicines but it is not a standalone solution—it is only meant to address certain specific access scenarios. Many eligible importing countries can still obtain cheap generic medicines from producing countries where the drugs are not patented, so compulsory licences are not needed for export. In fact, the system has been used only once, so far, for two shipments of AIDS medicines from Canada to Rwanda. Different reasons are put forward as to why it has been so seldom used: prices of many medicines have fallen sharply even without compulsory licences being issued (sometimes the simple prospect of a compulsory licence can induce price reductions); many front-line medicines are available as generic exports already (this may change in future as key exporting countries, such as India, have implemented TRIPS rules on patenting pharmaceuticals, potentially affecting the supply of generic versions of newer or second generation treatments); the mechanism is not self-implementing, but needs both notifications of need in importing countries and the introduction of legislative changes in potential exporting countries; and some critics argue that it is difficult to use the system, although the notification required to trigger the process is a very simple communication.

Traditional Knowledge, Biodiversity, and the Rights of Indigenous Peoples

The debate over biotechnology, traditional knowledge (TK) and genetic resources (GR) is still more complex than the public health debate—at times it takes on the character of a contentious dialogue between different cultures, expressing diverse values and interests, that reach dramatically beyond the conventional scope of IP law and policy. We see initiatives to curtail existing IP (for instance, calls to ban patenting of life forms); proposals to reform the patent system (notably by requiring source or origin of genetic resources and TK used in an invention to be disclosed by a patent applicant); and ideas for entirely new forms of IP protection (collective rights of indigenous and local communities over their TK). These technical questions mark a deeper debate about the values embedded in IP law; what kinds of innovation should be recognized and privileged by the IP system; and what it means to distribute equitably the benefits from the use of TK and GR, with due recognition to the ongoing contribution of traditional custodians and those who innovate within a traditional context. This far-reaching debate overlaps with international endeavours to strengthen protection for folklore and traditional cultural expressions (TCEs), as for many traditional communities and indigenous peoples it is artificial or even offensive to split these aspects of their holistic intellectual and cultural heritage into separate categories.

The issues

What forms of TK and TCEs does TRIPS recognize already as the subject of IP protection—directly or indirectly? What form does this protection take? Are the benefits of protection enjoyed by the right people—the true innovators and creators—or by intermediaries who adapt or simply misappropriate traditional materials?

'Defensive protection' means safeguarding against improper or erroneous IP rights that third parties seek to take out on TK, TCEs or GR. What kinds of defensive protection, if any, are considered to be lacking and should be included in TRIPS?

'Positive protection' means recognizing that traditional holders of TK, TCEs, and GR have exclusive rights over this material; if this is not as strong as absolute veto rights, it may at least entail having a say in how that material is used and an entitlement to an equitable share of benefits derived. Does TRIPS facilitate the exercise of such rights, or get in the way of their recognition and exercise? Should it be amended to recognize these rights explicitly?

What are the kinds of knowledge and innovation that are currently recognized by patent law in line with TRIPS? How can or should this scope be extended to take account of TK systems?

The CBD establishes a clear international principle that the use of genetic resources—the useful elements of biodiversity—requires an equitable sharing of benefits of the use with the provider of the resources. Since one effect of TRIPS is to extend the possible scope of available patents to cover many inventions derived from access to and use of genetic resources, the past decade has seen a major debate about whether this state of affairs presents a fundamental conflict of international laws, policy objectives, and value systems; whether TRIPS and the CBD are already consistent, need to be carefully implemented so as to ensure TRIPS supports the objectives of the CBD, or inherently conflict with one another. With the goal of strengthening mutual coherence, some countries propose that TRIPS be revised to include a tailor-made disclosure obligation. This would require patent applicants to disclose specific details of TK and GR used in the claimed invention—the source or origin, or also details of the legal circumstances surrounding access to these materials—evidence of prior informed consent from the original community, and of agreements to share equitably with them any benefits resulting from use of their materials.

TRIPS provisions

TRIPS does not directly identify or protect TK, TCEs or GR as such, but several provisions indirectly cover this subject matter.

- TRIPS:14 may include protection of performances of TCEs.

- TRIPS:15 and Paris provide for the protection of trademarks, including certification and collective marks, which may be used by indigenous and local communities to protect distinctive names, signs and symbols associated with traditional products.
- TRIPS:22–24 geographical indications can also be used to reinforce the recognition the distinctive identity of traditional products.
- TRIPS:27 patentable subject matter can include inventions that use GR and TK, but equally provides scope for exclusion of TK/GR-based inventions either for lack of novelty or inventiveness, or
- TRIPS:29 a patent applicant must already disclose the invention sufficiently to enable others to carry it out.
- Paris:10 and Paris:10*bis* protection against false indications and unfair competition, which may include the suppresion of some false suggestions that products are of indigenious origin or bear the endorsement of particular communities.
- TRIPS:39 protection against misuse of confidential information can include secret and sacred materials held by traditional communities.

Areas of divergence and of reinforcement

Some writers criticize TRIPS for recognizing innovation and creativity very selectively, showing a cultural and economic bias towards more individualistic and formalized modes of intellectual activity that are found predominantly in the developed world—inventions, individual copyright works, and so on. They argue that TRIPS ignores significant forms of human creativity, especially the knowledge and creative expressions that are developed in a more collective, intergenerational manner by traditional communities.

By this view, TK can be highly inventive and useful, and worthy of recognition, even if it does not fit within the formal categories recognized by the conventional IP system covered by TRIPS. TCEs, too, are argued to be far more worthy of recognition and protection than the ephemeral works that make up the bulk of material legally protected by copyright. And the custodians of biological diversity argue that GR, potentially of inestimable value to humanity, are valued and treated as a raw material to be exploited freely, while researchers and commercial enterprises can secure patents on what they see as relatively minor technical developments making use of these same resources. Our principal food crops embody countless generations of selective breeding and innovation, which is only recognized by the modern IP system as part of the background to more recent incremental improvements to crops—so the debate has also seen criticism of conventional plant variety rights as overlooking the contribution made by past generations.

In this debate, downstream uses of TK, TCEs and GR—without paying due recognition to their original custodians—have been termed as 'misappropriation'. Misappropriation is alleged to occur through the patent system—either when I take out a patent over what I claim to be an invention but which is effectively your TK, or when I obtain a patent on a genuine invention, which was derived from your TK and GR without any recognition or fair sharing of the benefits I have reaped from your material. And critics have charged that TRIPS is predisposed to facilitate such misappropriation without adequate safeguards for custodians of TK, TCEs and GR—whether through positive or defensive protection strategies.

The foundational principles of the patent and copyright systems, enshrined in TRIPS but dating back to the early industrial age, do not aim to misappropriate the resources—intellectual or tangible—of others, but only to recognize some particular forms of innovation and creativity that genuinely build up on and add to what has been done before. The evolution of IP law has been, in essence, a long debate over how to recognize that true contribution, while avoiding any intrusion on the public domain and appropriation of the legitimate rights of others. TRIPS establishes minimum standards for protection— patents should be available for genuinely new and non-obvious inventions, for instance—but does not require measures to *ensure* that those standards are met in every case. National authorities need to implement search and examination procedures to ensure that patents actually granted comply as far as possible with accepted patentability standards. It is plainly good policy to do so—these standards are designed to serve the public interest by limiting patents to genuinely new contributions to human knowledge, and avoiding the encumbrance on the public created by patent rights over ineligible inventions. Yet there are no firm international obligations to apply patent standards rigorously to exclude 'bad' (ineligible) patents, such as those incorrectly claiming TK as an ostensibly novel invention that is already known within a community.

As it stands, TRIPS does have several forms of both positive and defensive protection for such 'traditional' subject matter—ranging across design protection, recorded performances, marks of authenticity and geographical origin, anonymous musical works, secret knowledge, and innovations within traditional knowledge systems. And national systems do allow for defensive protection through opposition procedures that enable illegitimate claims over TK material to be overturned—TRIPS requires these procedures to be balanced, fair and open to appeal. Many practical initiatives have explored these options in the interests of traditional communities. But TRIPS, and its practical implementation, do not directly address what many commentators see as the central issue—recognizing or giving effect to collective rights of traditional communities over their knowledge and cultural heritage—the kind of rights recognized by the UN General Assembly when it adopted the UN Declaration on the Rights of Indigenous Peoples: 'Indigenous peoples have the right to maintain, control, protect and develop their cultural heritage, traditional knowledge and traditional cultural expressions, as well as the manifestations of their sciences, technologies and cultures, including human and genetic resources, seeds, medicines, knowledge of the properties of fauna and flora, oral traditions, literatures, designs, sports and traditional games, and visual and performing arts. They also have the right to maintain, control, protect, and develop their intellectual property over such cultural heritage, traditional knowledge, and traditional cultural expressions'.

Reconciliation of TRIPS and the IP system with concerns about traditional knowledge systems and the rights of indigenous peoples takes three forms:

- More effective use of existing mechanisms to protect communities' interests—examples include protecting TK-based products through GIs, trademarks and certification or collective marks, protecting TCEs through copyright and performers' rights, and opposing contentious patents that claim inventions based on TK and GR.
- Adapting the existing principles of IP law and extending their effect to respect more effectively community interests—examples include protecting collective rights and interests through the copyright system, and the proposal (already introduced into a number of national laws) for a special disclosure requirement in the patent system for inventions using TK or GR.
- Creating altogether new, stand-alone ('sui generis') forms of protection for TK and TCEs, and strengthening the effect of CBD principles on the right to grant access to biodiversity and on the right to an equitable share of benefits when GR are exploited. The TRIPS Council has debated these possibilities, but current efforts are focused on WIPO negotiations towards new legal instruments to protect TK and TCEs, and the CBD's implementation of the Nagoya Protocol, which codifies and strengthens obligations on access and equitable benefit-sharing.

Climate Change

The issues

- Just as technology has been a major cause of anthropogenic (man-made) climate change, technology is equally relied upon to curtail our impact on the atmosphere and to deal with the consequences of climate change.
- Innovation, transfer and diffusion of green technologies are therefore central to efforts to *mitigate* climate change—to retard or reverse our impact on the environment.
- Technology is also required to *adapt* to the changed environment—climatic disruption will create stress on health systems, food systems, and ecosystems, requiring new technologies to be developed and disseminated.
- Some climate change policymakers have argued that the needs for accelerated green innovation and technology diffusion are too acute, too fundamental to our wellbeing, and too urgent to rely on 'business as usual', or the regular operation of the patent system. The model of access to medicines, and the Doha Declaration, have suggested to some that a direct analogy should apply, and similar steps should be taken for green technologies such as wind or solar power. Others have argued that there is no evidence of major bottlenecks in green technology dissemination, and that disrupting the current system could be counterproductive.

TRIPS provisions

- TRIPS:7—sets out a policy framework for innovation and access to technologies.
- TRIPS:8—clarifies the scope for domestic policy measures to promote the public interest in sectors of vital importance to their socio-economic and technological development and to prevent practices which unreasonably restrain trade or adversely affect the international transfer of technology.
- TRIPS:27—states there is to be no discrimination in patent law as to technological field; optional exclusions available for inventions when preventing their commercial exploitation is needed to avoid serious prejudice to the environment.
- TRIPS:29—patent applicants must disclose their inventions, enabling dissemination of information on green technologies.
- TRIPS:30— national laws may provide limited exceptions to patent rights, such as for research and regulatory approval processes.

- TRIPS:31— national laws may provide wider exceptions including for commercial scale production under compulsory licence or government use order, subject to procedural and equitable safeguards.
- TRIPS:16—distinctive certification marks may be used to certify environmental compliance of green goods and services.
- Paris:6*ter*—official signs and hallmarks indicating control and warranty, potentially applicable to environmental certification by government authorities.
- Paris:10*bis*—measures against unfair competition may be used to combat illicit 'greenwashing', ie false claims of environmental friendliness.

Areas of divergence and of reinforcement

Amidst a dynamic debate over TRIPS and climate change, three general sets of proposals can be identified:

- Keep the status quo, but implement it more effectively, such as through improved flow of information about patented technologies and licensing opportunities.
- Adopt initiatives akin to the access to medicines process, establishing specific measures to remove barriers to using TRIPS flexibilities, on the model of TRIPS 31*bis*.
- Implement more fundamental changes to rules on patents, such as revocation or refusal of patents on technologies needed for climate change adaptation or mitigation, and specific carve-outs for least developed countries and other countries vulnerable to climate change impacts.

These proposals reflect divergent philosophies and working assumptions about the interplay between the IP system and efforts to promote innovation and diffusion of green technology that have emerged in contemporary debate and international negotiations (such as at the Copenhagen conference in late 2009):

- A critical view, assuming the existence of a patent to be an inherent barrier to technology diffusion, and asserting patents over green technology should be restricted, revoked or prohibited.
- A legal view, laying priority on legislating for or directing access to patented technology, including through compulsory licensing or government use orders, with backing by international law and political statements.
- A disruptive innovation view, promoting new innovation mechanisms, such as open innovation and public private partnerships, with the aim of

ensuring innovation is done in new ways with a focus on access to technologies and leveraging new technology platforms to change the patterns of innovation.

- An administrative view, seeking actively to construct IP management mechanisms to facilitate pooling of patents and access to technology—measures that may be voluntary, but sufficiently attractive to deliver useful results.

- A transparency view, aiming to improve the flow of information about technologies and licensing interests and opportunities, including through technology brokering and more effective use of patent information systems.

- The view that providing stronger market incentives essentially within the existing legal framework would produce the necessary innovation and technology diffusion, and that undercutting existing incentives would be counterproductive.

Strategies and options

It is common ground that improved innovation cycles and rapid dissemination of low carbon technologies are essential to mitigate climate change. But a central question for policymakers is whether the existing framework of international IP law, epitomized by TRIPS, provides a sufficient basis for workable solutions. Should the scope of patentable subject matter be redefined or reduced; should powers of intervention to enforce technology transfer be strengthened? Or is it a matter of finding new ways for the existing system to be deployed, through more effective knowledge management and more active use of existing regulatory safeguards? Ultimately the debate concerns effective innovation policy—how to garner and focus the resources, private and public, needed for the innovation, adaptation, and practical development of green technologies, in fields as diverse as wind power and carbon sequestration. It is unlikely that a single, stand-alone intervention would make practical sense across a wide range of technological fields and patterns of development, ownership, dissemination and transfer of technology. Several possibilities present themselves:

- TRIPS currently allows for exclusions on patents for inventions that would damage the environment when commercially exploited. This gives the option of reducing incentives for environmentally damaging technologies. But, by contrast, to exclude from patentability environmentally beneficial inventions would reduce the incentive to invest in and to publish these technologies; it may create an incentive to conceal potential green applications of a new technology, and to refuse licences for environmentally beneficial uses of it, as such beneficial usage may create grounds for revoking a patent.

- Robust measures are already available within the TRIPS framework for governments to deal with attempts to suppress or restrict the flow of green technologies. Failure to make any use of a patented technology can expose the patent to compulsory licensing in some countries, as can anti-competitive abuse of a patent. TRIPS itself recognizes that licensing practices can impede the transfer and dissemination of technology, and identifies several forms of restrictive practices that may have to be remedied. It creates a mandatory consultative mechanism to enable cross-border cooperation for the enforcement of these remedies. Government use orders are available for public non-commercial use, subject to the safeguards of TRIPS:31.

- Most patented green technology is not covered by patents in many developing countries, and is increasingly accessible, as practical knowledge, through patent information systems—if the mere absence of a patent were sufficient to galvanize technology transfer, then there should already have been no difficulty for many countries. In fact, by and large, the obstacles to transfer and diffuse green technologies are linked to economic, infrastructure, and commercial factors distinct from the operation of patent law as such.

Geographical Indications (GIs)

The issues

- Many place names and other signs convey important information not only about the geographical origin of products, but also about the distinctive properties of goods. Traditional producers and artisans seek to maintain exclusive use of these signs as GIs to protect the integrity of their produce and to ensure they remain recognized as the origin of distinctive products. International IP law has long recognized that the public should be protected against misleading and deceptive practices in the marketplace; and producers argue that this protection should be strengthened to enable them to object to use of terms that evoke the reputation or general character of an original product, without necessarily deceiving the public.

- Yet language evolves. Many geographical terms have developed different descriptive significance over time, sometimes retaining an essential geographical reference in some cultures but losing it in others (evidenced by debates and negotiations over whether 'champagne' is strictly one preeminent winegrowing region in France, or describes a style of wine), and sometimes losing altogether any geographical reference (such as suede leather, or Arabica coffee). And the common language is an important public domain—traders and the general public are argued to have a positive right to use common descriptive terms in the course of their business (for example, French dressing).

- Equally, geographical terms can assume separate significance as distinctive trademarks (Mont Blanc pens or Fuji films). Sometimes both the trademark system and the GI system protect the same underlying term ('Roquefort' is a prominent example). And two separate regions may share a name, potentially creating a need for 'homonymous' protection of GIs—the recognition that two locations may lay legitimate claim to the same name.
- Such overlapping uses of language, and conflicting rights either to use, or to exclude others from using, specific terms and symbols, can readily set up a zero-sum case—two parties vying for exclusive use of the one term. The long contest over 'Budweiser' shows how the same term can be claimed both as a true trademark and as a GI.
- On what basis can one party's claimed rights over a term exclude altogether the interests of another; and what forms of coexistence may be either mandated by law or negotiated between competing right holders? How should the interests of the general public, of original producers, and of other legitimate traders be reconciled—according to a common, central set of principles, or through prag-matic negotiations?

TRIPS provisions

- Paris:10—obliges countries to seize goods on importation when they bear a false indication of their source, or of the identity of their producer. It confirms that anyone producing the original goods in the locality falsely indicated has a legal interest and a right to initiate legal action.
- Paris:10*bis*—under the broad heading of unfair competition, requires countries to repress a range of confusing or misleading representations about products in the marketplace.
- TRIPS:16—clarifies that a trademark consists of any sign, or any combina-tion of signs, that is capable of distinguishing the goods or services of one undertaking from those of other undertakings. This leaves open the possibility of a place name acquiring such distinctiveness through extensive use as a trademark.

- TRIPS:17—applies the familiar 'three-step' logic (see Appendix and related discussions above) to exceptions to trademarks; in *EC—Trademarks and Geographical Indications*, the dispute settlement panel interpreted this allowable exception to include some legitimate uses of geographical indications that would conflict with trademark rights. Unlike the other 'three-step' tests in TRIPS, this one provides a concrete example—fair use of descriptive terms.
- TRIPS:22.1—stipulates what a GI needs to do to be eligible for protection. It has to identify a good as originating in the territory of a country, or in a region or locality within that territory; the good should have a given 'quality, reputation or other characteristic' that can essentially be attributable to this geographical origin.
- TRIPS:22.2—sets the baseline for protection of a GI—legal remedies should be available if a good is designated or presented in such a way that misleads the public as to from where it originated, or any other use of a protected GI that amounts to unfair competition.
- TRIPS:22.3—helps to define the expected interplay between trademark and GI protection, requiring rules against registering trademarks containing or consisting of a GI for goods originating elsewhere, again if the public would be misled as to their true origin.
- TRIPS:23.1—mandates a stronger level of protection for GIs that identify wines and spirits—they are to be protected against use by others on the same kind of product, even if the public is left in no doubt about the true origin of the goods, or the term is used in translation.
- TRIPS:23.2—similarly applies this 'stronger' protection to the interplay between GIs and trademarks, barring registration of trademarks containing or consisting of GIs for wines or spirits, if these products do not come from the region indicated.
- TRIPS:23.3—allows for the coexistence of homonymous GIs (the same term referring to two different regions), based on 'practical conditions' such as distinct forms of labelling and presentation.
- TRIPS:24.4, 24.5, 24.6, 24.7—provide for a range of exceptions and limitations to GI protection which are much more specific than the conventional 'three-step' structure—enabling continuation of long-term or good faith prior use of a GI; a mandatory safeguard of good faith rights to use and register trademarks in the face of an identical or similar GI; and entitlements to use common descriptive language, grape variety names, and personal names.
- TRIPS:23.4, 24.1, 24.2—provide for further negotiation and review of GI protection, illustrating the still somewhat unsettled character of TRIPS provisions on GIs.

Areas of divergence and of reinforcement

The intensity of debate may surprise newcomers, but GI policy issues have provoked robust controversy for many years—today's international differences can be traced back to divergences within the Paris Convention in the 19th century. A rough and misleading caricature of the positions taken in this debate would divide the globe into two camps:

- The 'Old World' view—centred on the interests of traditional and original producers, stressing the value of absolute protection of GIs, arguing that the adoption of geographical terms by other producers and traders is an illegitimate practice that usurps or undermines the distinctive character of GIs, and seeking firm legal guarantees against the slide of geographical terms into generic descriptive use; often presumed to prefer tailormade ('sui generis') legislation and a more active role for the State in protecting GIs.
- The 'New World' view—arguing for a more liberal entitlement to use terms that are considered to have become legitimate descriptive terms, despite their earlier roots as place names or geographical references, conditioning GI protection on a test of public deception or confusion, and resisting any automatic protection against genericization of formerly geographical terms; generally characterized as preferring to protect GIs through the trademark system, such as by certification marks, and resisting any direct obligations on countries to protect specific GIs.

The debate is of course more diverse, nuanced and legally intricate than such simplifications would suggest. Many countries and regions wrestle with how to recognize authenticity in references to products' origins and characteristics, how to safeguard continuing fair use of descriptive terms, and how to deal with the multiple meanings that certain words can acquire. Equally, some GIs can take on the character of politically valued 'national champions', with a significance out-reaching their immediate commercial or legal imprint, and touching on questions of cultural diversity in an homogenized world. And the question is further complicated when we bear in mind that the trademark system is accepted as one means of protecting GIs, even while TRIPS defines trademarks as legitimate exceptions to GI protection and vice versa.

The division of the globe into distinct national jurisdictions and the principle of territoriality in IP law (decisions on protection and the legal reach of IP rights being strictly confined to the country concerned) can stand in tension with the globalization of linguistic references and global patterns of trade and promotion of local products, so that latent divergences over which use of a valuable term should trump all other uses can sharpen into more direct conflict. So these are concerns about how to maintain distinctive national approaches, even while the principles of national regulatory autonomy and territoriality of rights are firmly emphasized.

Strategies and options

TRIPS:24.9 is a vital reminder of a country's principal pathway to ensuring it derives benefits from GI protection—no other country has any legal obligation to protect a GI which is not actually protected in the country of origin, or which has fallen into disuse. Well-defined, established protection in the home market is a practical fulcrum to leverage protection in foreign markets, as well. GI protection concerns another form of 'IP'—identity preservation. It is practically incumbent on the source country to ensure clarity and precision in the link between the product and the GI which identifies it; the stronger this link continues in practice, the stronger the likelihood that protection will also be accorded elsewhere, although TRIPS leaves the choice whether to protect a particular term as a GI up to the authorities in each distinct jurisdiction.

As for other forms of IP, protection of GIs does essentially remain the responsibility of national legal systems—there is no truly 'international' protection of GIs as such under TRIPS, just a set of rules governing when and how GIs can be expected to be protected at the national level. Two general strategies are pursued to deal with the interplay between territoriality of law and the international reach of linguistic significance:

- A presumption that the significance of a geographical term in the country of origin should be given particular weight in other countries as well.
- Avoidance of any link between the legal status and use of a term in one country, and its entitlement to protection elsewhere—formal independence of rights, and the determination of a word's linguistic significance on the basis only of existing use in the domestic market.

Given that disagreement continues to simmer over the way in which competing uses of geographical terms should be managed, negotiators generally pursue two ways of settling on what amounts to legitimate use of terms in international trade:

- Agreeing on the international rules and standards that national laws should comply with, and then leaving it up to domestic authorities to work out how to apply those rules to individual claims for GI protection.
- Agreeing internationally on specific terms that should be protected as GIs, including agreeing to cease generic or descriptive uses of contested terms

which have their roots in place names or geographical references—the so-called 'clawback' approach.

The latter, more directly pragmatic, outcome-oriented approach has been explored in bilateral negotiations, notably in the area of trade in wine, in which two countries settle on an agreed list of terms that should be restored to exclusive use, sometimes specifying an agreed timetable for the cessation of generic use. Bilateral negotiators agree to phase out generic use typically as a trade-off against market access opportunities in other areas, such as rules on production standards and certification of wine. Generally, the former, 'fix-rules', approach has been preferred in multilateral negotiations, although there have been some mentions in multilateral discussions of possible generic 'clawback' or a stronger presumption of GI protection based on legal status in the home jurisdiction. Countries that see themselves as custodians of valued GIs naturally push for greater automaticity of protection, fewer legal tests and less of an evidentiary burden in foreign markets; other countries perceive their interests in terms of maintaining a more limited scope of what should be granted protection as a GI and of what forms of market behaviour should be constrained by GI protection, and claim an ongoing right to use established descriptive terms in export markets as a form of legitimate trade.

TRIPS does establish an unprecedented level of clarity and comprehensiveness in the coverage of international law governing GIs, and the broad principles that should apply, even if the continuing negotiation and review agenda under TRIPS demonstrates—together with the activity in bilateral negotiations and in WIPO— that the rules and their practical implementation are not yet beyond controversy. However, the two tiers of protection provided—a defence against consumer deception, and a stronger right over the protected term as such—do betoken an unresolved international debate over what uses of a geographically resonant term do or should count as 'legitimate' and 'illegitimate' trade.

Beyond Zero-Sum: Strategies for Reconciliation

Situating TRIPS in the context of public policy debates typically starts from a zero-sum assumption that IP protection serves private interests inherently at odds with the broader public wellbeing and that public policymaking should consist essentially of determining the right exclusions, exceptions, and limitations—the very idea of 'balance', in its simplest form, suggests a zero-sum trade-off. So by this view, innovation is promoted at the cost of access to technologies; a trade-off always exists between private industry interests and public health; a 'human rights' reading and a 'trade' reading of legal texts will contradict one another; IP rights are individualistic, privatized subtractions from the public domain, depriving the public of legitimate access; the IP system will operate routinely to misappropriate knowledge and cultural expressions legitimately held by traditional communities; trademarks, geographical indications and fair descriptive terms cannot cooexist equitably. Yet each of these outcomes would represent evidence of an IP system at odds with its policy rationale and in tension with its essential principles: the 'mutual advantage' of TRIPS:7.

The IP system—in each of the areas of IP law and policy covered by TRIPS—is plainly intended to move beyond these bare 'winner take all' characterizations. Instead, it is meant to be calibrated to progress legitimate private interests and at the same time to serve society by bringing into existence valuable public goods.

This is the paradox of the IP system: by its very character, the rights it defines are exclusive—rights to exclude—but they are established to promote inclusive public policy objectives. Policymakers over many years have wrestled with this conundrum, but ultimately conclude that legitimate, bounded exclusive rights—tailored, measured, time-bound exclusions from the public domain—are one way of producing public goods and advancing wider social welfare. For the most part, they remain utilitarian tools, rather than fundamental rights, and TRIPS recognizes these limitations, both at the level of general principles and in its legal details. Achieving actual public policy outcomes, however, remains the ultimate task of the domestic legislator and policymaker, who must sift through and select the best means of delivering in practice the 'social and economic welfare' and the 'mutual advantage' of TRIPS, across a wide range of policy domains such as those briefly charted in this chapter.

The following chapter therefore looks at this key figure, the national policymaker, who is charged with working towards delivering on the policy promise of the IP system within the bounds of the international framework defined in part by TRIPS.

7

TRIPS and the Promotion of National Interests

> How unreasonable people are! They never use the freedoms that they have
> but demand those they do not have.
>
> *Søren Kierkegaard, Either/Or*

This concluding chapter reviews the essential character of TRIPS as a legal
instrument within a trade law system, concentrating on the critical role of the domestic policy maker. The real-world impact of TRIPS depends on how its principles
are translated, and given actual effect, in national laws and their administration
and enforcement, and how the WTO dispute settlement system influences the
choices of national legislators and policymakers on IP matters. The essence of
the practice of TRIPS law consists in probing, understanding, and optimizing the
linkage between TRIPS as a legal system, governing international relations, and
the national layer of IP law and policy.

In retrospect, the idea of trade agreement on IP protection now seems a natural
consequence of the increasing knowledge content of international trade, and the
tensions and uncertainty that can result from disagreement over what constitutes an adequate or fair level of IP protection. TRIPS was thus intended to foster
greater certainty and stability in the management of trade relations concerning
IP, establishing an objective level of mutual expectations and offering the benefits of a rules-based system. Even so, TRIPS does have unsettled, contested
aspects. Its formal legal scope can still be unclear on key questions: it took a case

(*Havana Club*) to go to the AB, and a reversal of a panel's findings, to clarify whether TRIPS obligations covered the entire field of business name protection at all. And its actual effect on government behaviour and on legislative and administrative choices varies greatly: portions of some national legislation are taken directly, word for word, from the TRIPS text; in some cases, legislation is lacking altogether in certain areas of IP law, in tension with longstanding obligations; even a formal finding of non-compliance with TRIPS does not necessarily lead to immediate revision of the laws in question; but the more general experience is for legislation to be crafted according to specific national needs and interests, with a view also to respecting TRIPS and other international obligations.

Understanding how countries determine their national interests under TRIPS, how those interests feed into specific policy and legislative choices, and how they defend those choices, is essential for a thorough practical working knowledge of TRIPS. The 'trade' context of TRIPS—its situation within the broader body of trade law, transparency and review processes and dispute settlement administered by the WTO—clearly sharpens attention to international obligations. Even so, countries perceive and act upon their interests relating to TRIPS in diverse ways.

Beyond IP Producer versus IP Consumer?

Analysis of national interests under TRIPS frequently begins with a stark choice: a country is either a net consumer of IP protected material, and thus its interests consist in maximizing exclusions, exceptions, and limitations to the extent legally defensible under TRIPS; or it is a net producer of IP and thus may have an interest in 'strong' or 'TRIPS plus' IP protection, higher than the bare minimum required. Yet any country's perceived interests under TRIPS, as mediated through the WTO dispute settlement mechanism, will be more complex and variable than this monochrome picture suggests.

Most countries are net 'importers' of IP, however one measures the flow of IP—in almost all economies, whether developed or developing, IP is predominantly owned by foreign firms, and most report a net outflow of royalties and licence fees and net imports of trade in IP-based goods and services. Yet many countries look to more effective management of knowledge and deployment of IP law and policy as central to their economic strategies. The national treatment principle rules out the possibility of offering stronger IP protection only to domestic interests. And a 'stronger' IP system is seen as a means of attracting investment and the inflow of investment. TRIPS compliance can be used as a signal to this end. A country may seek to pursue interests both as consumer *and* as producer of IP, by accepting the systemic benefits of IP protection as essential infrastructure for the knowledge economy, regardless of whoever may own or exercise individual IP rights. Against this view, predominant foreign ownership of IP may induce a kind of mercantilist instinct—the idea that knowledge capital only benefits a nation to the extent that it is owned by its own nationals, rather than as a means of enabling mutually beneficial trade and commercial exchanges. Yet a low level of patent, trademark or design applications by foreign firms does not necessarily promote economic growth, and increased practical activity by foreign applicants can be both a cause and effect of improved technological and economic growth. Considering exceptions and limitations to IP rights, domestic nationals stand to benefit more from an expanded public domain than foreign nationals, simply by virtue of their physical location.

Figure 7.1 illustrates three ways of measuring national trade interests in IP.

- IP assets—proportion of local to foreign right holders.
- iTunes trade—exporting royalties or licence fees.
- iPod trade—exporting high technology goods.

These perceptions of IP-related interests flow into how countries manage their international trade relations. TRIPS and subsequent bilateral and regional deals on IP standards are, in effect, agreements to recalibrate the terms of trade in the intangible material recognized as IP, by negotiating the scope of subject matter that is protected, the scope of rights that flow from protection, and the scope for limitations or exceptions to those rights. But should a country see such deals as inherently a net trade concession to foreign interests, accelerating a net outflow of IP-related earnings, and for which a compensatory trade-off in 'traditional' market access should be negotiated? Or can such 'strengthening' of IP protection be inherently worthwhile, as an objective step towards laying the groundwork for a robust indigenous innovation economy? Are exports of royalties indicators of a sound investment in a knowledge economy, or a pay-off to foreign rent-seekers as the pragmatic cost of holding together an otherwise beneficial multilateral trading system? Or can they be both?

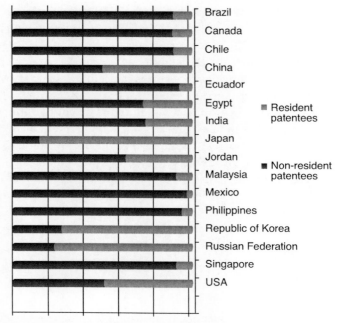

i. Proportion of Patents Granted to Domestic and Foreign Patentees, 2008
Source: WIPO

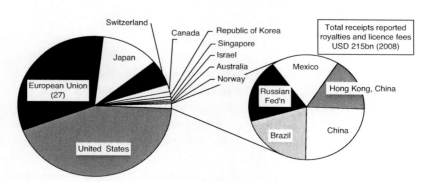

ii. 'iTunes Trade'? Top 15 Exporters of Royalties and Licence Fees, 2008
Source: WTO

Figure 7.1　Measuring 'Trade-Related Aspects' of IP

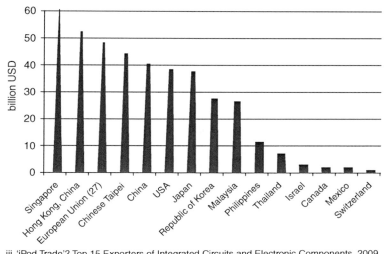

iii. 'iPod Trade'? Top 15 Exporters of Integrated Circuits and Electronic Components, 2009
Source: WTO

Figure 7.1 (*cont.*)

And Beyond Zero-Sum Trade-Offs?

Conventional trade negotiations are typically zero-sum in character. Deals on market access are considered as 'concessions' or trade-offs—so to gain market access in one country, you must pay for it by granting equally valuable access to your market. Yet classical trade theory tells us that liberalized international trade is mutually beneficial, and that trade 'concessions' towards reduction of trade barriers promote welfare even if they are made unilaterally. Even so, we need the two-way reciprocal dynamic to structure and to drive progress towards trade deals—the instinct to trade and barter is so deeply engrained. Negotiations on IP issues confront a similar paradox: a nation's IP laws should promote public welfare; TRIPS:7 itself enshrines this as the objective of IP protection. No advocate of stronger IP laws or higher IP standards argues that such revisions would actually damage the public's wellbeing. Yet IP negotiations—negotiations over the terms of trade in knowledge products—retain a strong zero-sum flavour, and are structured through trade-offs, especially through linkages with other sectors. The Uruguay Round package itself is the archetype of this phenomenon—without the logic of a 'single undertaking' involving commitments on trade in agriculture, textiles, and industrial goods, it is most unlikely that the majority of developing countries would have unilaterally accepted the standard of IP protection established in TRIPS. Yet, on the face of it, TRIPS-level protection of IP is intended positively to serve the interests of all those countries which apply its standards. Casting IP protection as a bare trade concession suggests a lack of practical confidence in systemic benefits from strengthened IP law and administration.

In fact, such orderly, mutually exclusive caricatures of national interests rarely do justice to the range and complexity of the actual interests of any country: few are, or aspire to be, exclusively either consumers or producers of IP. IP policy-making is a more complex game, involving the reconciliation of diverse, but intertwined, domestic and foreign interests. What is an incentive to foreign investment, technology-based commercial exchanges and technology diffusion, and what is a concession to foreign economic interests? The very same measure could be seen as both—and, often, the difference can seem more a matter of perception and ideology than a clear objective division. Similarly, when IP legislation is influenced by foreign models and international standards, is this submission to foreign interests, or is it a means of importing the benefits of policy development elsewhere, and facilitating mutually beneficial transactions? As in much of the world of working with TRIPS, both could be true: policymakers cannot construct a system of IP protection in total isolation from global standards; but, equally, they cannot ensure the optimal policy settings to promote national interests by uncritically importing foreign models.

In principle, policymakers should seek, objectively, to determine what their priority domestic interests are; then review at the domestic level what policy options would best further those interests; and only then to consider the international environment—trading and political relationships as well as legal obligations—which sets legal, political, and pragmatic bounds to domestic choices. But TRIPS also set a significant precedent—the idea that standards of IP protection can be used in trade negotiations to leverage market access in other sectors. Thus the cost of concessions made to purchase trade access in other sectors (typically agriculture and industrial goods such as textiles) may be measured by the degree to which preferred domestic policy options on IP matters are precluded by the legal constraints negotiated under TRIPS. Most countries did not enter the TRIPS negotiations having already concluded that their economic wellbeing objectively required at least a 20-year patent term and a three-step test to govern exceptions to patent rights; compulsory licensing of patents was effectively dormant in many countries yet had not been identified domestically as a priority need for legislative review or for the tighter procedural safeguards of TRIPS.

Assessing Impact in a Changing Context

The nature of IP protection means that it can be very difficult to predict the sub-sequent effects of negotiated changes in IP standards—both in terms of the actual legal scope of new standards agreed to, and the economic costs and benefits of such constraints on domestic policy choices. The effect of negotiated changes may only be fully felt or even become measurable years after the deal has been closed. By then, the constantly evolving international legal and political environ-ment may have shifted considerably, so that expected costs may be deflected, unlooked-for gains may be reaped, and new flexibilities explored. And, above all, with rare exceptions, international agreements such as TRIPS do not directly predetermine specific outcomes from IP protection at the national level, and these remain within the province of national sovereignty.

Equally, the initial calculation of interests prior to or during negotiations may overlook possible benefits from accepting certain obligations and renouncing independently preferable domestic policy choices. An autonomous search for domestic perfection in policy settings may drive out a more attainable second-best outcome that permits cooperation on the administration and enforcement of IP. Few countries have sufficient resources to meet in complete isolation the administrative challenge of ensuring high quality examination and registration of IP, and some convergence of criteria for IP protection may enable improved prac-tical outcomes even within a less than ideal set of legal standards. Equally, con-vergence in IP standards may facilitate trade and investment flows that outweigh losses from falling short from a theoretically optimal, autarchic regulation of IP.

An objective determination of national interests under TRIPS must take account of the dispute settlement dimension. Actual decisions made in dispute settlement under TRIPS provide an immediate imprint of the concrete trade inter-ests prioritized and pursued by a country. Disputes over IP norms and standards mostly do not concern a distinct knowledge economy, but are very much linked to the world of trade in goods. For instance, the United States and Australia pursued the 'TRIPS' dispute *EC—Trademarks and Geographical Indications* partly out of concern for effective future market access for agricultural products—'stuff you can drop on your foot'. The dispute dealt with fundamental non-discrimination rules under the GATT, the central agreement on trade in goods agreement, along-side the disputed provisions of TRIPS. The only fully successful defence against a TRIPS complaint in the WTO dispute settlement system was by Indonesia; the case, *Indonesia—Autos*, did not concern IP protection as such, but challenged trademark measures that were part of a national car programme, a conventional form of industry policy. And Antigua and Barbuda, Brazil, and Ecuador have explored cross-retaliation under TRIPS to leverage market access in agricultural goods and online gambling services.

Towards Richer Ideas of 'Compliance': Treaty Implementation as Good Policy, and Good Policy as Treaty Implementation

There is a rich academic debate about the precise legal character of WTO obligations, and TRIPS obligations in particular—the extent to which legal compliance is a multilateral obligation in itself, or whether TRIPS can be seen as a more pragmatic system of managing the IP dimension of bilateral trade relations. To take a conservative view of its legal character, TRIPS is strictly a legal regime between discrete legal entities, determining mutual expectations regarding protection of IP in national jurisdictions. In conjunction with the DSU, TRIPS provides a framework for determining compliance with those expectations and containing reactions to disappointed expectations. Complaints about failure to meet expected standards are initiated, pursued and ultimately sanctioned by other WTO Members through bilateral disputes, rather than by the WTO as such.

If what mattered to countries were not compliance as an end in itself, but rather concern about the costs of non-compliance, then the ultimate effect of TRIPS on domestic policymakers and legislators would be defined more by a pragmatic assessment of the likely impact of findings of non-compliance, including the political fallout from being found non-compliant and the cost of the coercive 'sanctions' that popular commentary attributes to the WTO as its distinguishing characteristic. The principles of the DSU stipulate that TRIPS should essentially function to prevent or settle bilateral disputes in a more objective, less divisive and predictable multilateral framework, and should set a fair ceiling to legitimate retaliation, in contrast to the more anarchic state of affairs that applied prior to the incorporation of multilateral standards on IP within the trade law framework. Ideally, TRIPS should objectify trade disputes over IP-related commercial interests, contain the escalation of disputes and limit their linkage with unrelated trade interests.

Early analyses of TRIPS as a multilateral regime emphasize trade sanctions and the heavy compliance costs for developing countries. Compliance with TRIPS, and willingness to bear the burden of compliance, are assumed to be motivated by the risk of 'sanctions', rather than acceptance of the inherent legitimacy of the agreed standards. This political background may suggest that choices actually to comply with TRIPS—its real influence on state behaviour—would be determined by an objective risk assessment as to the likelihood of a successful dispute or, to take a harder-nosed approach, the likelihood of a dispute in which the ultimate assessed compensation or withdrawal of concessions was costlier than compliance; in other words, compliance is no longer an end in itself. Yet many countries have sustained TRIPS-inconsistent provisions in their laws for years without legal repercussions, and formal determinations of TRIPS inconsistency may be unresolved for years. And limited non-compliance with TRIPS—'cross-retaliation'—is accepted as a legitimate means of pursuing trade interests in other fields.

So if TRIPS compliance were rooted in fear of sanctions, not from commitment to comply as a true legal obligation and acceptance of the inherent legitimacy of the obligations, this would suggest that a calculation as to the likelihood and impact of 'sanctions' would be the principal factor setting the bounds of state behaviour, and that a naïve reading of treaty obligations would be less influential. Yet the actual experience since 1995 has shown general willingness to comply with TRIPS, and a strong, consistent record of good faith endeavours to implement its standards (even if specific deadlines are not always met). We have seen how TRIPS dispute settlement has not unfolded as expected—the majority of TRIPS cases were filed against developed countries, and only three findings of non-compliance have been established against developing countries; no retaliatory sanctions have been approved, let alone implemented; developing countries have used TRIPS within dispute settlement system to leverage access for agricultural products and to defend their trade in generic medicines.

So what does 'TRIPS compliance' mean in practice: what pathway should a country take when confronting a difficult, borderline policy choice that may raise issues about TRIPS consistency in an area where the law is unclear? It might legislate according to how it best interprets its interests and a fair reading of its treaty obligations, scrupulously formulate sound policy reasons for taking that choice (avoiding discriminatory treatment or special pleading), and then, armed with that policy rationale and legal analysis, respond to any request for clarification or consultations posed by its trading partners. If the legislative choice were to trigger dispute settlement proceedings that flowed through to a panel or AB report, then this outcome would give clearer guidance on how to resolve a domestic policy dilemma; if the case led to finding of TRIPS inconsistency, the rules allow reasonable time to make the necessary revisions. The guidance provided by a dispute settlement panel would indeed be likely to reduce the risk of over correction and excessive restraint in domestic policymaking, more likely than choices made in the face of legal uncertainty.

Some countries have dealt with TRIPS along these essentially pragmatic lines, at least on some sensitive issues. Domestic policy choices may be guided by a practical, informed assessment of TRIPS implications. TRIPS 'compliance' and transparency processes, consultative mechanisms and formal settlement under TRIPS disputes then shades into the general management of domestic policy-making and bilateral trading relations; rather than being seen in terms of a stand alone, discrete regime compelling compliance as an end in itself.

Yet in wider policy debates TRIPS as a legal system is rarely analysed in this pragmatic, precisely legally informed manner. This means that its actual legal operation and its effective policy influence can diverge: in effect, there is a 'black letter law' of the actual provisions of TRIPS itself, and a more uncertain or contentious 'oral jurisprudence' of what it is argued or supposed to require. TRIPS plays multiple roles: as a benchmark for a level of IP protection needed to attract foreign investors; offering detailed policy guidance to domestic regulators (and setting boundaries to policy and legal); and a ghostwriter for national legislatures (in the late 1990s, 'implementing TRIPS' came close to defining the sum and substance of the workload of a generation of IP legislators in many countries; more recently, its opposing bookend, 'implementing TRIPS flexibilities' define an IP reform agenda in reaction to that process). Many officials in developing countries were relieved to find, as they approached the deadline for compliance with most substantive provisions in January 2000, that there were no automatic 'sanctions', nor even any formal determinations of non-compliance, apart from the 'rite of passage' through the TRIPS:63 transparency process. Compliance with TRIPS was not, after all, on the model of parking tickets issued routinely in response to each formal breach. In practice, it transpired that compliance was more to do with establishing a formal and objective framework for organizing trade relations on IP matters between states.

Political economic analysis of TRIPS concentrates on how the dynamics of the Uruguay Round's single package of negotiations had the effect of imposing upon developing countries a set of developed country policy choices on how to manage the knowledge economy when it was assumed that developing countries would mostly have chosen different pathways for IP policymaking and norm setting in the absence of the deal making of the Uruguay Round and the economic and political coercion that lay behind it. Objectively, comparing the laws that legislators had drafted relatively freely prior to their incurring TRIPS obligations, most developing countries had considerably more work to do than almost any developed country to bring their laws into line with TRIPS. So TRIPS became for many critics of conventional IP law and policy a symbol for a wider range of developments, notably the privatization of knowledge resources on a neo-liberal Western model. Yet the assertion that legislation is 'TRIPS compliant' also served as a metonym—a brand, even—of a country's willingness and capacity to provide a regulatory regime that is receptive to the trade interests that defined 'new economy' or innovation-based models of growth and prosperity.

For the sake of analysis only, if we assumed, improbably enough, that the assessment of options for domestically initiated IP legislation were insulated from broader political and legal influences beyond the border, and could be undertaken from an immediate perspective of domestic self-interest, then a country could, in principle, take one of four different approaches to treaty standards:

- Neutrality to international standards: draft and implement national IP laws without choosing to work towards compliance with international standards, even while drawing on international texts and foreign laws as benchmarks for standards of protection.
- Planned limited compliance: develop national laws consistent with domestic interests and constitutional constraints, compliant as far as possible with TRIPS and other international standards, conscious that some limited elements of the law may remain technically inconsistent with certain TRIPS provisions while giving effect to its objectives and principles, and calculating that the consequences of such non-compliance will not outweigh the benefits of the approach taken.
- Domestically responsive full compliance: craft IP laws consistently with domestic interests and constitutional constraints, with the express aim of complying with TRIPS obligations as they are understood in good faith to apply to the country; use actual policymaking experience in developing a workable national IP regime that meets domestic concerns from the point of view of practicality, constitutionality, and equity as the basis for promoting an approach to implementation that does justice to the treaty text while providing a positive model for other countries dealing with similar implementation issues and seeking to find an equitable balance of interests in practice.
- Reactive compliance: implement national IP laws essentially to conform with agreed international standards and with external judgements, in particular those of trading partners, as to what amounts to an adequate level of protection, possibly making use of external legislative models including the text of TRIPS itself, with limited tailoring or adaptation in view of distinct domestic needs and priorities.

These distinctions are not, in practice, entirely exclusive. For instance, there is considerable potential overlap in terms of the scope of actual outcomes between the second and third options, precisely because of the scope of discretion in national implementation and because of the inevitable subjectivity that arises when assessing the intent of national administrations in the context of treaty obligations. A trading partner's expectations as to detailed TRIPS implementation will typically reflect their own domestic settings which, in turn, may provide the background for treaty interpretation. Of course, one country's proper exercise of sovereign discretion can be argued, by its critics, to be a defiance of international standards. Even so, the second approach (planned limited compliance) is inherently undesirable for legal, policy, and immediate pragmatic grounds:

- The formal obligation to implement treaty obligations in good faith (*pacta sunt servanda*) and the ongoing systemic interest in an international culture of compliance with treaty obligations in the IP domain.
- The general policy interest in supporting the predictability, clarity, and equity that flows from a strengthened trend to interpret and implement treaties consistently prima facie with their text and with their objectives. An approach of planned limited compliance in one expedient case may be used to justify a comparable approach by other economic partners in ways inimical to core interests.
- The need to limit friction in trade relations, and reduce the prospects of trade-based retaliation based on a claimed failure to abide by international standards.
- The need to ensure continuing input into the interpretation and application of treaty standards, including serving as a potential model, and the commensurate loss of influence and credibility that would flow from planned limited compliance.
- Potential for influence in future negotiations if a country has a track record of reasonable and effective implementation of international standards.

The fourth option—passing laws solely as a reactive means of complying with international standards—is clearly suboptimal, and ultimately unworkable. TRIPS is silent on some basic questions at the heart of IP policy, questions that lie at the heart of national assessments of social and economic interests and the advocacy of sectoral interests, such as the very nature of an invention, the doctrinal basis of copyright and ideas of originality, the nature of distinctiveness that defines a mark as a trademark, and the function of a geographical indication as a means of denoting a product and connoting its properties. It does not touch on key areas of IP law, such as the entitlement to apply for and to hold IP, and issues such as inventorship and authorship. It only establishes general principles in other areas, requiring detailed elaboration and application under national law—for example, the definition of exceptions and limitations to rights; the substantive grounds for compulsory licences; the specific mechanism required to protect test data against unfair commercial use; the regime of exhaustion of rights and the entitlement of right holders to curb parallel impor-tation; and the expectation that trade in counterfeit and pirated goods would be eliminated. And in other areas critical to maintaining a dynamic balance of interests, TRIPS is permissive of regulatory action but does not impose obliga-tions—for instance, in curbing abusive licensing practices. So a purely reactive, text-driven approach to compliance is unlikely to deliver on the expected ben-efits for both domestic *and* foreign interests.

The formal legal aspect of TRIPS compliance is, nonetheless, practically important—as it provides a certain safeguard against external leverage, in deter-mining objectively what can and cannot be a legitimate complaint about the level and effectiveness of IP protection. A wide range of legitimate and defensi-ble policy options remain open within a TRIPS-compliant framework. But a richer approach to TRIPS compliance entails taking the broad principles it sets out, and putting them to work in practice—in determining what makes legal and policy sense as a 'legitimate interest', 'unreasonable prejudice', a 'balance of rights and obligations', 'fair and equitable procedures', valuable concepts enshrined in TRIPS but with limited direct benefit in the more rarified air of the multilateral legal system. Thus the domestic policymaker, in establishing a fair, effective, and balanced IP system under national law, while complying formally with TRIPS, is, in a way, engaging in a higher form of 'treaty interpretation'. The actual choices taken and implemented at the domestic level ultimately shed light on the real effect and import of the treaty language, and can provide practical guidance and an informal benchmark to others addressing the same challenges. The expectation of 'social and economic welfare' articulated in TRIPS:7 is a constant reminder of why this challenging and exacting task—giving effect to the broad principles of treaty language in more tangible form on the domestic plane—is also an essential one.

Appendix

Practical Jurisprudence from TRIPS Disputes: Exceptions to IP Rights

Determining the proper scope of exceptions and limitations to exclusive rights is a central task of IP policy, a vital means of maintaining balance in the IP system. TRIPS sets general standards for such exceptions and limitations to patent, trademark and design rights, as well as copyright, using criteria that are similar but not identical to one another. These shared concepts were originally derived from the text of Berne:9(2), which defines allowable exceptions to one single right under copyright (the right of reproduction), the 'three-step text'. The relevant TRIPS provisions can be consulted in Table 4.1.

This table gives an outline of the way dispute settlement panels have interpreted and applied the central legal ideas used in these tests. The table reveals both convergence and divergence. First, the specific 'steps' in question are defined differently in TRIPS—the standards differ for different IP rights. Second, the policy objectives and the nature of the rights differ markedly between the different fields of IP. The panel in *EC—Trademarks and Geographical Indications* said 'whilst it is instructive to refer to the interpretation by two previous panels of certain shared elements . . . it is important to interpret Article 17 [on trademark exceptions] according to its own terms'. But the ways of dealing with the broader issues—what is a legitimate interest, what is unreasonable prejudice, and so on—were developed in similar ways that reinforced the systematic, equitable and predictable character of dispute settlement.

The general elements under consideration (summarized in the left-hand column) are:

- general nature and scope of exceptions and limitations ('limited' or 'certain special cases');
- conflict with normal exploitation of the IP right;
- effect on right holder's legitimate interests; and
- taking account of third parties' interests.

	Copyright	Trademarks	Patents
TRIPS text	TRIPS:13: limitations or exceptions [confined] to certain special cases which do not conflict with a normal exploitation of the work and do not unreasonably prejudice the legitimate interests of the right holder.	TRIPS:17 limited exceptions . . . such as fair use of descriptive terms, provided that such exceptions take account of the legitimate interests of the owner of the trademark and of third parties.	TRIPS 30: limited exceptions . . . . . . [that] do not unreasonably conflict with a normal exploitation of the patent and do not unreasonably prejudice the legitimate interests of the patent owner, taking account of the legitimate interests of third parties.
General interpretation	Effective treaty interpretation requires a distinct meaning for each of the three conditions, avoiding a reading that could reduce any of the conditions to redundancy or inutility. The three conditions apply cumulatively, each is a separate and independent requirement. Failure to comply with any one results in the exception being disallowed. Notions of 'exceptions' and 'limitations' partly overlap: an 'exception', derogation from an exclusive right provided under national legislation in some respect; 'limitation', reduction of a right to a certain extent.		The three conditions are cumulative, each a separate and independent requirement that must be satisfied. Failure to comply with any one results in the exception being disallowed. Each must be interpreted in relation to each other, and must be presumed to mean something different from the other two. An exception complying with the first condition can violate the second or third, and one complying with the first and second can violate the third. Existence of the provision amounts to a recognition that the definition of patent rights in TRIPS:28 would need certain adjustments. The three limiting conditions testify strongly that TRIPS negotiators did not intend the equivalent of a renegotiation of the basic balance of TRIPS. The goals and limitations in TRIPS:7 and 8.1 must be borne in mind as well as those of other TRIPS provisions which indicate its object and purposes.

Nature of exceptions or limitations	TRIPS:13 has a narrow or limited sphere of operation. Its tenor (consistent with Berne:9(2)) discloses that it was not intended to provide for exceptions or limitations except for those of a limited nature.	Adopts interpretation of 'exception' from patent case (*Canada—Pharmaceutical Patents*): the term 'exception' by itself connotes a limited derogation, one that does not undercut the body of rules from which it is made.	The word 'exception' by itself connotes a limited derogation, one that does not undercut the body of rules from which it is made.
'limited exceptions'/ certain special cases'	'Certain special cases': Certain: exception or limitation in national legislation must be clearly defined. No need to identify explicitly each and every possible situation to which the exception could apply, provided that the scope of the exception is known and particularized, a guarantee, a sufficient degree of legal certainty. Special: more is needed than a clear definition; an exception or limitation must be limited in its field of application or exceptional in its scope. Exception or limitation should be narrow in quantitative and qualitative; narrow scope as well as an exceptional or distinctive objective. Given second condition ('no conflict with a normal exploitation'), exception or limitation should be opposite of a non-special, ie, a normal case.	Addition of the word 'limited' emphasizes that the exception must be narrow and permit only a small diminution of rights conferred by a trademark. May be 'limited' whether or not the exception affects few trademarks or few trademark owners. Necessary to examine the exception on an individual 'per right' basis. It requires a *legal* assessment of the extent the exception curtails that right, not an economic assessment, although economic impact can be taken into account.

Relevant trademark right is the right to prevent uses resulting in a likelihood of confusion. 'Fair use of descriptive terms' illustrates what is considered a 'limited exception': it is inherently limited in terms of the sign which may be used and the degree of likelihood of confusion which may result from its use (purely descriptive term is not distinctive and not protectable as a trademark). Fair use of descriptive terms. | 'limited': must be given a meaning separate from the limitation implicit in the word 'exception' itself. 'limited exception' connotes a narrow exception—one which makes only a small diminution of the rights in question. Limited effect to be assessed case by case.

'limited' is measured by the extent to which the exclusive patent rights have been curtailed, not by size or extent of the economic impact. condition of 'limited exception') is neither designed nor intended to address the issue of economic impact directly. Following two conditions ask more particularly about the economic impact of the exception, and provide two sets of standards by which such impact may be judged.

Curtailment of legal rights not measured simply by counting the number of legal rights impaired by an exception. There is no hierarchy of patent rights. If there is no curtailment of right to sell, this does not in itself mean there is a 'limited exception' with respect to rights to make and to use. |

(cont.)

	Copyright	Trademarks	Patents
	No need to consider whether limitation or exception pursues a special purpose whose underlying legitimacy cannot be discerned. No need for judgment on legitimacy of exceptions, but the stated public policy purpose can guide assessment of scope and clarity, from a factual perspective. 'Certain special cases' should not lightly be equated with 'special purpose.' No need to justify this element of the test in terms of a legitimate public policy purpose. AB rejected interpretative tests based on the subjective aim or objective pursued by national legislation.	not limited by number of third parties who may benefit, nor by quantity of goods or services for which descriptive terms are used. Applies to third parties who would use those terms in the course of trade and to those goods or services which those terms describe. Number of trademarks or trademark owners affected is irrelevant, although implicitly it would only affect those marks which can consist of, or include, signs that can be used in a descriptive manner.	
Normal exploitation	'exploitation': employment of exclusive rights over copyright works to extract economic value from the rights 'normal' is empirical (descriptive of what is usual) and normative (conforming to a type or standard), with a dynamic element responding to changes in market and in technology. Harmonious interpretation uses *both* connotations.	Scope of allowable exceptions influenced by *absence* of any reference to a 'normal exploitation' of the trademark and any reference to rights to exclude legitimate competition. Trademark confers right to prevent uses that would result in a likelihood of confusion, without otherwise restraining the manufacture, sale or importation of competing goods or services. Some conflict with such normal exploitation may therefore be legitimate.	'exploitation' refers to the commercial activity by which patent owners employ their exclusive patent rights to extract economic value from their patent. The term 'normal' used in a sense that combines two meanings: an empirical conclusion about what is common within a relevant community, and a normative standard of entitlement.

	'normal' exploitation is less than full use of an exclusive right: Forms of exploitation that currently generate significant or tangible revenue (empirical sense) and forms of exploitation which, with a certain degree of likelihood and plausibility, could acquire considerable economic or practical importance (normative sense).	Normal exploitation by patent owners . . . is to exclude all forms of competition that could detract significantly from the economic returns anticipated from the grant of market exclusivity. specific forms of patent exploitation are not static. To be effective exploitation must adapt to changing forms of competition due to technological development and the evolution of marketing practices.
	Extent of exercise or non-exercise of rights relevant for assessing normal exploitation, but may not be *sufficient* for assessing potential impact, e.g. if lack of affordable enforcement makes it not worthwhile or practical to exercise rights.	'normal exploitation' is not the same as protection of exclusive patent rights as such. All gains from the mere existence of the patent owner's rights to exclude do not flow from 'normal exploitation'.
Conflict with normal exploitation	Conflict with normal exploitation to be assessed separately for each exclusive right, not all rights clumped together.	Normal exploitation: patent owner's right to exclude all forms of competition that could detract significantly from economic return expected from market exclusivity.
	Conflict with normal exploitation occurs when uses allowed under a copyright exception enter into economic competition with the ways right holders normally extract economic value from the right to the work and deny significant or tangible commercial gains.	More than just the right to sell products; normal exploitation includes all regular commercial benefits from exclusivity.

	Copyright	Trademarks	Patents
Right holder's legitimate interests	'interests' not limited to actual or potential economic advantage or detriment	'legitimate interests' contrasted with the 'rights conferred by a trademark'; something different from full enjoyment of legal rights conferred by trademark.	'legitimate interests' is a normative claim calling for protection of interests that are 'justifiable' in the sense that they are supported by relevant public policies or other social norms.
	'legitimate' has two aspects, meaning lawful but also with a broader sense of justifiable in the light of the objectives of protection.	TRIPS sets out what WTO Members consider adequate standards and principles concerning trademark protection—these are legal standards but also WTO Members' shared understandings of legitimate interests of trademark owners. Function of trademarks is to distinguish goods and services. Trademark owner has a legitimate interest in preserving the distinctiveness, or capacity to distinguish, of trademark. This includes its interest in using its own trademark in connection with the relevant goods and services of its own and authorized undertakings.	'legitimate interests' cannot be equated with full respect of legal interests pursuant to patent rights under TRIPS:28. If they were equated, any exception under TRIPS:30 would cause 'prejudice' to some legal rights under TRIPS:28, reducing this condition to a simple requirement that the exception not be 'unreasonable'.
	There was no question as to the 'legitimacy' of the interest of right holders to exercise their rights for economic gain.		Equating 'legitimate interests' with legal interests makes no sense when referring to the 'legitimate interests' of third parties, who have no legal right to perform the tasks excluded by TRIPS:28 patent rights. The 'limited exception' condition already takes care of legal rights.
			The concept of 'legitimate interests' should not be used to decide, through adjudication, a normative policy issue that is still obviously a matter of unresolved political debate.

| Prejudice to or account taken of right holder's legitimate interests | 'prejudice' connotes damage, harm or injury. A certain amount of 'prejudice' has to be presumed justified as 'not unreasonable'. 'Not unreasonable' connotes a slightly stricter threshold than 'reasonable'. The latter term means 'proportionate', 'within the limits of reason, not greatly likely or appropriate', or 'of a fair, average or considerable amount or size'.

Prejudice to the legitimate interests of right holders reaches an unreasonable level if an exception or limitation causes or has the potential to cause an unreasonable loss of income to the copyright owner.

Need to consider information on market conditions, taking into account, to the extent feasible, actual, and potential prejudice caused by the exemptions, as a prerequisite for determining whether the extent or degree of prejudice is of an unreasonable level. Take into account not only the actual loss of income but also the loss of potential revenue from other similar sources. Taking account of actual as well as potential effects is consistent with past GATT/WTO dispute settlement practice. | Exceptions only need to 'take account' of the legitimate interests of the owner of the trademark, no reference to 'unreasonabl[e] prejudice', unlike tests for copyright, designs and patents—suggesting a lesser standard of regard for the legitimate interests of the trademark owner. 'Take account of' is less than 'protect'.

Includes taking account of the trademark owner's interest in the economic value of its mark arising from the reputation that it enjoys and the quality that it denotes.

Possibility that distinctiveness will be affected by permitted exception. The provision permits exceptions to the exclusive right to prevent uses that would result in a likelihood of confusion, so a certain degree of likelihood of confusion can be permitted. | Not considered—interests concerned were not legitimate in the first place. |

(*cont.*)

	Copyright	Trademarks	Patents
Third parties' legitimate interests	No reference to third parties' interests.	Not only refers to the legitimate interests of third parties but treats them on a par with those of the right holder. 'legitimate interests' of third parties differ from the simple enjoyment of legal rights. 'third parties' include consumers. Trademark functions to distinguish goods and services of undertakings in the course of trade, a function served for consumers as well as owners. Consumers have a legitimate interest in being able to distinguish the goods and services of one undertaking from those of another, and to avoid confusion. Third parties include persons using a geographical indication (GI). TRIPS definition of GI reflects a legitimate interest a person may have in identifying the source and other characteristics of a good by the name of the place where it is from, if the name would serve that purpose. But legitimate interests of users as third parties differ from legal protection of GIs under TRIPS.	Compared with its source (Berne:9(2)) this provision requires that account be taken of 'the legitimate interests of third parties'. The reference to the 'legitimate interests of third parties' makes sense only if the term 'legitimate interests' is construed as a concept broader than legal interests. By definition, third parties have no legal right at all to perform the tasks excluded by TRIPS:28 patent rights. Research exceptions have been justified in legal analysis on the basis of both society and the scientist having a third party 'legitimate interest' in using patent disclosure to support the advance of science and technology.

Index